HIGH-STAKES LEADERSHIP IN TURBULENT TIMES

Why Stakeholders Are Your Greatest Assets ... in Good Times and Bad

D1593744

PRAISE FOR
HIGH-STAKES LEADERSHIP
IN TURBULENT TIMES

"Managing through adversity and turbulent times is the 'new normal' for leaders at every level in every organization. Dr. Barger's amazing background and experience make him uniquely qualified to teach us lessons that will make us more effective and resilient leaders during times of uncertainty and/or crisis. I highly recommend this book!"

David Brandon
Past CEO and Current Chairman, Domino's Pizza, Inc.

"High-Stakes Leadership in Turbulent Times is an illuminating and unique book on leadership in crisis — a book in which Mike Barger draws upon his extensive military and businesses background to untangle complex leadership theories to offer digestible, real-world applications. Mike has made it his life's work to develop these ideas and to inspire seasoned and aspiring leaders through his nuanced and engaging insights. This book should be essential reading for all leaders — in organizations big or small — who want to be prepared for managing uncertainty."

Jennifer Sherman
President and Chief Executive Officer, Federal Signal Corporation

"This book is a MUST-READ for business leaders in today's fast-moving world, where real-time global connectivity makes crisis preparedness a MUST-HAVE survival skill. Dr. Barger shares his lessons on crisis leadership based on real, first-hand knowledge and experience — providing valuable insight for leaders of any organization."

Russell Chew
Former Chief Operating Officer, Federal Aviation Administration

"The volatility of today's business environment requires leaders who are ready to perform at the top of their game. Dr. Barger's lessons are perfectly suited to anyone looking to become a more effective leader ... in good times and in bad. Dr. Barger's 360-degree approach to the situation, solutions, and stakeholders is invaluable because — often during a crisis — the tendency is to move forward without this holistic perspective, particularly that of *all* stakeholders."

Marcy Klevorn
Board Member and Advisor, Former EVP and President, Mobility, Ford Motor Co.

"Having worked with Mike to start JetBlue, I was delighted to see that this book solidifies the importance we found in building solid partnerships with all stakeholders — which will serve organizations well in both normal and crisis times. This is real leadership, by real people, in the real world. The book will allow you to determine your personal and corporate readiness for the crisis that will undoubtedly come."

Captain Al Spain
Co-founder, JetBlue Airways

"A must-read for anyone with leadership responsibilities. Dr. Barger's experiences as an accomplished military and business leader helped him develop many exceptionally practical lessons that you could — and should — implement today."

Vice Admiral DeWolfe "Chip" Miller, US Navy (Retired)
Former Commander, Naval Air Force, Pacific

"Having served as a guest lecturer in Mike Barger's classroom, I know first-hand his incredible perspective on leadership in times of crisis, and I assure you that this book is a MUST-READ. Times of crisis can make leaders or break them, and Mike charts an excellent path for achieving the former."

Cathy Bessant
Chief Operations and Technology Officer, Bank of America

"Once in your professional career, if you're fortunate, you might encounter a leader as impactful as Dr. Mike Barger. With a rare intuition for navigating through chaos, Barger draws on his impressive military and business background to create in this book a template for crisis management that is both highly engaging and spot-on for leaders of any modern organization."

Lang Sias
Attorney; Former State Representative, Colorado General Assembly; Commercial Airline Pilot; Former Navy TOPGUN Lead Instructor

"I have had the good fortune to participate in Mike Barger's crisis management class at Ross, seeing first-hand how he teaches the value of leading by serving stakeholders with skill, grace, transparency, and accountability. This book brings that wisdom to life in a clear, dynamic way that will benefit the leader in each of us as we prepare for life's next crisis, professionally or personally. Leave it to Mike to shatter the axiom that 'there is no substitute for experience.' Whether you are preparing to face your first inevitable crisis as a leader or have navigated through countless storms, this book will give you a roadmap to lead confidently and humanly, come what may."

Tom Lewand
Chief Executive Officer, Marygrove Conservancy; Former Chief Executive Officer, Shinola Detroit; Past President, Detroit Lions

"Leaders today must learn to manage crises. The challenges are ever present — whether they're related to a global pandemic, natural or human-induced disasters, supply-chain disruptions, product malfunctions, or emerging public relations SNAFUs. Dr. Barger's careful analysis of crisis case studies, coupled with useful and easy-to-adapt frameworks, makes this a must-read for any leader who must manage an emerging catastrophe."

Philip Price
Director – Peer Learning Community, Grads of Life

"*High-Stakes Leadership in Turbulent Times* is THE leadership book we need today. It provides research-based practical solutions to help leaders face these unprecedented times. Its author is the rare true 'scholar practitioner' who has both researched the topic and lived it."

Doug Lynch, PhD
Professor and Senior Fellow, Rossier School of Education, University of Southern California

"If you really want deep insights into crisis or high-stakes leadership, then look no further than this book. Mike is the go-to guy on the topic and he nailed it! From understanding the VUCA environment to the necessity of being prepared, it's all covered and then some. An absolute MUST-READ for today's aspiring (and seasoned) leaders."

Robert "Bo" Brabo
Former Presidential Communications Officer for Presidents Bush and Obama, and Author of *From the Battlefield to the White House to the Boardroom: Leading Organizations to Values-Based Results*

"The ability to view the world from a different perspective is a gift in any situation, but the ability to do so as a leader in a crisis situation is a necessary skill. Mike's framework for managing stakeholders is both brilliant and obvious, and also a missing link to leadership effectiveness today. This book is a MUST READ for leaders everywhere."

Teresa Mackintosh
Chief Executive Officer, Trintech

"The lesson of 2020 — which can and should guide us far into the future —is that today's business leaders must be prepared to manage crises both in the markets where they compete and the communities where they live and work. Mike's practical, people-centric approach gives you the tools you need to not only survive but *thrive* in this challenging environment."

Derek Newberry
Affiliated Faculty, Liberal and Professional Studies, University of Pennsylvania

"If ever there was a time to rethink your leadership approach, this is it — post-2020 and in a world that is forever changed. Dr. Barger teaches us that, when the stakes are highest, the most effective leaders don't just manage their stakeholders — they serve them ... and even inspire them. There's no more important lesson for leaders to embrace in this moment. *High-Stakes Leadership in Turbulent Times* is impressive, authentic, and practical."

Pope Ward
Chief Research Officer, The Advisory Board for the Arts

"Creating and evolving a world-class culture where employees are motivated and committed does not happen by accident. Today's business environment requires leaders who are capable of effectively leading their organizations in a way that engages, aligns, and inspires their employees. Dr. Barger's lessons are perfectly suited to anyone looking to increase their effectiveness and consistency as a leader ... regardless of the state of the world within and outside their four walls."

Dave Almeda
Chief People Officer, UKG (Ultimate Kronos Group)

"Today's leaders must be ready to perform at the highest levels, especially during crisis. Through his experience as both an accomplished leader in the military and in business, Dr. Barger offers highly valuable lessons to anyone looking to become a more effective leader ... in good times and in bad. This is an incredibly important and valuable piece of literature."

André V. Branch
Senior Vice President and General Manager, MAC Cosmetics North America (The Estée Lauder Companies); Independent, Public Company Board Director

"The rate of change in business today is accelerating at an unparalleled pace and it is vital for leaders to adapt to this rapidly changing environment. Dr. Barger provides valuable insights into the critical attributes for today's successful leaders."

John Sznewajs
Chief Financial Officer, MASCO

"As a *leader*, you must first *lead*. The formula is simple: know your business and know your people and then provide clear, consistent direction. Dr. Mike Barger's vast experience in the military and corporate world has afforded him the insights to write a remarkable book that will provide readers the tools to lead with their stakeholders in mind!"

Andy Kozak
General Manager, Technical Operation Line Maintenance and Materials for the Southeastern USA and Puerto Rico, JetBlue Airways

"Leaders around the world should have approached the COVID-19 pandemic as Dr. Barger recommends in this wonderfully instructive book. The lessons, frameworks, and strategies offered here will help you to prepare yourself and your company for the next crisis."

Ram Krishnan
Global Chief Commercial Officer, PepsiCo

"Today's business environment in increasingly unpredictable and requires that leaders can step up at a moment's notice when crisis strikes. Mike's lessons on high-stakes leadership teach you to do just that — to be ready for the inevitable and to lead effectively, in good times and in bad."

Derek Kerr
Chief Financial Officer, American Airlines

"This book is a remarkable accomplishment for leadership expert Mike Barger and a unique opportunity for readers looking to prepare for the worst-case scenarios that might await them. *High-Stakes Leadership in Turbulent Times* is a must-read for anyone with leadership responsibilities, full of practical lessons and recommendations that you would be wise to implement immediately."

Warren Christie
Senior Vice President for Safety, Security and Fleet Operations, JetBlue Airways

"The modern world accelerates everything, including crises. Dr. Barger's book will help you prepare for and lead through turbulence with a people-centric, human approach to high-stakes leadership. His experience as a business leader of extraordinary ability, combined with his scholarly research and teaching at a world-class institution, takes you on a journey from theory to practice that will prepare you to lead through an unimaginable future. This book is a MUST-READ!"

Alan Todd
Founder and Chief Executive Officer, CORP/U

HIGH-STAKES LEADERSHIP IN TURBULENT TIMES

Why Stakeholders Are Your Greatest Assets ...
in Good Times and Bad

MIKE BARGER

JetBlue Airways Co-founder and Former Navy TOPGUN Chief Instructor

SILVER TREE
PUBLISHING

Editing by:
Kate Colbert

Cover design and typesetting by:
Courtney Hudson

Proofreading by:
Gwendolyn Blanc

First edition, March 2021

ISBN: 978-1-948238-35-9

Library of Congress Control Number: 2021902738

Created in the United States of America

DEDICATION

For Anne, my inspiration and the love of my life.

For Mom, who suggested that military service just might be the start of something wonderful.

For Amanda, Joseph, Brendan, Hannah, Kate, and Sam, who are just beginning to appreciate the wonderful messiness of life.

And for high-stakes leaders everywhere who strive valiantly to navigate these turbulent times.

TABLE OF CONTENTS

INTRODUCTION

Turbulent times — we have all known them and some of us have known the privilege (and terror) of leading people and organizations through them. Crisis leadership is not for the faint of heart nor the uninitiated, and it's certainly not for the unprepared. Perhaps this book will be *your* initiation to organizational crisis. Or perhaps you are already battle-weary from turbulent times, and this book will serve as a refresher of what can and will go wrong ... and a dose of new perspective as you prepare for the next disruption, crisis, or scandal. The truth is that significant organizational disruptions have become increasingly common in today's fast-moving, constantly evolving business environment. Regardless of your industry or the size of your organization — whether you lead inside a Fortune 1000 company, a university, a nonprofit organization, a small business, or a start-up — challenges lie ahead, and the better you prepare, the better you (and your stakeholders) will fare.

> Crisis leadership is not for the faint of heart nor the uninitiated, and it's certainly not for the unprepared.

Why Take the Time to Read This Book?

The answer is simple. Organizational crisis is "the new normal." I wrote this book in 2020 and released it in March 2021, nearly a year to the day from the moment the global coronavirus pandemic was declared by the World Health Organization. Whether you are reading this book while the pandemic still rages on or have picked it up several years hence, you know that 2020 was a remarkably challenging year — for everyone. It changed us, it taught us, it inspired us, and sometimes it took us to our breaking points ... personally and professionally. Businesses shuttered, balance sheets turned red, leaders stepped up and stepped down, millions of workers lost their jobs. Some of us survived, and some even thrived. But no one was left untouched by the lessons.

How would you rate the effectiveness of the leadership you witnessed or personally experienced during 2020 — an incredible and unprecedented year? While I saw a few shining examples of exceptional leadership, I saw many more examples of horrific leadership failures or non-existent leadership when people and communities desperately needed leaders to show them the way, do the right thing, and provide stability and hope. We were all looking to leaders in businesses, governments, nonprofits, and communities to see us through a painful era. Some of us were led and inspired, and others were let down.

Reflecting on my own pandemic observations, I believe that poor leadership was either a result of an *unwillingness* to step up and lead or an *inability* to do so. My purpose in writing this book is to help you with the latter and, in doing so, perhaps I can help you build some confidence to address the former. The evidence tells us that crisis leadership — what I call *high-stakes leadership* — is difficult and rare. But it can be done well and it can be prepared for, by those who are willing and able. We simply cannot afford to wait and learn from our experience in the next major crisis. *The time to prepare is now.*

- -

> Crisis leadership — what I call *high-stakes leadership* —
> is difficult and rare. But it can be done well and it can be
> prepared for, by those who are willing and able. We simply
> cannot afford to wait and learn from our experience in
> the next major crisis. *The time to prepare is now.*

- -

What to Expect from This Book

I wrote this book for you — for the developing or veteran leader   so you can more effectively navigate the challenges of significant organizational disruptions. In the pages that follow, you will learn how to become a more effective crisis leader. Regardless of your current organizational role, the extent of your leadership experience, the size of your team, or the number of people directly reporting to you (even if this number is zero), this book will help you understand the best way to prepare for, deal with, and recover from a crisis. You will also quickly discover that many of the steps necessary to effectively lead through a crisis are the same steps necessary to run a thriving business. So, taking the time to read this book will not only prepare you for the inevitable crisis that will impact your organization, it will also help you build and run a better company, even in the best of times.

Ultimately, this book is about people and our interactions with them — people who depend on us and the organizations we lead to make their lives better. These are people who need us to be at the top of our leadership game, particularly when times are tough, because they have a tangible stake in our performance. Accordingly, we will spend a great deal of our journey together thoroughly exploring what has been termed the *stakeholder theory of management* — a leadership philosophy that emphasizes an organization's relationships with those who are counting on its success. Along the way, we will discover how and why an understanding of these *stakeholder perspectives* — not just our own or those of our leadership team — can inform and dramatically improve a leader's response to events that threaten an organization's very survival. In fact, the subtitle of this book (*Why Stakeholders Are Your Greatest Assets … in Good Times and Bad*) underscores the extent to which our relationships with our stakeholders are so vitally important — before, during, and after a crisis.

Unfortunately, for many reasons we will examine together, we are going to occasionally let our stakeholders down by failing to meet their expectations or perhaps even causing them harm. When we do, we are going to have to take extraordinary steps to recover not just their business, but their confidence, their trust, their loyalty. This is why much of this book will also help you develop an improved capacity for individual *and* organizational resilience, which we will define as the ability to anticipate potential threats;

to cope effectively with adverse events when they occur; and to adapt to changing conditions to ensure a viable path forward for yourself, your team, your organization, *and* your stakeholders.

Now is the time to develop an improved capacity for individual and organizational resilience, which we will define as the ability to anticipate potential threats; to cope effectively with adverse events when they occur; and to adapt to changing conditions to ensure a viable path forward for yourself, your team, your organization, and your stakeholders.

As you begin to wonder if the book in front of you might be overly academic, let me assure you that our journey together will be remarkably practical. We won't examine stakeholder perspective and resilience as research constructs. We will explore them through dozens of examples that will all feel quite familiar — several of which probably impacted you and your family. During our explorations of these examples, our lessons will be informed by such topics as how stakeholders react to crises (Chapters 3, 4, 6, and 8); crisis varieties and options for appropriate responses (Chapter 9); the unique and challenging nature of the crisis environment, which makes high-stakes leadership so difficult (Chapters 1, 3, and 10); the fundamentals of effective crisis leadership (Chapters 4, 5, 6, 11, and 12); and how best to build a plan that can prepare you, your team, your organization, *and* your stakeholders for your next major crisis (Chapters 3, 9, and 12) — which, in today's world, is not an "if" but a "when."

Who Am I to Write This Book?

That's a question that business-leaders-turned-business-authors, like me, ask ourselves when we first put pen to paper or fingertips to keyboard, hoping to pass along meaningful insights to our contemporaries and to future generations. It's also a question you might be wondering as you look to invest your time in reading this book (for which I am humbled and grateful). I wrote this book for you because I have some unique perspectives to offer on this topic and some stories that are both instructive and entertaining. And when it comes to leading during turbulent times, I have "been there and done that," as they say.

Over my professional career, I have spent a great deal of time leading teams through particularly challenging circumstances. After completing my undergraduate degree at the University of Michigan back in the mid-1980s, I spent 13 years as a flight instructor in the United States Navy, flying and teaching in the F/A-18 Hornet. I even had the privilege of serving as the lead instructor pilot at the Navy Fighter Weapons School, better known as TOPGUN, for a period of time. The high-speed, high-pressure nature of military fighter aviation offered some of the most complex environments you can imagine, but they also provided some great opportunities to develop resilience — to experiment with new and innovative tactics, to constantly look for better ways to execute, and, perhaps most importantly, to analyze and learn from mistakes.

As it turns out, combat aviation and organizational crisis leadership have quite a bit in common: no two scenarios are exactly the same, there is never enough information to make perfect decisions, and the participants engaged in the scenario rarely behave as you would expect. With regard to these similarities, I am reminded of a military axiom that has served me well over the years — "No plan withstands contact with the enemy." I have found that notion quite useful in crisis leadership as it has helped remind me to tell my team that, "Overcoming these challenges is going to be hard. Along the way, we're not going to have all of the answers, and we're going to run into some situations that we didn't expect. So, let's keep our objective in mind and do our best to keep moving forward."

> As it turns out, combat aviation and organizational crisis leadership have quite a bit in common: no two scenarios are exactly the same, there is never enough information to make perfect decisions, and the participants engaged in the scenario rarely behave as you would expect.

After more than a decade in the Navy, I joined a small group of experienced airline executives, including my brother Dave — who had been a senior leader at Continental Airlines for many years — and started an airline that we named JetBlue Airways. I suspect you have heard of it, and I hope you have had the pleasure of being a passenger aboard a JetBlue plane at least once. Over my 13 years with JetBlue, I held many roles and led in various ways. I was our senior pilot; I launched and led the corporate training and development department — what we called JetBlue University; and I ran our strategy office and headed up all flight and maintenance operations for the company. During my time as a co-founder and executive at JetBlue, I learned a lot about stakeholders and resilience, and I saw (hundreds, if not thousands of times) that a plan rarely withstands contact with anyone.

As an executive at JetBlue, I experienced dozens of crises. What do I think are the chances that you will also find yourself, in the not-too-distant future, as part of a leadership team dealing with a crisis of your own? I believe the odds are 1 in 1. It *will* happen. When it does, will you be ready? Could it be that this next crisis will offer you the greatest opportunity imaginable to play a critical role in the future of your business? I think it just might. So, let's take peek around the corner and learn from others who have been in the danger zone before you as we examine a vast collection of practices, strategies, and people-focused commitments that will help you weather whatever storms await. If you are looking for ways to become a more effective high-stakes leader, this book is a great place to start.

I applaud your commitment to exploring a topic that is exciting, daunting, and almost impossible to master. But I am absolutely certain that with some time and effort, you can develop an exceptional set of crisis-leadership tools that are not only customized to your own style, your strengths, your role, and your industry, but that are ready to deploy the instant they are needed. I believe you'll discover during our time together that while high-stakes leadership inherently involves situations that could (and perhaps will) go horribly wrong, the benefits of being effectively prepared for these challenging scenarios will make your personal journey feel well worth the effort. You will find that opportunities to lead people and organizations through their most difficult and pivotal moments will bring with them a great sense of achievement, pride, and satisfaction.

High-stakes leadership in turbulent times is a topic that is exciting, daunting, and almost impossible to master. But I am absolutely certain that with some time and effort, you can develop an exceptional set of crisis-leadership tools that are not only customized to your own style, your strengths, your role, and your industry, but that are ready to deploy the instant they are needed.

Welcome to *High-Stakes Leadership in Turbulent Times: Why Stakeholders Are Your Greatest Assets … in Good Times and Bad.* Let's get started.

01

A CHANGING WORLD
The Perfect Breeding Ground for Crisis

High-stakes leadership is about leading in times of crisis — when the interests of many are threatened, when the potential for significant loss is great, when there is no clear path to resolution, and when the need for leadership is greatest.

High-stakes leadership is about leading in times of crisis — when the interests of many are threatened, when the potential for significant loss is great, when there is no clear path to resolution, and when the need for leadership is greatest.

Throughout this book, you will discover why there are few more challenging environments for a leader than navigating the turbulent and dangerous waters of an organizational crisis. As you read, you will not only learn why high-stakes leadership is so incredibly difficult and challenging, but you will learn many practical skills to prepare for these situations and to more effectively manage them when they appear.

How can I be so certain that you will be called to face some sort of team, unit, or organizational crisis? Because we live and operate businesses in a world where the pace of change is accelerating, where advances in technology are happening faster than ever before, where customer expectations are changing more quickly than businesses can respond, where a nearly infinite supply of information is available at the click of a button, and where competitive pressures often force businesses to launch new products and services before they are 100% complete. This is the new normal.

Thriving in the VUCA World

The business environment of today can be difficult to describe. Perhaps the best way to do so is with a term that was introduced by leaders of the United States Army back in the early 1990s to describe the battlefield of the 21st century — a battlefield where decision-making would be immensely challenging due to the nature of the environment in which those decisions had to be made and then executed. The term used was VUCA — an acronym for the four unique but related characteristics of all future combat environments that military leaders should expect to encounter:

- Volatile
- Uncertain
- Complex
- Ambiguous

As a business leader in the 21st century, you will be faced with these same characteristics on the battlefield of competition. Today, we all lead in volatile, uncertain, complex, and ambiguous environments.

Why is this important in the context of this book? Because the VUCA environment in which you live and work has become the perfect breeding ground for organizational crisis. So much so, in fact, that business leaders can no longer afford to think about a crisis as a rare, once-in-a-lifetime event. Now, and going forward, a crisis at some scale is no longer an "if" but a "when." The combination of the new business environment and the evolving intensity of competition for smarter, savvier, better informed, and more demanding customers requires leaders to be ready for the inevitable day when some aspect of the business goes sideways in a major way. When it does, exceptional high-stakes leadership will be required.

- -

The VUCA environment in which you live and work has become the perfect breeding ground for organizational crisis.

- -

What is it about the VUCA environment that is creating such challenges for combat decision-making and, similarly, is increasing the likelihood of crises for business leaders? Consider each characteristic of the VUCA environment and the challenges it creates for you and your business.

The business environment is *volatile*. Things are changing continuously. As we see daily in the news, there seems to be no limit to the possible impact of seemingly minor events or decisions or actions. When a public figure makes a statement or does something unique, social media erupts with charged responses both in support of and opposed to the act. In a business context, our markets seem to fluctuate wildly, sometimes based on changes in fundamentals and other times based purely on emotion. Commodities markets are demonstrating volatility unlike any other time in recent history, impacting our ability to predict and manage the cost of our materials and their availability. Supply chains — whose effectiveness and efficiency have become such vital elements of our business processes — can implode in an instant, effectively bringing production, distribution, or delivery to an immediate halt. Severe weather systems, international tension, and now, global pandemics, headline the inventory of factors that create volatility for business leaders around the world. This volatility has become a primary cause of many business crises.

The business environment is *uncertain*. More than ever, we live in an environment that offers a great deal of uncertainty. It has become much more difficult to accurately make predictions about the future. What we knew for sure yesterday may not be true today and has a better chance of not being true tomorrow. Goods and services that our customers loved yesterday — offerings that have served as the cornerstones of our brands — are being copied, improved, produced at lower cost, and delivered more quickly by competitors. Add to this that now, more than ever before, our competition can come from anywhere in the world. The products, services, trends, and substitutions that can put you out of business aren't just threats from down the street or across town (consider, for example, how Amazon put so many independent, local bookstores out of business). So, our threat-sensing radars must be kept at their highest settings and our minds have to be open to the full extent of what might occur. As our ability to make accurate predictions about the future declines, we will find ourselves making decisions that are less reliable and, therefore, less likely to produce the outcomes that we expect. As our decisions become less reliable, both the likelihood and the scale of our miscalculations will increase. Unfortunately, with greater levels of miscalculation comes a greater likelihood of crisis.

It has become much more difficult to accurately make predictions about the future. What we knew for sure yesterday may not be true today and has a better chance of not being true tomorrow.

The business environment is *complex.* In all aspects of our businesses, we see increasing levels of complexity. Where we were once able to clearly identify how and why individual components of a system functioned and contributed to the greater whole, increasing levels of complexity have made these connections almost impossible to see (much less understand or control). An entire field of study — systems engineering — has evolved to help us better understand component interactions within a system, because in many of our increasingly complex business processes, the system itself has as much of an impact on the contribution of a component as the component does on the system. These increases in complexity have made it exponentially more difficult for high-stakes leaders to truly understand a situation or to be able to predict the impact of the decisions they are asked to make within it. Because of this, even seemingly obvious decisions can produce unintended consequences that can rapidly deteriorate and manifest a crisis.

In many of our increasingly complex business processes, the system itself has as much of an impact on the contribution of a component as the component does on the system.

The business environment is *ambiguous*. Are vitamins good or bad for you? Is it worth investing in solar power for your home? Has social media been a benefit or a liability for society as a whole? For each of these questions, and so many more, you can easily find convincing but contradictory information and opinion. Throughout the summer of 2020, the COVID-19 pandemic raised many questions about the appropriate steps to take in support of *human lives*, on the one hand, and the health of local and national *economies* on the other. Is one or the other more important? The practical reality is that leaning too much toward one side or the other of this tension could have catastrophic long-term results. The broad availability of unfiltered information has created a situation where, some would argue, it has become increasingly difficult to identify clear solutions to our planet's most challenging problems.

What we *do* know about conducting business in a VUCA environment is that things can go wrong and, in doing so, can create significant risks and challenges for high-stakes leaders and those they serve. We have seen situations where things have gone wrong in an instant:

1   Rob McLean, "A Hacker Gained Access to 100 Million Capital One Credit Card Applications and Accounts," CNN.com (July 30, 2019; accessed July 11, 2020), https://www.cnn.com/2019/07/29/business/capital-one-data-breach/index.html.

2   Evan Perez, Jeremy Herb, Geneva Sands and Priscilla Alvarez.,"Law Enforcement Missed Key Signs Ahead of Riot on US Capitol," CNN.com (January 7, 2021; accessed March 3, 2021), https://www.cnn.com/2021/01/07/politics/police-capitol-riots-response/index.html.

3   Shep Hyken, "Nike: A Real-Time Lesson In Crisis Management," Forbes.com (February 22, 2019; accessed July 11, 2020), https://www.forbes.com/sites/shephyken/2019/02/22/nike-a-real-time-lesson-in-crisis-management/#55a0b48e2206.

And we have seen situations where things have gone wrong over time:

A common lesson from every crisis, irrespective of its onset rate, is that the requirement for exceptional leadership will be imperative. In response to our increasingly VUCA world, there has never been a more important time for a vast supply of competent, capable, and well-prepared high-stakes leaders.

There has never been a more important time for a vast supply of competent, capable, and well-prepared high-stakes leaders.

The Implications of COVID-19 on Your Reading of This Book

The COVID-19 pandemic has become one of the most challenging global crises in the history of our humankind. I offer this observation not because the consequences of the pandemic have been the most devastating ever

---

4   Josh Sanburn, "The Poisoning of an American City." *Time*, Vol. 187 (February 1, 2016), https://time.com/magazine/us/4188304/february-1st-2016-vol-187-no-3-u-s/.

5   Jef Feeley, "J&J's Oklahoma Opioid Fight May Signal Drug Industry Liability," Bloomberg.com (August 26, 2019; accessed July 11, 2020), https://www.bloomberg.com/news/articles/2019-08-26/j-j-s-oklahoma-opioid-fight-may-signal-drug-industry-liability.

6   Constance Grady, "R. Kelly's Music Label Has Reportedly Dropped Him," Vox.com (January 18, 2019; accessed July 11, 2020), https://www.vox.com/culture/2019/1/18/18188618/r-kelly-sony-music-rca-records-dropped-mute.

recorded (although far too many lost their lives to this terrible virus — more than 2.4 million deaths as of the time this book went to press) nor simply because of its scope (which clearly became a global concern within weeks of the very first case). COVID-19 developed into one of the most challenging global crises in history because it placed a spotlight on the effectiveness of our leaders.

Around the world, people watched, with great interest, government leaders, business and community leaders, and even leaders of families as they assessed the situation, considered the advice of trusted advisors, made decisions, implemented actions based on those decisions, and then were forced to deal with the consequences of their choices. In most cases, these leaders were not doing this in the privacy of their own homes; their actions were very public. The blessing and curse of our ability to leverage technology for vast and rapid communication has created a reality where the decisions made by leaders at any level can be broadcast, analyzed, scrutinized, spun, and manipulated quickly and consequentially to audiences of millions. But even more importantly, the COVID-19 pandemic highlighted the need for improved crisis readiness — for better ways of planning for crisis, for better ways of managing a crisis, and for better ways of communicating during a crisis. The coronavirus pandemic left us clamoring for better high-stakes leadership. COVID-19 tested our readiness for a global healthcare threat and taught us that unprepared, uninformed, and incompetent high-stakes leadership is lethal. Clearly, we have so much more to learn.

- -

COVID-19 developed into one of the most challenging global crises in history because it placed a spotlight on the effectiveness of our leaders; it tested our readiness for a global healthcare threat and taught us that unprepared, uninformed, and incompetent high-stakes leadership can be lethal.

- -

As you begin your exploration of the principles and suggestions in this book, you may find it helpful to keep in mind something that all of us experienced during the COVID-19 crisis. We are all naturally wired for self-preservation; our instincts and physiology have developed over millions of years to make sure that we are always focused first and foremost on protecting ourselves from threats. Because of this, it's extremely difficult for us to recognize and remember that our thoughts and deeds in response to threats can have a significant impact those around us — those who could benefit from our support and those who may actually need our help to navigate these complex and uncertain times.

Adults around the world during the pandemic (and even many yet to reach adulthood, who also endured significant life disruptions during the outbreak) spent an extraordinary amount of time thinking about the many ways that the COVID-19 crisis impacted us as individuals. This is how we *all* tend to respond to crises when they appear. "What does this mean for *me*?" "How does this impact *me*?" Think about how you processed the plethora of information, guidance, and regulation directed at you in what seemed like a continuous heavy stream. Did you feel as though you knew how to interpret this information and guidance? Did you know what to do as a result? Even as an individual — as a single member of a community — it was and will continue to be challenging to know how to deal with the COVID-19 pandemic going forward. New information is constantly changing our attitudes and behaviors, and emotional fatigue is challenging our judgment. As we finalize the edits of this book, I am a pilot — and an airline industry insider — who remains hesitant to fly because I haven't yet been able to get a SARS-CoV-2 vaccine. If you are or were feeling overwhelmed, I am right there with you. Times like these can be very, very difficult to navigate.

So what do these challenges we have as *individuals* tell us about the critical need for crisis leadership in organizations and institutions? I believe the lesson is that because we are hard-wired to serve our own interests during a crisis, we must purposefully and deliberately develop our capacity to also serve others. I'm not suggesting that taking care of ourselves first during a crisis is wrong. Quite the contrary. If we're not operating at 100%, our leadership effectiveness will suffer. What I'm suggesting here is that we must do our best to look beyond our own self-interests because, in any crisis, we have the opportunity — sometimes the responsibility — to serve others. If we can project the way we feel about our own concerns on those around us, we will have a sense of what they might need from us. This, I will argue throughout the book, *is* the purpose of leadership — the ability to understand, appreciate, and respond to the needs of those who depend on or could benefit from actions that *you* could take with *their* interests in mind — actions that *you* could take that would benefit *others*.

In any crisis, we have the opportunity — sometimes the responsibility — to serve others. This *is* the purpose of leadership — the ability to understand, appreciate, and respond to the needs of those who depend on or could benefit from actions that *you* could take with *their* interests in mind — actions that *you* could take that would benefit *others*.

You will certainly be counting on yourself to make it through the next crisis. Will *others* be able to count on you as well? Hopefully, with what you are about to learn in this book, they will indeed.

02

DEEPWATER HORIZON
Setting the Stage for Exploration of High-Stakes Leadership

Image Credit: US Coast Guard, Wikimedia Commons

On April 20, 2010, a surge of natural gas blasted through the concrete oil well core of the Deepwater Horizon (DH) drilling platform, positioned on the ocean's surface some 5,000 meters above, about 41 miles off the coast of Louisiana in the United States' Gulf of Mexico. The gas that passed through the fractured core traveled up the Deepwater rig's riser to the platform where it ignited and exploded, causing 11 deaths and 17 injuries. The resulting oil spill took several months to fully contain, and forensic analysts believe that almost 210 million gallons (five million barrels) of oil was released into the Gulf, devastating the ecosystem, creating a public relations nightmare, and all at a cost of almost $62 billion for the responsible company.

For most readers, this story will ring a bell — maybe even a loud one. But do you remember the name of the company responsible for Deepwater Horizon? Would you consider this a crisis for BP? They were the oil and gas company responsible for operating the Macondo Prospect, where the disaster occurred. I think it is fair to categorize this event as a crisis, and a big one at that. Do you remember who was actually managing the work on the platform (i.e., the Deepwater Horizon drilling rig)? It was not BP. It was a company called Transocean. Was Deepwater Horizon a crisis for Transocean? Of course it was. And bonus points if you know who actually manufactured the DH platform — it was the heavy engineering arm of Hyundai. Was DH a crisis for them as well? If something you manufactured is the source of a raging fire and getting attention from every media outlet on the planet, then yes, this is a crisis. BP, Transocean, Hyundai — all managing a disaster soon known to the masses as simply the "Deepwater Horizon oil spill." Why call out these three companies in this example? Because it serves as a useful illustration of the challenges crisis leaders can have when trying to determine who has been impacted by a critical event. In the case of DH, most people associate the crisis with BP. Very few, however, realize how challenging this event was for Transocean and Hyundai as well.

I'm not about to suggest that crises must be this visually dramatic for them to qualify as the kinds of disruptions that could determine the future of a company. In fact, some crises are almost imperceptible to anyone other than the internal teams or people attempting to manage them. But regardless of their size, scope, duration, onset rate, or long-term impact, crises threaten the future of any business that finds itself amid one, and they require the full attention of the leadership team, often for an extended period of time. As we dig deeper into the art and science (and even politics) of crisis management in this book, we'll explore why crises can be so devastating and so challenging to manage.

Regardless of their size, scope, duration, onset rate, or
long-term impact, crises threaten the future of any business
that finds itself amid one, and they require the full attention of
the leadership team, often for an extended period of time.

The Far-Reaching Implications of a Crisis

A core lesson that I will reiterate frequently during our journey together is that crisis situations are not only of vital concern to the businesses going through them, but to everyone around them as well. A crisis produces outcomes that are likely to have significant and material impact on the lives and well-being of a broad range of different people, inside and outside of the organization that owns the crisis. Therefore, I will do my best in the pages that follow to build a case for high-stakes leadership as a people-centric endeavor. It is my firm belief that much of crisis leadership is about understanding and engaging with people whose interests are threatened by the potential outcomes of a crisis at hand. We will refer to these people as stakeholders and I will do my very best to help you see why caring for stakeholders is so important. Together, we will explore how to provide the leadership necessary to effectively care for *everyone* impacted by a crisis. If it would be helpful to have a pithy phrase to remind you of our goal in this regard: Love your stakeholders, in good times and in bad. If you can embrace this notion, you'll be heading down the right path.

During my 35+ years in leadership positions helping guide organizations through crises, I can tell you what you will *see* in a crisis. Unpredictable as they may be, they evolve somewhat formulaically:

First, during a crisis, everyone involved – *all* impacted stakeholders – will look to organizational leaders for tangible evidence of leadership.

- *Who is in charge?*
- *What actions are they taking?*

- *How serious is the trouble we are in?*

Second, these stakeholders want and need leaders who they can believe in.

- *Will everything be OK?*
- *Will the company survive?*
- *Will I still get the product or service or value that I expected?*
- *Will I still have a job?*

And third, as high-stakes leadership is about addressing stakeholder concerns and fears as effectively as possible, the very best way to gain or regain trust is to truly understand and appreciate each stakeholder's perspective. Be asking yourself:

- *How do the perspectives of each stakeholder group line up with ours as a leadership team? Where do our expectations and concerns diverge?*
- *How can we make decisions for the "greater good" — serving all of us, as best we can?*

Throughout this book, we will explore how engaging with these stakeholders should become a priority for enterprise leaders. Why and how should they be engaged, in good times and bad? What will they want to hear? How should we, as enterprise leaders, engage each of them in a way that delivers the information they need and establishes or restores their trust in our ability to lead? While this might sound somewhat common-sensical, far too many business leaders discover that they should have given these questions much more thought prior to finding themselves into the midst of a major crisis.

Looking back at the Deepwater Horizon crisis, what stakeholder groups do you think were impacted by the crisis? What distinct groups of people can you think of that had specific and unique interests in the outcomes of the crisis? Certainly, the executive teams of BP, Transocean, and Hyundai — they were all completely engaged in the situation. What do you think they were most concerned about?

How about the *employees* of these organizations? What were they most concerned about? Do you think that their concerns were identical to those of the executive teams? Or were they slightly or even vastly different?

Now consider the customers of these companies — and their investors, government regulators, the media, and their competitors. If you give these groups some thought, you will see that while their interests might have overlapped to some extent, they were clearly not the same. Some members of these groups were concerned about their jobs. Others were concerned about their reputations or even legal action. Yet others were wondering whether they should look elsewhere for the fuel they would normally have bought from BP for their car. The differences in the interests and concerns of various stakeholders will serve as the foundation of this book. Attending to those interests, I believe, is the primary responsibility of a high-stakes leader.

The good news is that stakeholder management isn't an abstract or academic exercise. If leaders appropriately prioritize their attention and resources, they can better understand the desires and concerns of all stakeholders with an interest in their organization. And this improved understanding will help them lead a better business. The relationships that leaders and brands build and maintain with their stakeholders (during good times) can help those leaders identify opportunities for improvement when the stakes are low; and, as luck would have it, those relationships provide a foundation of trust and open communication when things are *not* going so well. These stakeholder relationships can, if we're strategic and compassionate and disciplined, actually improve our capacity for resilience.

Crisis Definition and Expectation Management

Our brief exploration of the Deepwater Horizon crisis gave us an opportunity to appreciate the challenges of understanding the full spectrum of stakeholders who could be impacted by a crisis. Without exception, the ability to identify and engage stakeholders during a crisis is one of the most important and valuable skills a high-stakes leader can possess. The reason for this can be drawn from the very definition of a crisis, which can tell crisis leaders a great deal about the purpose of stakeholder engagement.

There are many definitional variations of the term "crisis." For high-stakes leaders, the following definition can be particularly informative:

CRISIS — *noun* — cri·sis \ krī-səs \: an unstable or crucial time (or state of affairs) in which a decisive change is impending, especially one with the distinct possibility of a highly undesirable outcome

Two crucial messages can be taken from this definition. The first is that the situation at hand — the crisis — is going to create an environment that will not be pleasant for anyone involved. Both inside and outside the organization, there will be a growing sense of anxiety that has the potential to last for an extended period. For those impacted by the events as they run their course, there will be increasing concern about how the crisis will lead to change — about how things will be different in the wake of the catastrophe. This foreboding sense of change for the worse will make it nearly impossible for members of the organization to do anything other than worry about what the future may bring. *Things will be different* — and people decidedly do *not* like the thought of things being different — particularly when it's impossible to predict with confidence what lies ahead. "What will things look like once this is all over?" they will wonder. "I have a sense that things will be different, very different."

> For those impacted by the events as they run their course, there
> will be increasing concern about how the crisis will lead to
> change — about how things will be different in the wake of the
> catastrophe. This foreboding sense of change for the worse will
> make it nearly impossible for members of the organization to do
> anything other than worry about what the future may bring.

The second key message from this definition is the strong possibility that the future will not only be different, but that it will also be worse. Nobody likes the idea of uncertainty in the days ahead. We all know that we can't predict the future, but we do find a certain degree of comfort in believing that today will probably be quite similar to yesterday. There is a calming sense of predictability in the notion that "I made it through yesterday, so I should be able to make it through today." But the crisis environment removes this element of predictability. There's no calming sense of normalcy. The ongoing crisis tells us that not only will we be unable to confidently predict how today or tomorrow will play out, but it's also quite likely that however it plays out, it won't be good.

For all stakeholders impacted by a crisis — not just those inside an organization, but all stakeholders, inside and out — a crisis creates anxiety about the unpredictability of the future. It also raises questions about who has their hands on the wheel and is going to provide leadership. Therefore, high-stakes leaders must understand and remember the following universal truths

Three Universal Truths About Stakeholder Expectations During a Crisis

1. In a crisis, stakeholders will look to leaders for tangible evidence of leadership.

2. Stakeholders want and need leaders they can believe in.

3. While stakeholders don't expect their leaders to be perfect or omni-scient, they do expect them to be visible, courageous, and committed to the best possible path forward ... with a sense of urgency.

Let's take a moment to consider each of these truths.

In a crisis, stakeholders will look to leaders for tangible evidence of leadership. Because stakeholders will be anxious about the uncertainty and likelihood of an undesirable outcome, they will want to see that someone, or some team, has stepped up to lead. Of course, they will hope that this leader or leadership team will immediately resolve the issue and that things can quickly return to normal. But they will recognize that the developing situation will take a while to resolve. Given this recognition, they will want to see tangible evidence that leadership is taking place.

When they look, stakeholders want and need leaders who they can believe in. In addition to being able to identify evidence of leadership, stakeholders will want and need to see leaders who are demonstrating actions that appear worthy of their trust. The situation has created tension and anxiety. People are concerned about their lack of control and the unpredictability of the future. They don't simply want to see leaders taking random action; they want to see leaders taking action that demonstrates an appreciation for *their* specific interests. Stakeholders want and need to believe that crisis leaders understand how the situation is impacting them, and they want some assurances that their interests are being served through the organization's actions.

***While stakeholders don't expect their leaders to be perfect or omniscient,
they do expect them to be visible, courageous, and committed to the best
possible path forward ... with a sense of urgency.*** High-stakes leaders
must understand that while some stakeholders will behave irrationally
during a crisis, most will recognize that fully resolving a crisis takes time (in
some cases, a great deal of time). While stakeholders will *hope* for miracle
solutions, they will *expect* steady progress. Stakeholders would *prefer* crisis
leaders to be perfect and all-knowing, but they know, at the end of the day,
that we are all human beings, doing our best to serve a wide variety of interests. High-stakes leaders should recognize, however, that all these "reasonable" expectations must be met with reassuring messages and action — then
reinforced frequently to preserve stakeholder confidence. Even the most
rational, patient stakeholders will quickly revise their expectations if they
aren't seeing leaders stepping up, taking charge of the situation, and clearly
demonstrating a commitment to the best possible path forward.

Most stakeholders recognize that fully resolving
a crisis takes time. So while they will *hope* for miracle
solutions, they will *expect* steady progress.

These universal truths of stakeholder expectations during a crisis are useful
concepts for every high-stakes leader to remember. Crisis leadership is hard.
Situations will be tense, anxious, unpredictable, and often lengthy. To make
the best of these very challenging times, leaders must be willing and able to
step up and provide tangible leadership, worthy of stakeholder trust, with
a clear commitment to everyone's best interests.

03

PERSPECTIVE MATTERS
Using Different Vantage Points to Inform Your Leadership Priorities

In a crisis, perspective matters.

When we considered the Deepwater Horizon crisis, I raised some questions about the broad reach of the situation. How would executives at BP, Transocean, and Hyundai Heavy Engineering be viewing this crisis? As you would expect, the incident became their primary focus — not for days, but for months. These leaders had one very important perspective on the crisis, but it was not the only perspective that mattered.

We know from research and, for that matter, from our own experiences, that leadership teams of organizations must respond to other stakeholders — other perspectives — looking to leadership for information, for guidance, and for some level of assurance that their interests will be protected. These concerns can be significant and they will require attention — often immediate and sometimes nearly continuous attention — for the duration of a critical situation.

Another important aspect of crisis leadership is the challenge leaders will face because of the limited time and resources at their disposal during a crisis. Given limited time and resources, how will leaders be able to address the needs of all stakeholders impacted by a crisis? Sometimes, there literally aren't enough hours in the day, people on your team, or money in the bank to do everything you know you ought to do (e.g., the phone calls, the emails, the press conferences, the private meetings). To effectively navigate a crisis, leaders will *eventually* have to engage all their stakeholder groups, but with limited time, especially in the early stages of a crisis, leaders have to make difficult tradeoffs, choosing which stakeholders to address first — and how to address them — knowing that some will receive immediate attention and others will simply become lower priorities.

How can crisis leaders navigate this challenge? This is where some pre-planning can be really helpful. Planning for certain categories of crisis can actually help high-stakes leaders identify which stakeholder groups are most likely to be impacted by certain scenarios. But research tells us that very few organizations bother to do this planning. So, to give you a bit of experience in the identification of key stakeholder groups impacted by different types of crises, we're going to conduct a short exercise. Over the next few pages, I would like you to consider four different actual crisis situations, conduct a quick assessment about the nature of the crisis, and determine which stakeholder groups you would consider to be the highest priorities for engagement.

Real-World Crises, Ripe for Your Monday-Morning Quarterbacking

When considering the scenarios that follow — most of which will be familiar to you — I'd like you to think about a few key questions for each.

1. First, **does the event fit our definition of crisis?** ("An unstable or crucial time or state of affairs in which a decisive change is impending — especially a change with the distinct possibility of a highly undesirable outcome.") If so, then the event should be worthy of executive time and energy.

2. Second, **what stakeholder group(s) will be impacted to a significant degree by the event, and which stakeholder groups should the leadership team identify as "priority stakeholders?"** Once again, while

it is accurate to claim that *every* stakeholder group will be impacted to some degree by an organizational crisis and deserve your attention in some way and at some time, the reality is that certain crises will impact some stakeholder groups more significantly than others. Your job as a high-stakes leader will be to determine which of these groups require the greatest share of your time (and which deserve it now versus later).

3. A third question worthy of your consideration is: **What do these priority stakeholders want and need from me?** High-stakes leaders who can effectively answer and act on this third question are the true rock stars of crisis leadership.

Apply the three questions to the three scenarios that follow.

- - - - - - - - - - - - - - - - - -

Scenario 1

On April 9, 2017, after passengers were seated on United Express Flight 3411, scheduled to depart Chicago's O'Hare airport for Louisville, Kentucky, a United gate agent announced that four passengers would need to deplane to accommodate four higher-priority company employees. When nobody volunteered, the agent randomly selected four passengers for involuntary removal from the flight. Three of these passengers agreed to leave. The fourth selected passenger was 69-year-old Dr. David Dao, an Asian-American physician from Elizabethtown, Kentucky. When approached, he pleaded with the manager not to remove him and explained that, as a doctor, he could not miss his return flight home. His patients were waiting for him.

Well-known leadership expert Tom Peters has always referred to leadership as a liberal art — a soft skill about a leader's ability to engage with people. This, in my view, is the essence of crisis leadership. It *is* a liberal art, a soft skill. It's the ability to understand how groups and individuals are thinking and feeling, and the ability to address these thoughts and emotions in ways that build and restore trust.

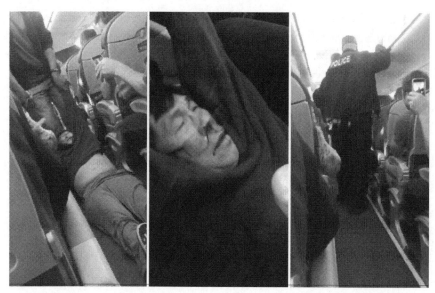

Image Credit: Jayse Anspach

Security officers from the Chicago Department of Aviation were called to forcibly remove Dr. Dao from the plane. In the process, they struck Dao's face against an armrest, then pulled him, apparently unconscious, by his arms along the aircraft aisle past rows of onlookers. Dr. Dao suffered a broken nose, lost two teeth, and was treated at a local hospital for a concussion. As the event took place, passengers on the flight recorded the extraction on their smartphone cameras. The videos were then widely circulated on social media.

The next day, United CEO Oscar Munoz issued a brief statement that justified the removal of Dr. Dao, underscoring the airline's right to "re-accommodate customers under certain conditions." He also released an internal message to United employees, commending the crew's actions. These statements were harshly criticized by the media and the public. Days later, Mr. Munoz released an additional statement apologizing to Dr. Dao and promising that such a traumatic and unnecessary situation would never happen again on a United flight.

Was this a crisis for United Airlines (UAL)? Absolutely. Some say that any media coverage is good media coverage, but in this case, it's hard to see how the saying could be true. This event did not play well for UAL. In fact, dragging a bloodied customer from the plane was only crisis number one for United. The subsequent public relations statements — which were poorly timed and executed — created a second crisis for the company.

Given what you know about the airline business (which may not be much, but that's OK for the sake of the exercise), which stakeholder groups would you expect to have been most significantly impacted by this event and most deserving of the company's attention? An argument could probably be made for any number of them (e.g., customers/passengers, investors, employees, media, public). But if you were forced to choose just one or two, which would you choose? Keep in mind that there is really no single "right" answer here. But in most crises, you will find that some groups are clearly impacted to a greater extent than others. Your ability to identify these will greatly help you focus your crisis leadership efforts.

In this case, I suggest that the *customer* group was arguably the most significantly impacted by this crisis. Customers — not just those on the flight but across the airline, if not across the entire airline sector — were apt to be outraged, disappointed, and even fearful of doing business with United in the wake of this event. If you were a leader at UAL, knowing that you couldn't turn back the clock and prevent Dr. Dao's trauma and the company scandal, what should have been done in response to these concerns? To win customers back? To regain their trust? We won't answer these questions here, but they are wonderfully illustrative of the types of difficult questions that every high-stakes leader must be prepared to address.

What would you say was the second-highest priority stakeholder group during this United crisis? You have many options to consider. You could imagine the *media* broadcasting the story and having great impact on consumer confidence in the company. Perhaps your next step as a leader should be to engage the media with a statement and a plan to make things right. There was also a great deal of mobile video produced by other passengers, and the bloodied face of Dr. Dao was horrific enough to generate lots of social media comments, reactions, and shares. Maybe a social media response should have been UAL's most appropriate next step. *Regulatory authorities* might also be a good guess as the second-highest priority group. Events like these can lead to both fines for the offending company and the possibility of new rules and regulations that could significantly impact the company and the entire sector (i.e., all airlines) going forward. Considering this, should United executives have proactively contacted their regulatory authorities even before the first news story aired? I would have.

How concerned do you think United's *investors* were about this crisis? In this case, I would expect investors to be extremely unhappy about the story. But as United's ability to grow and make money over the long-term would not likely be impacted much by this event, I wouldn't expect investors to demand immediate attention. (Fact check: UAL stock lost 2% early the following week, largely attributed to this event, but shares rebounded shortly thereafter.) Sure, they would eventually want to hear of any financial implications — particularly if the incident resulted in large fines or expensive lawsuits — but I wouldn't have reached out to investors before I engaged customers, regulators, and the media.

How would you have planned to communicate with UAL *employees* in the wake of this event? Should they have heard about this crisis immediately, or could leaders have waited on their internal communications while attending to other, higher-priority groups? In this case, employees were a priority for the CEO as they received one of the first official communications from the leadership team. Based on the message, they should have felt well-supported. Unfortunately for UAL, because communications were slow to reach other stakeholders, it appears that early efforts should have been directed elsewhere, perhaps simultaneously or in exchange for the immediate communication to employees.

What is the lesson here? For this particular crisis, while all stakeholders were very interested in how this situation would be resolved, company leaders should have addressed the needs of the customer, media, and regulator groups immediately to demonstrate their awareness of and concern for the crisis, to address causal factors and prevent a re-occurrence, and to begin their recovery efforts. Once these groups had been engaged, time could then have been dedicated to other groups. Suffice it to say, these were not great days for United Airlines.

- - - - - - - - - - - - - - - - -

Scenario 2

On August 19, 2016, Samsung officially launched the Galaxy Note 7 smartphone. It debuted to an eager marketplace with raving reviews

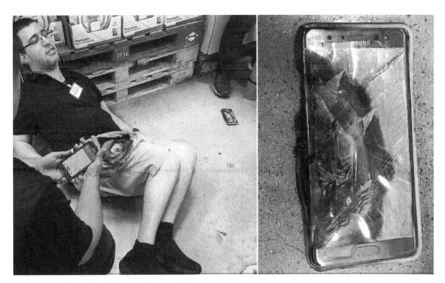

Image Credit: Kieth Pierro, Gold & Gold PA

and great demand. But by September 2, 2016, two weeks after the launch, Samsung suspended sales of the phone and announced an informal recall after reports alleging that manufacturing defects in the phones' batteries had caused some units to overheat to the extent that they were bursting into flames and exploding, on occasions, in customers' purses and pockets. During the informal recall period, Samsung was replacing faulty phones with like units, some of which were also catching fire. By October 10, Samsung recalled all Galaxy Note 7s and ceased production. Analysts reported that the financial impact of the product launch, recall, and termination was approximately $17B.

Was this a crisis for Samsung? Absolutely! Which stakeholder groups were impacted most significantly by this event? Again, there are many correct answers to this question, but which two would you argue were the most important to engage as quickly as possible? As with the UAL crisis, the first-priority group was probably Samsung mobile phone customers. Exploding devices are clearly a safety issue and images of melted phones are not good for consumer confidence. If you were a leader at Samsung, what could and should your team have done to regain the trust of this group?

What was the second-highest priority stakeholder group during the Galaxy Note 7 crisis? In this case, there is an argument to be made for the investor group. While employees, regulators, and the media will all need some attention as soon as is practical, the investor group would want to know Samsung's plans immediately. If this group was not engaged right away, it was possible that the financial markets would sour so significantly on the company that the resultant impact on market capitalization might be irrecoverable.

The lessons in this scenario? Once again, customers became a critical stakeholder group to engage as quickly as possible. Very shortly thereafter, investors and regulators would have been on my list of key groups to engage. It's also worth noting that while many people remember this situation and can generally attribute it to Samsung, there is typically a recollection that Samsung handled the crisis pretty well. This is a result, I believe, of Samsung's exceptionally rapid, transparent, and thorough response to customer concerns.

- - - - - - - - - - - - - - - - - -

Scenario 3

On April 12, 2018, two black gentlemen were sitting in a Philadelphia Starbucks waiting for a friend. They chose not to make a purchase yet, as many restaurant or café diners are apt to do while they wait for their entire party to arrive. Because they were sitting in the store and had not bought anything — yet — an employee asked them to leave. When the customers didn't leave, the police were summoned. The men were arrested and detained for several hours before they were released without being charged. News of this incident went public quickly. In fact, it went viral. Questions of racial bias were raised and the Starbucks brand was immediately under fire. Consumer advocacy groups stepped in quickly to use this bias incident to illustrate a larger problem that not only required, but demanded, attention. Starbucks was now under a global spotlight.

Was this a crisis for Starbucks? Yes, it was. Which stakeholder groups were impacted most significantly by this event? Do you think this is another example of customers being the top priority stakeholder group? Do you believe that customers around the world would stop purchasing their Venti Carmel Macchiatos if Starbucks didn't make things right immediately? Post-event analysis suggests that while customers did not support the way

Image Credit: Melissa DePino

the situation was handled, the event led to very little downward pressure on demand for Starbucks beverages.

So, if not customers, which stakeholder group *did* require immediate attention from Starbucks leadership? In this case, customer advocacy groups, which are non-governmental organizations (NGOs) but worth considering as a subset of the broader regulator group, should have been the priority. Which was the next-highest priority group? An argument can be made for the employee group, with communications about what happened, what the company expects of them, and how to behave if they ever believe individuals or groups in their stores are loitering rather than acting as true customers. The employees of this particular Starbucks location caused the scandal through their behaviors and words, and company employees — worldwide — were the only people who could restore customer confidence, improve race relations in their stores, and prevent a similar incident.

In this case, almost immediately, Howard Schultz, Starbucks' Chairman, stepped up and owned the issue. He assured everyone watching this event play out via the news media and social media that he was personally embarrassed and ashamed. He made it clear that what had happened was reprehensible and that the company was committed to making things right. Among the steps Starbucks took to do so was to shut down the entire company for the better part of a day on May 28 (just weeks later) to conduct racial bias training for 175,000 employees. This was training that would cost the company millions of dollars, but it would clearly send the message to the marketplace that this incident was an isolated one that Starbucks would not repeat. Today, this response is viewed by many as an exceptional case of doing the right thing in the face of a crisis.

Scenario 4

On October 29, 2018, a Lion Air Boeing 737 MAX passenger plane crashed after departing Jakarta, Indonesia, killing all 189 passengers and crew. Boeing's subsequent investigation was inconclusive, but their public response suggested two potential issues: with the angle-of-attack system (i.e., the system that helps pilots maintain a safe airspeed), as well as possible shortcomings in pilot training and experience.

The airline industry and the flying public hoped and assumed this tragedy was an isolated one. But less than five months later, on March 10, 2019, another 737 MAX aircraft operated by Ethiopian Airlines crashed six minutes after takeoff from Addis Ababa airport in Ethiopia, killing all 157 passengers and crew.

Image Credit: (From Top Left) Reuters/Stringer; Lion Air; Ethiopian Airlines; Associated Press

The very next day, on March 11, Ethiopian Airlines grounded all 737 MAX aircraft in its fleet. Later that day, the China Civil Aviation Administration grounded all 737 MAX aircraft operating in China. On March 12, the US Federal Aviation Administration stated that it had "no basis to order grounding the aircraft" in the United States and no data from other countries to justify such action. The next day, however, regulators in both Canada and the United States announced that they had received new information that supported the grounding of all 737 MAX aircraft.

By March 14, Boeing stock had lost 11% of its value. By March 23, the stock price had dropped 18%, which equated to approximately $40B in market value.

Was this a crisis for Boeing? Yes, in every sense of the word "crisis." Which stakeholder groups required immediate attention? In this scenario, it would be difficult to eliminate many from our typical list of candidates. Regulators were under as much scrutiny as Boeing, so they needed immediate engagement. Customers and investors were panicking as orders were being canceled and market capitalization was falling rapidly. Employees were concerned not only about the future of their jobs but were devastated by the lives lost to mechanical failure — the lives of co-workers who were the crews of the airplanes that crashed and the lives of the passengers they were entrusted to keep safe. The media was using their various channels for raising awareness of the crisis and most of the world was following the story. All of these stakeholders required attention at the earliest opportunity.

Perhaps you are wondering: "Why didn't you mention the families of those lost in the two crashes? Clearly, these would have been critically important stakeholders!" Yes, they were. In these cases, however, at least in the early stages of the two crises, these stakeholders would have been the responsibility of the respective airlines to support. Our focus here was on Boeing, the aircraft manufacturer, but we certainly could have explored these two crises from the perspectives of the airlines operating the fatal flights. They clearly had their hands full in the wake of both events. Given the dynamic here, it would be a worthwhile exercise for you to give this some thought. How would our Scenario 4 be different if we viewed these two crises from the perspective of the airlines? Furthermore, how would these airlines' crisis responses evolve as more was learned about Boeing's contributions to the fatal events? High-stakes can be immensely complex as well as challenging.

From these examples, you can begin to understand why it's vitally important to know your stakeholders: what they expect from their relationship with an organization and how those expectations are threatened when the organization is struggling through a crisis. An appreciation for stakeholder perspective in this way is perhaps the most valuable tool a high-stakes leader can have at hand.

It's vitally important to know your stakeholders: what they expect from their relationship with an organization and how those expectations are threatened when the organization is struggling through a crisis.

Crisis Happens! It's Not "If" But "When"

The nature of today's business environment is truly remarkable. The speed of business, driven largely by the ubiquity of technology-aided access to goods and services, has forced companies to accelerate business processes and product availability beyond traditional limits — all to secure "first access" to prospective customers. Meanwhile, there seems to be a shift away from offerings that are 100% ready for market to something closer to "good enough" to test customer response, get feedback, and iterate toward the next right answer. (Why this "good enough" go-to-market strategy has become so popular is debatable. Perhaps it's a result of changing customer expectations, the evolving practice of co-creation between businesses and their customers, or some combination of these phenomena.) This air of "fail fast, fail small, fail cheap, learn, and move on" is built into the fabric of many business sectors today — especially those providing offerings that don't have to be perfect when they enter the market. If yours is not one of these, perhaps it should be. If it is, how are you providing leadership to help navigate the turbulence that is produced by your "good enough" product or service strategy? In the end, a decision to "fail fast" is a decision to flirt with risk, and to invite disruption or crisis; we must be careful (and prepared for) what we wish for.

This evolution in today's business environment has increased our need for resilience — our ability to resolve issues as they occur and emerge from these disruptions having learned from the experience. Unfortunately, this is much easier imagined than managed. Business disruptions are more common than ever, but that doesn't mean we are better at managing them. I think it's important for leaders at every level to examine why today's business environment requires resilience and to identify some steps that we can take to improve our capacity for it. As the COVID-19 pandemic proved to all of us (through all the businesses disrupted or destroyed and all the organizations and governments brought under fire), there is great value to be found in further developing this capacity. Survival after a crisis is not a given.

Business disruptions are more common than ever, but that doesn't mean we are better at managing them.

As a testament to the changing business landscape, it is interesting to note that through the latter part of the 20th century, business schools around the world taught the latest techniques for disaster *avoidance*, rather than the best ways to *manage* crises when they appeared. The emphasis in these programs was placed on how to build relationships with members of key stakeholder groups to maximize the probability of identifying early warning signs of a pending crisis and how to extinguish the glowing ember of peril before it erupted into a full-blown firestorm. Through several decades, there even seemed to be an undercurrent of judgment that would be cast upon any leader who, probably because of insufficient oversight or simply a failure to effectively manage, allowed a crisis to develop on his or her watch. When crisis happened, we pointed fingers at leaders instead of accepting that "crises happen." In days gone by, perhaps these messages of focus and accountability helped solve a particular collection of leadership performance issues. But I am reminded of a former faculty member at the University of Michigan, Mr. Gerry Meyers, who created the first crisis-leadership course at the Ross School of Business. He shared a prophetic philosophy at the beginning of every class for more than 35 years: "Maybe it is time to stop trying to plan our way out of problems and consider an alternative — managing them." He knew from first-hand experience that no matter how much time and energy are devoted to crisis avoidance, a significant disruption at some point in the not-too-distant future is simply inevitable.

> "Maybe it is time to stop trying to plan our way out of problems and consider an alternative — managing them."
>
> — *Gerry Meyers*

Now, well into the 21st century, we see the nature of today's business environment changing. There are still some quality lessons to be learned from 50+ years of management research and how great relationships can help leaders spot a potential issue before it becomes a raging crisis, and we'll explore this practice as we learn more about applying the principles of stakeholder theory to early phase crisis identification. But today's leaders aren't facing the business environment of the past. We see indications of the *new* business environment all the time on magazine and book covers: "Fail Fast, Then Succeed" and "How to Really Learn from Failure" and "The 10 Commandments for Business Failure." Our new reality rewards risk-taking, getting new products into the market before competitors, and launching minimum viable products (MVPs) with a co-creation strategy where we ask users and customers to define which features or improvements they really care about. Ultimately, we are seeing a commitment not to perfection but to a strategy of getting things right at least as often as we get them wrong.

You and I may have different perspectives on the merits of this new business reality. I think we can all, however, embrace the notion that this reality means two things:

- We (i.e., our teams and organizations) are going to make mistakes, and
- We will be forced to deal with the consequences.

Hopefully, those mistakes will be minor. In these cases, we will fail small, learn fast, and advance our businesses through the benefits of these lessons. Realistically, though, some mistakes will be massive, the consequences will be significant, and the stakes will be high. In these situations, we will be faced with the harsh, unenviable task of having to lead our teams through the disruption, crisis, or scandal with a focus on preserving whatever confidence our stakeholders have in us and rebuilding whatever faith we lose along the way.

> We will be faced with the harsh, unenviable task of having to lead our teams through the disruption, crisis, or scandal with a focus on preserving whatever confidence our stakeholders have in us and rebuilding whatever faith we lose along the way.

Crisis leadership challenges us to accept that what we face is not a question of readiness "*if* we encounter a major problem" but rather a question of preparedness for "*when* we encounter one." All of us, as business leaders, will be asked at some point in our careers — probably sooner, rather than later — to help lead a team through a set of circumstances that threaten the future viability of our business. To be truly effective leaders, we should be spending time and energy considering what to do, and what our teams and stakeholders need from us, when such a scenario presents itself.

Establishing Goals for Your Reading of This Book

With our conversation of high-stakes leadership well underway, you may want to set some goals for yourself in terms of what you would like to accomplish by working through this book.

Based on what you have read so far, what would you like to learn about crisis leadership?

- Perhaps you're interested in better understanding your stake-holders and how to engage with them before, during, and after a major disruptive event.

- Perhaps you would like to learn about specific steps you can take to prevent crisis-level events and better prepare for situations that could blossom into crises.

- Maybe you're interested in the crisis environment itself, or the types of crises your organization may have to navigate.

- Or perhaps you have more of an action orientation, and you are interested in crafting a set of steps that you can complete as a formally designated crisis leader.

Well, while any one of these may sound daunting, we're going to cover all of these topics in the chapters to come. But right now, grab a pen or a notebook or a digital annotation tool and commit to yourself some goals for your exploration of crisis leadership. You were drawn to this book for a reason, perhaps several. So ask yourself: *Why am I here? What do I hope this book will allow me to learn or to do?* Given your answers to these questions, take a few minutes to formalize a set of goals. The prompts below may be helpful.

- "When I have finished this book, I want to be able to _____."

- "When I have finished this book, I plan to have developed skills in these areas: _____."

- "When I have finished this book, I will have the tools necessary to _____ for my organization."

- "By reading this book, I want to develop the skills or capability to: _____."

- "By reading this book, I want to learn all that I can about _____ so that I will be able to _____."

04

PEOPLE FIRST
Focusing on Stakeholders Before, During, and After a Crisis

Most leaders focus on their own perspective during a crisis, attending to the fires that are casting the greatest amount of personal heat. They work to reduce their own pain, to save face, to make the trauma of the crisis subside from their vantage point first. To be fair, as we established earlier, this isn't an unreasonable approach; the crisis environment typically requires a great deal of high-pressure decision-making that will inform the future of the organization. The CEO finds himself or herself in the hot seat (as do the head of operations, the public relations leader, and others). But focusing solely on a singular point of view will limit the effectiveness of crisis leaders in the eyes of their various stakeholder groups, all of whom are thinking about the crisis from *their* perspective and wondering: "What about me?"

To deliver a holistically effective crisis response, leaders must consider the perspectives of *all* stakeholder groups. To accomplish this effectively, they must first understand the importance of stakeholders to their organization. Understanding your stakeholders is the first step to engaging them — in good times and in bad.

To deliver a holistically effective crisis response, leaders
must consider the perspectives of *all* stakeholder groups.

Who Are Your Stakeholders?

Effectiveness in high-stakes leadership depends largely on a leader's ability to understand and appreciate the perspectives of various organizational stakeholders. To engage these stakeholders effectively, during good times or amid an organizational challenge, leaders must have a good sense of the value each stakeholder population derives from their relationship with the organization. While this should make intuitive sense to any business leader, the reality is that organizations don't typically excel at this practice — as they tend to be more internally preoccupied than externally focused. Even when leaders do have a good sense of these value propositions, the relationships with individual stakeholder groups tend to reside in specific functions. The Sales and Marketing department tends to own the customer group. Human Resources tends to own the employee group. Finance tends to own the investor group. Government affairs owns the regulator group. And so on. But as an effective high-stakes leader, it's *your* job to understand the interests of *every* stakeholder group – at least, to some degree – as these interests will form the foundation of your response to any crisis or imperiled situation.

In a high-stakes leadership scenario, it is critical that enterprise leaders can effectively engage all stakeholder groups in ways that recognize how each stakeholder's value proposition is being threatened by the evolving crisis or disruption. Not surprisingly, the leadership teams who have demonstrated an ability to do this successfully didn't have to waste time doing so during a crisis; long ago, they figured out which stakeholder groups are interested in what, allowing them to quickly assess the potential impact of a developing situation and respond accordingly. They had taken the time to learn about these stakeholders well before a critical event, had established relationships with key members of these groups, and had built a foundation of dialogue and trust that would serve them under any circumstance. Having done these things proactively, when a crisis or disruption is making times tough, these leadership teams can jump right to the heart of the matter — communicating with and serving the needs and interests of their key stakeholders.

You might be reading this argument and thinking: "OK, so as I think about my company, here's what I understand to be true. Our CMO knows our customers. Our CHRO knows our people. Our CFO knows our investors. Our Government Affairs Officer knows our regulators. Our PR team knows the media. Our entire C-suite knows the competition. What else is there to know? Let's just get all of these people together when we have a crisis and let them manage it collaboratively."

This is not flawed thinking. But it *does* beg a few questions about the logistics of leading a company through a crisis:

- What is the composition of the crisis management team?
- What will this team do?
- How will team members work together?
- Which stakeholder groups will receive what kind of care and information?
- Who keeps the company running — assuming the company continues to operate while managing the crisis — if the entire C-suite is focused on all these different stakeholders and not on the company's core business?

- -

> Who keeps the company running — assuming the company continues to operate while managing the crisis — if the entire C-suite is focused on all these different stakeholders and not on the company's core business?

- -

The answers to these questions will be explored throughout this book. For now, suffice it to say that rarely does the C-suite dedicate their entire bandwidth to managing a crisis. It does happen on occasion (e.g., think back on financial institutions during the US sub-prime mortgage crisis of 2008 — for quite some time, crisis management was the only thing on these leaders' minds), but most of the time the C-suite assigns a team of enterprise leaders to manage the effort. Will they know everything they need to know about the different stakeholder groups? Will they know how to organize and execute the crisis management plan? Not if they are unprepared for their new roles. Not if they haven't done the crucial work well *before* the crisis.

This chapter is about understanding the needs and interests of typical stakeholder groups for just about any organization. Not all of these groups will necessarily have a significant interest in your company (your firm, for example, might operate in an industry that doesn't have regulators, or you might work in a private company that doesn't have investors or shareholders). But, generally speaking, an organizational leader should be considering each of the following groups, both to run a thriving business and to effectively manage through crises.

Primary Stakeholders

- Enterprise Leadership
- Customers
- Employees
- Financiers/Investors
- Suppliers
- Local Communities

Secondary Stakeholders

- Media
- Competitors
- Government Officials and Regulators
- Special Interest Groups
- Consumer Advocacy Groups
- Non-Governmental Organizations (NGOs)

Understanding What Your Stakeholders Value About Your Organization

By their very definition, "stakeholders" have a stake in your business — financially, emotionally, and/or practically. Maybe their ability to retire at age 60 depends upon how your stock performs. Or perhaps they collect a paycheck from your organization to feed and house their family. Or maybe they buy your products and services so frequently that a disruption in your business would inconvenience or even devastate theirs in some way. Every group of organizational stakeholders brings a unique perspective to their relationship with a business, and every perspective matters before, during, and after turbulent times strike. Let's take a few minutes to explore, in a bit of detail, this concept of organizational stakeholders and the best way for high-stakes leaders to characterize relationships with these groups and their individual members.

At the simplest level, organizations exist because of their ability to create valued goods and services that provide acceptable outcomes for a collection of stakeholders. These stakeholders, typically considered in large groups rather than as individuals, have an interest, claim, or stake in the organization, in what it does, and in how well it performs. Business is ultimately about the creation of value through the interactions between and among these stakeholders. To understand a business is to know how these relationships work. An executive's or entrepreneur's primary function is to create, manage, and shape these relationships and the value propositions that result from them.

> Business is ultimately about the creation of value through the interactions between and among stakeholders. To understand a business is to know how these relationships work.

Stakeholders are motivated to engage with an organization if, and only if, they receive benefits that equal or exceed the value of the contribution they are required to make in exchange for them (e.g., if your company makes athletic shoes, it's imperative that your customers think the shoes are worth as much or more than the price you charge for each pair — that they are comfortable, attractive, durable, or even unique). While it is easy to see why *customers* are stakeholders, it's important to recognize that not all stakeholders are customers. The "benefits" a stakeholder derives from your business might not have anything to do with the product or service you provide. Benefits, loosely defined, can be thought of as rewards — such as goods, services, money, power, satisfaction from association, the support of shared beliefs or values, or organizational status. Maybe your customers get great athletic shoes, your employees get excellent career development opportunities, your board members build their own resumes by being affiliated with you, and your investors get an outstanding return on their financial investment.

Your organization provides the benefits, and your stakeholders offer contributions in exchange for access to these benefits. Contributions might take the form of money, goods, services, opportunities, time, effort, loyalty, or the skills, knowledge, and expertise that organizations require of their members during task performance. There is always some "cost" to doing business with or being affiliated with any organization. These costs or contributions are borne by stakeholders and they will vary by stakeholder group.

To survive a crisis, you must adequately engage your stakeholders — and engaging them requires first understanding them. In the end, understanding them is about understanding what they value. High-stakes leaders must fully appreciate the range of potential sources of value that are available for exchange. Why? Because during a crisis, it is precisely these benefits and contributions — informed by the extent to which some part of a value exchange has already commenced — that become threatened (e.g., the employee worries she'll lose her job; the customer worries he'll have to find a new brand of running shoes; the investor worries she'll have to take a loss on her stock and move on). Understanding stakeholders means understanding their perceptions of the contributions they have made (or are making) in exchange for the benefits they expect to receive. In other words, understanding stakeholders means understanding their perceptions of the "value proposition" they have (or could have) with your organization. Ultimately, understanding stakeholder value propositions is about fully recognizing and appreciating "what's in it for them."

To survive a crisis, you must adequately engage your stakeholders — and engaging them requires first understanding them.

Stakeholder value propositions would be sufficiently challenging to calculate even if they were simply the result of an economic formula (e.g., Value = Tangible Benefit - Cost). Unfortunately, a fundamental premise of this book is that organizational stakeholders are *not* simply emotionless automatons who perform their value proposition calculations using only the material components of an exchange. Rather, stakeholders will *always* include their humanity — their aspirations, expectations, and emotions — in their calculus. And that makes it incredibly complicated to fully know and flawlessly serve your stakeholders.

Consider, for a moment, the last time you made a purchase that failed to meet your expectations. Did you simply recalculate the value of the exchange in the context of the reduced benefit you received, chalking it up to a "forfeited sunk cost" or saying to yourself "well, it's not always going to be what I expected?" Or was your reaction to the disappointing purchase as much *emotional* as it was economic? There was almost certainly an element of emotion in your reaction — perhaps a sense of disappointment, or sadness, or frustration, or anger. This is simply an element of the human condition. When someone or something does not meet our expectations, we have feelings about it. In the context of crisis leadership, this human element must be a primary area of focus for high-stakes leaders. Crises don't just happen to organizations ... they happen to the *people* who care about the organization. And that makes things messy. To engage stakeholders in the most effective ways possible — before, during, and after any crisis event — leaders must be able to recognize and respond to the psychological implications of a crisis in addition to the implications of a material nature.

- -

Crises don't just happen to organizations ...
they happen to the *people* who care about the
organization. And that makes things messy.

- -

This idea of stakeholders and the relevance of their humanity is not new. In his book, *Stakeholder Theory: The State of the Art*, researcher Ed Freeman describes a business's relationships with stakeholders this way:

> "To create value for stakeholders , executives and entre-preneurs must see business as fully situated in the realm of humanity. Businesses are human institutions populated by real live complex human beings. Stakeholders have names and faces and children. They are not mere placeholders for social roles. Most human beings are complicated. Most of us do what we do because we are self-interested *and* interested in others. Business works in part because of our urge to create things with others and for others. Working on a team, or creating a new product or delivery mechanism that makes customers' lives better or happier or more pleasurable all can be contrib-uting factors to why we go to work each day. And, this is not to deny the economic incentive of getting a pay check. The assumption of narrow self-interest is extremely limiting, and can be self-reinforcing — people can begin to act in a narrow self-interested way if they believe that is what is expected of

them ... We need to be open to a more complex psychology
— one any parent finds familiar as they have shepherded the
growth and development of their children."[1]

The key lesson here is that we have relationships with our stakeholders
not simply to extract economic value, but to make their lives better — to
make the execution of their responsibilities or the challenges of their daily
routines more meaningful, satisfying, and enjoyable. And when value propositions are threatened during a crisis, there is not simply a material impact
... there is a personal impact as well.

A Closer Look at Different Stakeholder Groups

A few pages back, we identified two lists of stakeholders — groups of people
we might consider as primary stakeholders and those we might consider as
secondary stakeholders. They are listed again here.

Primary Stakeholders

- Enterprise Leadership

- Customers

- Employees

- Financiers/Investors

- Suppliers

- Local Communities

Secondary Stakeholders

- Media

- Competitors

- Government Officials
  and Regulators

- Special Interest Groups

- Consumer Advocacy Groups

- Non-Governmental
  Organizations (NGOs)

Primary stakeholders are relevant to just about every organization, regardless of industry or state of maturity. These are also the stakeholders who
will be most significantly impacted by an organizational crisis. Secondary
stakeholders represent other groups of people who may or may not have
a relationship with your organization. Some of the groups listed in the
"secondary" column here may, in fact, be primary stakeholders for some

---

1   R. Edward Freeman, et al., *Stakeholder Theory: The State of the Art* (Cambridge, UK:
     Cambridge University Press, 2014).

companies, depending on the nature of the organization's operations. A great example of this is the relationship between JetBlue Airways and Regulators at the Federal Aviation Administration (FAA). I can assure you that nobody at JetBlue considers that FAA to be a secondary stakeholder. Throughout this book, when I reference primary stakeholders, I will ask you to assume that I've already completed some calculus that places each stakeholder in the primary category, even if they appear here on the secondary stakeholder list. I hope this won't seem confusing. Ultimately, this book has been written to help you understand general concepts so that you can determine the best answers for your organization. When you apply these concepts to your own circumstances, your primary stakeholders will become clear.

If this generic approach to differentiating primary and secondary stakeholders doesn't feel particularly satisfying (or if I've confused you with my disclaimer), you may prefer to conduct the following mental exercise to determine the primary stakeholders for your organization. Australian business book author and corporate strategy expert Graham Kenny offers these five questions to help you "direct your organization's energy and resources to the right relationships." If your responses match those required below when considering a particular stakeholder, then they deserve your attention as a *primary stakeholder.*

- ☐ Does the stakeholder have a fundamental impact on your organization's performance? *(Required response: yes.)*

- ☐ Can you clearly identify what you want from the stakeholder? *(Required response: yes.)*

- ☐ Is the relationship dynamic — that is, do you want it to grow? *(Required response: yes.)*

- ☐ Can you exist without or easily replace the stakeholder? *(Required response: no.)*

- ☐ Has the stakeholder already been identified through another relationship? *(Required response: no.)*[2]

---

2   Graham Kenny, "Five Questions to Identify Key Stakeholders," *Harvard Business Review* (March 6, 2014), https://hbr.org/2014/03/five-questions-to-identify-key-stakeholders.

Answer "yes, yes, yes, no, no" and you've identified a primary stakeholder group that deserves your significant attention — in good times and bad.

- - - - - - - - - - - - - - - - - -

Typical Primary (and Priority) Stakeholders

The following groups are the most common and important stakeholders for organizations of all types and sizes. As you work through this book, it is safe to assume that when I mention *primary stakeholders*, I will be referring to *all* of the following groups.

Enterprise Leadership

Enterprise leaders are your executives: CEO, COO, CFO, CHRO, CMO, CIO and others. This group has a unique set of responsibilities and, in exchange for their leadership, they often extract a great deal of value from the enterprise. These leaders are expected to create, manage, and shape relationships with all other stakeholders. When the organization is performing as expected, these leaders tend to receive the credit. When the organization is not performing, they tend to be held responsible. Also, because stakeholder interests typically conflict (for instance, employees want high pay while investors want low costs and high margins), enterprise leadership must find ways to resolve these conflicts in the best ways possible. Depending upon the size, governance structure, and operational norms of your company, your Board of Directors/Trustees may also be a vital part of your enterprise leadership team.

Employees

Employees are the primary internal stakeholder group in any organization (and are a group that is generally much larger in scale, cost, and complexity than enterprise leadership). These stakeholders often have a desirable set of specialized skills; a value system aligned with the organization's values; and are willing to provide time, energy, and a commitment to the enterprise. In return for their labor, employees expect job security, fair wages, employee benefits, personal respect, and meaningful work. Most employees also expect an opportunity to grow professionally and increase their own value or profile over time (within the organization and in their career).

Customers

Customers and suppliers exchange resources for the products and services of the firm and, in return, receive the benefits of those products and services. In short, you provide something that customers buy from you. These stakeholders will be expecting value in exchange for something of value that will be (or may have already been) exchanged for it, such as the types of currency mentioned earlier (e.g., money, goods, services, opportunities, time, effort, loyalty, etc.). Not all customers are called "customers" by the organizations that serve them; colleges and universities have student customers, charities have philanthropic customers, and healthcare organizations have customers they call "patients."

Financiers/Investors

Owners or financiers have a financial stake in the business in the form of stocks, bonds, and other currencies. They expect a financial return from their investments. Financiers typically expect these returns in a specific timeframe (e.g., short-, medium-, or long-term) and are typically doing so at a predictable and predetermined level of risk.

Regulators

For many organizations, governmental officials are considered a secondary stakeholder. In most of the businesses that I have led, however, they were clearly a primary stakeholder. Typically, these officials play one of two different roles in their relationships with an organization. While all regulatory officials are elected or appointed to serve the interests of their constituents, some (like mayors and governors) are expected to look after the interests of the communities they serve, while others (like safety or legal officials) are expected to oversee enterprise compliance. The value propositions of all regulators can be found in the organization's ability to perform as it is *expected* to perform. When an enterprise serves a community well, community leaders will tend to highly value it. When an enterprise complies with regulations and meets or exceeds regulatory standards, officials responsible for compliance will be satisfied.

Media

The media, while often viewed as a secondary stakeholder, can easily become a primary stakeholder for an organization, especially in today's environment, in which social media and traditional media outlets maintain a 24/7 commitment to share the news. While the value proposition of the media group is quite different from the groups previously mentioned, members of the media will look to an organization for stories that serve the interests of their audiences. The more interesting the stories, the greater the value proposition for the media. Also, when stories of great interest can be reported *exclusively* by a single outlet (i.e., when your firm calls and offers to give its only interview on a particular subject or crisis just to that station, website, or publication), this increases the value proposition for the specific outlet significantly.

Competitors

Why might competitors be viewed as a primary stakeholder for an organization? Not surprisingly, there are many ways an organization can behave that impact the decision-making and performance of its competitors. When you think about the fundamentals of competition, it's hard to argue against the fact that competitive forces inevitably influence all companies in each industry. When you manage one hotel in a town that has just three, it matters significantly if one of them goes out of business or if one undertakes a massive remodeling and expansion. What is not so clear to most leaders when it comes to competition, however, is the extent to which an organization can influence the way its stakeholders view other competitors in that industry. For example, when a single manufacturer produces an unsafe product, there is often increased regulatory scrutiny across the entire sector. Because of this potential to influence different groups with both strategic and tactical organizational choices, high-stakes leaders should always think of competitors as primary stakeholders that can be significantly influenced by its performance.

EXERCISE #1
Identifying Your Key Stakeholders

Welcome to the interactive portions of this book. Grab a pen (and a notebook too, if you're reading the Kindle edition or prefer not to write in your paperback book). It's time to get you in the crisis leadership "simulator" for some flight time!

You have just learned why high-stakes leaders like you are wise to understand and appreciate the importance of stakeholder perspective. Thinking about what you've just explored regarding the different types of organizational stakeholders and the typical interests of each, let's put some of those insights to work.

Take several minutes to identify the primary stakeholders of your current organization (or the organization you are perhaps planning to establish) and briefly describe what you believe to be the value proposition for each stakeholder group. What value do you think members of each group will find in their relationship with your organization?

Your list should include a minimum of five stakeholder groups, though you may have several more.

Stakeholder Group: _____

Their Value Proposition (i.e., what's in it for them): _____

_____

_____

Stakeholder Group: _____

Their Value Proposition (i.e., what's in it for them): _____

_____

_____

Stakeholder Group: _____

Their Value Proposition (i.e., what's in it for them): _____

_____

_____

Stakeholder Group: _____

Their Value Proposition (i.e., what's in it for them): _____

_____

_____

Stakeholder Group: _____

Their Value Proposition (i.e., what's in it for them): _____

_____

_____

Now take a moment to reflect on the extent to which you feel adequately aware and informed of each of the groups that you identified. Consider making note of where you can improve when it comes to stakeholder understanding, acknowledgment, communication, and engagement.

A Crisis Is a Crisis for Everyone: Appreciating How a Crisis Threatens Stakeholder Value Propositions

"Value proposition" is a term that admittedly sounds academic, but when you think about the unique relationships that stakeholders have with the organizations that offer them value, there is no better term for these vital connections. In the context of high-stakes leadership and the inevitability of crisis or disruption, I cannot think of a better way to conceptualize these relationships. It's all about creating value for those who value you, and understanding how to manage the tough conversations when the confidence of stakeholders is shaken.

> **It's all about creating value for those who value you, and understanding how to manage the tough conversations when the confidence of stakeholders is shaken.**

When a major disruption of some sort occurs at an organization, it is these very value propositions that are threatened by the crisis (e.g., the employee who worries about her job; the airline customer who wonders whether he'll make it to his destination on time; the competitors who fear that scandal or problems at your organization will reflect negatively on all organizations in the industry.) As such, it can be incredibly useful for crisis leaders to organize their thinking into a stakeholder-centric framework — to imagine a crisis from the perspective of different stakeholder groups and then strive to treat stakeholders as they would wish to be treated if they were in their shoes.

During Exercise #1, you did some list-making about *all* the stakeholders of your own organization and the value propositions you believe they hold. In the next exercise, at the end of this chapter, you will be asked to identify, the best that you can, one or two ways that each of these value propositions could be threatened. The exercise will inform not only how you should start to think about engaging these stakeholders during a crisis, but it will also challenge you to confirm your understanding of these groups and individuals during your "normal" business operations. Most companies wish they understood their stakeholders better. This wish becomes regret during a crisis — something we will explore in great detail later on.

> **Most companies wish they understood their stakeholders better. This wish becomes regret during a crisis.**

For now, I'd like you to ask yourself some crucial, insight-generating questions about stakeholders:

1. How would I formally define the value proposition of each of my
    company's stakeholders? *(Refer to your responses in the previous exer-
    cise. If you didn't complete the exercise, then take a moment to consider
    questions 1 and 2 here before moving to questions 3 and 4.)*

2. How does each stakeholder group perceive the value and what are they
    willing to exchange for it?

3. What is the mechanism for enabling the value exchange?

4. Do they pay/invest/work/commit ahead of time and wait for the value?
    Or do they "pay" when a good or service has been delivered?

In thinking about that final question, you might wonder: "Why does it
matter when they 'pay'?" Well, it can matter immensely. Imagine these two
different scenarios — pay ahead or cash on delivery — in the context of
a crisis where your company cannot deliver the goods or services expected
by your customers. What is the perceived threat to the customer value proposition if they have already paid for a good or service and you cannot deliver
it? How is this different from the second scenario? We tend to be a little
more forgiving when being asked to wait for something if it hasn't become
a debit in our bank account just yet.

The detail underlying the questions above is critically important to truly
understanding the perceptions of your stakeholders during a crisis. Your
stakeholders have expectations of you — perhaps they have even contributed their component of the value exchange — and now your organization
may not be able to live up to its commitment to delivering your side of the
value equation. This creates a problem, perhaps a significant problem — for
your stakeholders and ultimately for you. It's one thing to screw up or to
be seen in a negative limelight by your stakeholders, and it's another thing
to have them feeling like you have failed them, betrayed them, or come up
short to them personally.

Customers, of course, are just one kind of stakeholder to attend to before,
during, and after a crisis. What do your employees value in their relationship
with your organization? At JetBlue, we spent an incredible amount of time
thinking about ways to create unique value for our crewmembers (this is
the term JetBlue uses for its employees). We discovered that different work
groups had different interests and that we could improve the quality of each

group's value proposition by addressing these interests. For example, many of our early applicants for flight attendant positions (we referred to these individuals as "inflight crewmembers") wanted to commit to JetBlue, but couldn't accept full-time positions. So, our remarkable HR team found a way to create a job-share opportunity where two people could fill one full-time role. We were able to hire many of these part-time inflight crew and they were unbelievably committed to the company because we understood and responded to their most valued interests — flexibility and time.

What do your investors value in their relationship with your organization? What value proposition does your company offer to your regulators? The communities that you serve? Your suppliers or value chain partners? All these groups are typically referred to as your primary stakeholders — and every single one of them will feel threatened when your enterprise is facing a crisis.

What about the list of *secondary* stakeholders? How might a crisis threaten their value proposition? Your competitors? The media? Special interest or action groups? You may be shocked by the number of "other parties" that feel threatened by something that is creating such a major problem for your organization. And this is exactly the point here. You have *many* stakeholders. Each of them think about their value proposition with your company in a different way. When your company is facing a crisis, each of these stakeholder's unique value propositions is threatened. Your job, as a high-stakes leader and executive problem solver, is to not only understand this, but to be able to do something about it. (And in a crisis, sometimes the "doing" has to happen quickly.)

EXERCISE #2
Facing the Facts About Your Key Stakeholders and Value Proposition Threats

In the previous exercise, you created a list of stakeholders for your current or future organization. Refer to that list of stakeholders and the value positions you identified. Now, list one or two ways or situations during which the value position for each stakeholder might be threatened. Take some time to imagine various situations in which each stakeholder group might perceive a threat to their value proposition.

Stakeholder Group: _____

Possible Perceived Threat(s): _____

_____

_____

Stakeholder Group: _____

Possible Perceived Threat(s): _____

_____

_____

Stakeholder Group: _____

Possible Perceived Threat(s): _____

_____

_____

Stakeholder Group: _____

Possible Perceived Threat(s): _____

_____

_____

Stakeholder Group: _____

Possible Perceived Threat(s): _____

_____

_____

Did anything surprise you as you identified possible perceived threats from the vantage points of your key stakeholders? This exercise, repeated periodically over time as your stakeholders change and your business evolves, is a great way to frame your early thinking about how and why you should engage each of these stakeholder groups before, during, and after a crisis. Take your time with this brainstorming and consider asking your fellow leaders to help you identify threats you haven't yet considered.

Anyone who knows me well knows that I'm constantly talking about "loving your stakeholders." I believe this idea is the foundation of a successful enterprise and the chief responsibility of its leaders. There is nothing you can't survive if you keep your stakeholders' interests foremost in your minds when you encounter turbulent times. Throughout the stories and lessons in this book, the perspectives of these stakeholder groups will be the focus of our attention. Even now, with just simple descriptions of these stakeholders and their value propositions, it should be relatively easy for you to see how they are threatened during a crisis.

As we bring this chapter to a close, let me offer a final recommendation that might serve as a reminder of the critical importance of your relationships with your stakeholders. As a high-stakes leader, you will continuously need to find ways to effectively manage, mitigate, and recover from value proposition threats *and* thoughtfully, purposefully, and genuinely engage your stakeholders every step of the way — not as instruments of economic value, but as members of your extended organizational family.

05

OPERATIONAL TURBULENCE
The JetBlue Airways
Valentine's Day Crisis

I'm passionate about a few things when it comes to business: ethical leadership, stakeholder engagement, employee empowerment, coherent and thoughtful strategy, and — of course — everything about the world of aviation. So what better way to illustrate the nature of leadership in turbulent times than to take you behind the scenes — right into the heart of darkness — during one of the most demoralizing, frustrating, and humbling moments in my professional career? It would become known as JetBlue's Valentine's Day Massacre.[1] The product of a once-in-a-century ice storm and the decisions of an overly optimistic leadership team, JetBlue suffered an epic operational meltdown that required every executive at the company to flex their high-stakes leadership muscles non-stop for nearly a full week. The story provides a wealth of lessons about crisis leadership and, for our purposes here, creates an exceptional platform for connecting our earlier discussions of stakeholder value propositions; how those

---

1   The JetBlue operational crisis that started on Valentine's Day 2007 and extended beyond President's Day is now famously known by both names. For this reason, you'll see me use "Valentine's Day" and "President's Day" somewhat interchangeably throughout the remainder of this book.

propositions are threatened during a crisis; and how engaging stakeholders before, during, and after a crisis can be the difference between long-term success and total failure.

In February of 2007, seven remarkably successful years after JetBlue commenced its commercial operations, the United States' youngest and most innovative airline experienced its first major operational catastrophe. All company stakeholder groups were impacted to some extent by JetBlue's spectacular failure. While it eventually became a moment in JetBlue's history that served as a great opportunity to learn, grow, and become the airline it is today, the more than six days of the Valentine's Day Massacre forever changed the way I — and many leaders at JetBlue — think about crisis readiness and the importance of stakeholder engagement. I am so proud to have co-founded JetBlue with a remarkable team of exceptional people, and I was equally thankful for the opportunity to dedicate myself to serving our stakeholders' interests, in good times and — as the following story will so vividly illustrate — in bad times too. Buckle up, readers; the seatbelt sign is now illuminated, and the ride is about to get a little bumpy.

> In February of 2007, seven remarkably successful years
> after JetBlue commenced its commercial operations,
> the United States' youngest and most innovative airline
> experienced its first major operational catastrophe.

Clear Skies — Setting the Stage for JetBlue's First Operational Disaster

Throughout JetBlue's first seven years of operations, which began in February of 2000, we enjoyed an incredible track record of successes, despite some remarkably challenging times for our industry as a whole. We were able to make a profit in our first full year of operations. And after the tragic events of September 11, 2001, we were one of only three airlines that didn't close out the year with a loss: Southwest, AirTran, and JetBlue — the low-cost, high-efficiency carriers in North America.

In 2002, JetBlue earned *Ad Age*'s Marketer of the Year award and was recognized for having created a unique identity in an industry with companies that, on average, were disliked slightly more than the postal service and slightly less than the IRS. In 2003 and 2004, JetBlue ranked at or near the top of most operational performance categories, filled planes more completely and effectively than any other US carrier, and, by the end of 2004, had amassed 16 consecutive quarters of profitability. In 2005, JetBlue had the highest customer satisfaction of any low-fare airline according to JD Power. And by 2006, it had the highest satisfaction score of any airline on the continent.

> In 2002, JetBlue earned *Ad Age*'s Marketer of the Year award and was recognized for having created a unique identity in an industry with companies that, on average, were disliked slightly more than the postal service and slightly less than the IRS.

Financially, although we were among the top performers for the entire US airline industry, we suffered earnings losses in both 2005 and 2006 ($20.3M and $1M respectively), primarily due to rapidly rising jet fuel costs. Despite the difficult operating conditions, JetBlue's other performance metrics in almost every major category were number one or two among its peers. JetBlue was the airline every competitor was watching, and we were incredibly proud of our ability to compete. Also in 2006, our operating revenue totaled almost $2.4B, which represented growth of nearly 39% over the previous year. We were, by far, the fastest-growing (and arguably the best-performing) airline in North America at the time.

By the beginning of 2007, JetBlue's fleet of Airbus 320 and Embraer 190 jets served 52 destinations with more than 575 daily flights. While critics continued to ask about and warn us of possible growing pains, JetBlue was expanding rapidly and with a purpose — in people, planes, and destinations — at a rate not seen for many years in the industry.

For more than seven years, JetBlue had brought humanity back to air travel — our company's vision statement — and *New York's Hometown Airline* had become what many called the darling of the industry. But, as is so often the case, staying on top is often more challenging than getting there in the first place.

Staying on top is often more challenging than getting there in the first place.

The large-scale disaster that would eventually become known as JetBlue's Valentine's Day Massacre — a horrific operational meltdown that took place amidst one of the worst winter storms the New York metropolitan area had ever experienced — was on the horizon. In handling it, we would make many mistakes and at least as many timely and meaningful corrections. Most importantly, however, we would survive and eventually thrive, largely because we were able to learn so very much from the experience. So, please allow me to first tell you the story, then I'll share how JetBlue executives viewed the interests of their stakeholders before the events of the storm played out — as well as how JetBlue executives tried to address their failure to serve these interests as the crisis progressed. I think you'll find this candid and detailed account of the crisis useful, relatable, somewhat entertaining, and wonderfully illustrative of the application of stakeholder theory. We learned a tremendous amount from this crisis, and so can you.

The Calm Before the Storm

It was 2007 and the year had begun with great enthusiasm for JetBlue. Despite a small loss in 2006, leaders across the airline were committed to overcoming the rising cost of jet fuel with a collection of efficiency initiatives that would ensure JetBlue's return to profitability. The key for turning a profit in the first quarter of '07 would be to perform exceptionally well over the President's Day weekend holiday. JetBlue, you see, was primarily a leisure airline, which means that we mostly carried what we called VFR traffic (an acronym not for Visual Flight Rules, a term pilots and aviation enthusiasts would know, but rather an abbreviation for customers who were Visiting Friends and Relatives). VFR. It was where we excelled.

From a revenue perspective, this meant that JetBlue made money during peak leisure travel periods. JetBlue had always done very well over the summer months because so many families traveled for vacations when their children were out of school. JetBlue also tended to make money on long holiday weekends. In the *first* quarter of 2007, President's Day weekend was the only long holiday because Easter, typically a first quarter holiday, fell in April of that year (i.e., in second quarter). So, coming off a small loss in 2006, we felt a sense of urgency to operate a full and productive schedule over the long weekend that encompassed the President's Day holiday. That year, the holiday began on Valentine's Day, February 14, falling on the Wednesday before the long holiday weekend. We were ready to delight travelers and investors alike.

But as Valentine's Day approached, so did the weather. A winter nor'easter barreled toward the New York metropolitan area and landed, full-force, on JetBlue's primary base of operations — John F. Kennedy International Airport (JFK or Kennedy airport) — on Valentine's Day morning. The next seven days would be, by far, the most trying in our eight-year history.

February 14, 2007 — Valentine's Day: The Bitter Truth

Weather predictions for the winter storm approaching the New York area had prompted all airlines — except JetBlue — to cancel their flight schedules in and out of the area for the coming two days. Based on some conflicting temperature forecasts, leaders at JetBlue, myself included, had reason to believe that we might just be able to operate, even though every one of our competitors had decided not to. It wouldn't be a question of pushing the boundaries of safety (for our passengers or our crew), because we knew that airports would be closed (by the FAA) if the conditions weren't safe for operations. The question was really about how we could — and should — deliver on our corporate raison d'être. The choice to operate during the developing storm would be difficult, but we were willing to go to a lot of trouble to do what we thought was generous and courageous for our stakeholders. If there was even the smallest chance that conditions might allow the airports to remain open on Valentine's Day, JetBlue wanted to deliver on its commitment to help customers get to their holiday destinations. After all, that's why we started the airline in the first place — to serve the interests of our stakeholders. Approaching the long President's Day weekend, every seat on every one of our flights had been sold. If there was a chance that we could operate, we thought, then we should try. So we tried.

If there was even the smallest chance that conditions might allow the airports to remain open on Valentine's Day, JetBlue wanted to deliver on its commitment to help customers get to their holiday destinations. After all, that's why we started the airline in the first place — to serve the interests of our stakeholders.

Early on Valentine's Day morning, as we had hoped, the weather allowed Kennedy airport to open. The temperature was near freezing and there were brief periods of rain, but expectations were such that everyone — airport officials and JetBlue leaders — expected the airport to remain open. We were thrilled. Our competitors had canceled their flights and it looked like we were poised to have a busy, happy, profitable holiday weekend. Undaunted by what was just cold rain at that point, and emboldened by an open airport, JetBlue decided to begin boarding planes for the early morning launch.

At that time, JetBlue was operating out of Terminal 6 at JFK, with 14 primary operational gates, and a small satellite facility that supported another 7 gates. As the day began — and as it was the first day of the extended holiday weekend — there was an aircraft on every gate *and* every one of these planes was expected to be full. At sunrise, each of these airplanes would be ready to push off their gate, almost simultaneously, ahead of their departures scheduled for takeoff between 6:00 a.m. and 7:00 a.m.

At the risk of significantly oversimplifying the hundreds of details and plot twists of that weekend, let me paint a picture of what happened next.

At 5:30 a.m., as JetBlue leaders had hoped, weather conditions were such that the airport could open on time. So, it did. The green light was given by JFK Operations (JFK Ops) for airplanes to push off their gates, as scheduled, and proceed to the de-icing pad for treatment, which would be required for all departing aircraft that morning. JFK Operations was the responsibility of the Port Authority of New York and New Jersey (PANYNJ), who operated all the major airports in the greater New York area. They were certified to do so by the FAA.

With approval from the airport, *all* 21 JetBlue planes moved from Terminal 6 to the de-icing area, located at a remote location on the airport, a good distance from JetBlue's gates. Due to space constraints, only two planes could be de-iced at the same time, so imagine a pair of queues through which aircraft would proceed to be treated with fluid (a process that required 5 to 10 minutes to complete) prior to making their way to the operating runway. That morning, as pairs of aircraft completed de-icing, they headed for the departure runway and requested clearance for takeoff. Initially, a few of these aircraft were released and ultimately made it to their planned destinations. But most were trapped in the following, very unfortunate sequence of events.

At some point during that very first block of departures, with many JetBlue airplanes that had completed de-icing lined up on the taxiway near the active runway — awaiting clearance for takeoff — the weather deteriorated such that an "ice pellet condition" developed. This condition, as defined by the FAA, meant that there would be an increased likelihood of aircraft icing on takeoff. To ensure the adequate safety margin required by regulators, this condition meant that the airport would no longer be authorized to conduct flight operations until either: 1) the temperature increased to above freezing, or 2) the "pellets" (frozen or semi-frozen supercooled water droplets) were no longer present.

The airport closure wasn't a subjective judgment call on anyone's behalf; it was a product of the law that had been written and implemented by the FAA. The law had been established in the interest of safety. As such, JetBlue leadership never viewed the decision to attempt operations in the face of a possible storm to be a question of safety; we knew that if conditions were such that it was *unsafe* to operate, the law would require the airport to close. It's important to me now, as we reflect on what happened that fateful day, that readers don't take my previous comments as JetBlue falsely attributing responsibility for the Valentine's Day crisis somewhere else. FAA rules are written for safety. JetBlue knows the rules and has its own additional rules for ensuring safety. At the intersection of FAA rules and JetBlue procedures is a double layer of safety, which is exactly where JetBlue found itself on Valentine's Day morning: doubly safe and unable to operate flights. JetBlue planes, full of anxious customers and dedicated crewmembers, were now forced to sit and wait.

As JetBlue leaders communicated with JFK Operations to determine the anticipated length of the delay, conversations focused on the projected weather conditions. Would the ice pellet conditions dissipate, or would the temperature rise above freezing? If either of these changes were to happen, airport operations would resume. According to JFK Ops, while the rain was likely to continue, the temperature was projected to rise "within the next hour or two."

So, JetBlue leaders decided to press on. Customers continued to arrive at JFK for their late morning flights, while JetBlue aircraft sat on the taxiways, unable to move. Also — and this would become a significant contributor to JetBlue's crisis situation — as JetBlue aircraft sat on the ground waiting for the airport to open, other JetBlue aircraft were *arriving* at JFK from other JetBlue cities and were holding overhead the airport (i.e., circling in the air, unable to land) — also waiting for the airport to re-open.

Within about an hour of the airport closure, JFK Ops announced that the temperature had increased such that the airport could resume operations. There was much rejoicing! The JetBlue aircraft on the taxiways now had to proceed back to de-icing for another application. (They couldn't just take off right away because the conditions required another fluid treatment.) JetBlue *hadn't* been keeping airplanes moving through the de-icing area as they awaited the temperature increase, because the treatments have a very short effectiveness period (and, frankly speaking, these treatments aren't cheap!) Therefore, not having approximate takeoff times made it unreasonable to just cycle aircraft through the de-icing pads. It was time to start over with the process we'd just completed an hour ago.

As JetBlue aircraft on the ground at JFK headed back to de-icing, the aircraft that had been holding overhead were cleared to land. More than a dozen airplanes full of JetBlue customers landed and pulled into the gates at Terminal 6, where they unloaded — and then *re*loaded. It appeared that the airport would stay open so we were "back in business," getting passengers headed to their holiday destinations.

Some of the aircraft that were sent to the de-icing queue were de-iced, made their way to the active runway, and departed. Others, however, spent their time waiting in queue. Meanwhile, JetBlue's reloaded aircraft pushed back and made their way to the de-icing pad.

Just about the same time that all the reloaded JetBlue aircraft had made it to the de-icing area, but well before more than a few of the aircraft from the first wave (which had now been de-iced twice that day) had the chance to takeoff, we received more bad news from JFK Operations. The temperature had dropped again to below freezing and the airport was required to close. Ugh.

"How long do you expect the airport to remain closed?" we asked.

"Unknown", said JFK Ops, "but we do expect it to reopen soon."

Once again, we waited. Some aircraft from the first launch bank of the day had now been waiting more than three to four hours for departure, with no clear sign of relief in sight. If you were an airline passenger with this much time invested and the hope of actually making it out at some point, would *you* want to keep waiting? Or would you give in and go home? Most of our passengers were hopeful and committed to making it to their destinations. So, we kept trying on their behalf.

Sadly, in a final wave of "you just can't make this stuff up," after about an hour of the airport being closed, the temperature, once again, rose to above freezing. Airplanes on taxiways made their way back to the de-icing queue. Third time's a charm?

And *another* wave of JetBlue airplanes that had been holding overhead were able to land and fill the gates at JetBlue's JFK Terminal 6.

So, let's pause to do the math here. A handful of aircraft from the very first wave of JetBlue flights had still yet to take off. A whole second wave of JetBlue flights had loaded, pushed from their gates, and were now waiting at de-icing — behind the remaining first-wave flights. And now a third wave of JetBlue flights had parked at JetBlue's terminal, unloaded their customers, and, because the airport was now open — and expected to stay open — these aircraft were being filled with customers for flights that were already one, two, or three hours behind schedule.

The JetBlue leadership team thought that the logjam at JFK was about to break loose. But then, we received the worst news of the day. The temperature had dropped yet again, and the airport was closing — for a third (and what would turn out to be final) time that day. The ice pellets then became heavy freezing rain, which increased in intensity and began to form a thick layer of ice on everything it touched.

JFK Operations informed us that the airport would now be closed for the rest of the day because of the heavy icing. In an instant, our irrational sense of hope became an overwhelming sense of disappointment and dread. Cleaning up the mess we had created for ourselves was not going to be easy or pretty. But, as USA Hockey coach Herb Brooks so famously said before the Miracle on Ice game during the 1980 Winter Olympics, "Great moments are born from great opportunity." This was certainly going to be a great opportunity for the high-stakes leaders at JetBlue.

In an instant, our irrational sense of hope became an overwhelming sense of disappointment and dread. Cleaning up the mess we had created for ourselves was not going to be easy or pretty.

It was time to send the passengers home, but that was easier said than done. JetBlue's gates were all occupied with planes full of customers, which now all needed to be unloaded. JetBlue aircraft that were somewhere else on airport property but not on a gate — and there were more than 21 such airplanes on the ground, which meant there were more planes than we had gates to serve — had to wait their turn for deplaning. And while they waited ... ICE. Up to a half inch of solid ice covered the New York area. At JFK, everything was frozen. Airplanes couldn't move under their own power, as the icy taxiways were too slippery to use. Ground equipment couldn't move for the same reasons. Many of our planes and our people were now stranded.

JFK was shut down. JetBlue was unable to move. Customers and crews were stuck on airplanes, and there was no way to get to them. In fact, nine JetBlue aircraft, full of customers and crew, waited on taxiways — away from their gates and unable to access terminal facilities — for more than six hours. On some these aircraft, lavatories became unusable and tensions began to run very high. In terminals across the JetBlue system (i.e., in other states and even far away from the weather woes of New York), passengers awaiting flights suffered lengthy delays with little helpful information to guide them, as JetBlue was unable to predict when it could resume operations. It was a truly horrible day for the airline that promised to "Bring Humanity Back to Air Travel."

Add up all these events and what do you get?

- Multiple JetBlue airplanes, full of understandably tired, angry, and emotional customers, stuck on taxiways around JFK with no way to deplane.
- A JetBlue terminal full of confused, frustrated, and very vocal customers.
- JetBlue crewmembers who were doing everything they could for customers, but without any good answers or satisfying ways to serve their needs.
- And a JetBlue organization that found itself in its worst-ever operational crisis.

It would take us another five days to get the airline ready to resume operations at full speed again.

Storm Damage

By February 19, because of our attempt to operate through the storm, we suffered outcomes far worse than we had ever imagined. We ultimately canceled more than 1,000 flights (more flights than all our competitors *combined*). We stranded thousands of customers and crews on planes, in terminals, and in cities away from their homes and away from their loved ones. And we incurred tens of millions of dollars in losses. Perhaps even worse, JetBlue's sterling reputation was now seriously tarnished — perhaps permanently — because of bad luck, flawed decision-making, and multiple systemic and leadership failures.

JetBlue found itself in its first, true, operational crisis. And the way we dealt with that crisis would change the airline forever.

THE JETBLUE AIRWAYS VALENTINE'S DAY CRISIS

BY THE NUMBERS

32°F / 0°C

The outside temperature that precipitated the disaster, producing freezing rain and ice pellets that left half an inch of ice across the NYC area.

3

The number of decision-makers calling the shots that day: the FAA, JFK operations, and JetBlue Airways.

3

The eventual number of times JFK shut down operations that day before they they decided to remain closed.

21

The number of JetBlue gates at JFK, each filled with aircraft moving in and out due to additional flights landing in between airport closures.

9

The number of fully occupied aircraft stuck on the tarmac for more than 6 hours. Other flights experienced an average 3-4 hour wait before they were able to depart or were forced to return to their gates.

5-10 minutes

The amount of time it took to de-ice each waiting airplane, two aircraft at at time, every time the airport tried to reopen — some of which were de-iced up to three times before the airport finally closed.

1,500

The number of JetBlue flights eventually canceled during the six-day crisis, beginning on February 14, 2007.

More than 150,000

The number of JetBlue customers unable to complete their travel plans during the five-day period. Tens of thousands more were significantly delayed.

More than 100

The number of JetBlue executives who personally went to JFK to assist with the crisis. JetBlue's CEO made 14 TV appearances on February 20 to apologize to customers and announce the new BOR.

$44M

The amount of JetBlue's lost revenue — $20M in flight cancelations and an additional $24M in credit vouchers issued to customers — due to the crisis.

JetBlue found itself in its first, true, operational crisis. And the way we dealt with that crisis would change the airline forever.

As of the publishing of this book, it's been 14 years since the Valentine's Day Massacre and, as I'm sure you know, JetBlue survived the crisis to become the sixth largest airline in the United States.[2] They have done so by learning from their mistakes. They have succeeded by viewing failures as opportunities to grow, to improve, and to become increasingly resilient.

But in February 2007 and shortly thereafter, we had no idea whether there would be silver linings to those storm clouds. We were "in it" and we were all-hands-on-deck to handle the crisis. Of course, how it played out had as much to do with what we did *before* the storm as it did with how we responded, but we didn't know that at the time. We had made a choice that depended on flawless execution and a little luck, but we ultimately experienced neither. In thinking about our Valentine's Day crisis, you might be wondering why we — the leadership team at JetBlue Airways — would have attempted such a thing. As you'll see, the decision was ultimately made because it actually served the best interests of our stakeholders.

Ahead of the Winter Storm: JetBlue Leadership's View of Stakeholder Interests

Unlike some crises, a nor'easter gives you some warning. At JetBlue, we'd been tracking the weather reports and knew it didn't look good for air travel that holiday weekend. But unlike other businesses, we couldn't just pack an umbrella and carry on. The Valentine's Day winter storm was approaching and JetBlue leadership was facing some very difficult decisions in support of a large collection of stakeholders. We wondered:

---

2   JetBlue Airways was the fifth largest US carrier until 2016, when Alaska Airlines acquired Virgin America.

- **What would our customers want us to do?** Would they want us to attempt to fly? Or would they want us to cancel and have them forego their vacation plans?

- **How about our investors?** Would they want us to preemptively cancel much of our flying on the *only* holiday weekend of the fiscal quarter if there was even the slimmest chance that the weather might improve and we might be able to operate as originally planned?

- **What would our crewmembers expect us to do?** We had their safety, their paychecks, and their schedules to consider. Interestingly, our employees all owned equity through our crewmember stock purchase program and were all entitled to profit-sharing (if we were able to earn any), which means they were an interesting group to consider — part employee and part shareholder.

- **How would the Federal Aviation Administration (FAA), our regulatory authority, want us to be thinking about our operations?** They held an important stake in aviation safety, in airport operations, and in the reputation of the industry as a whole.

- **How about the media?** What kind of stories would they want to capture during JetBlue's departure from convention? "JetBlue flies against all odds and embarrasses their much more experienced competitors!" Or … "JetBlue's holiday plans collapse tragically … illustrating the overconfident, flawed logic of an adolescent startup."

- **Speaking of our competitors, what were they thinking as they dutifully closed up shop ahead of the weather, leaving vacation-bound customers at home, bags packed, with nowhere to take them?** Surely, our competitors grappled with the same questions we were facing, though we all approached those questions differently.

Each of these questions was vital and none came with easy answers — particularly in the face of a developing winter storm. The thought of trying to satisfy all stakeholder interests, even when everything *is* going according to plan (e.g., when it's sunny and 72° F), can be daunting. Add in some bad weather and the pressures of two years of rapidly rising sector costs because of a global energy crisis … and you have a perfect storm (literally!). The conditions we faced weren't going to be easy for even the most effective high-stakes leaders to manage.

Over the next few pages, I'll describe for you the ways in which JetBlue leadership was thinking about our primary stakeholders as we entered this fateful week in February 2007. I'll begin with a short, high-level summary of our understanding and then I'll provide a much more detailed explanation of our perceptions of stakeholder interests. I'm hoping that these descriptions will serve as useful illustrations of the extent to which I believe high-stakes leaders should understand their stakeholders. As you read about each of the following groups, you may find it helpful to consider the extent to which you understand stakeholder interests in the context of your *own* enterprise. I believe JetBlue was uniquely in tune with its stakeholders and their interests – and this crisis was still monumental. Had the company been less aware or engaged with them, the results could have been catastrophic.

- - - - - - - - - - - - - - - - - -

Our Customers

Our customers, as they packed their luggage and finalized their vacation plans, were surely also watching the weather and understood (and felt) the implications of the approaching winter storm. The likelihood of commercial flight operations was not high, and our customers were typically quite pragmatic. But this was JetBlue, and JetBlue is not like every other airline. We had promised and proven that, time and again. So our customers were also hopeful. As a leadership team, we knew that our customers would understand if we canceled operations and waited out the storm. But we also knew that if there was a chance to operate, if we could do so safely, we should try to live up to the commitment we made to our customers when they purchased their tickets. We felt that it was our responsibility to operate our schedule and to try to get our customers to their destinations to visit friends and families. So, torn a bit by the tension between canceling and attempting to operate, and knowing that our customers would understand if we canceled (but also knowing that we could be heroes if we operated when nobody else did), we decided to try to fly our schedule.

- -

If there was a chance to operate, if we could do so safely, we should try to live up to the commitment we made to our customers when they purchased their tickets.

- -

Our Investors

We were a leisure airline looking at the only holiday in the fiscal quarter — the first quarter to redeem ourselves after two consecutive unprofitable years because of rising fuel costs. As such, our investors were clearly very interested in having us attempt to fly — if, of course, we could do so safely. Yes, it would have been easy to cancel flights and try to move customers to other flights that operated after the storm had passed, but that would likely mean a two- or three-day delay, so many of our customers would likely miss their ocean cruises or lose their rental properties because they failed to show up on time. And when kids need to return to school and adults need to return to work, it's over; a holiday weekend has an expiration date. Investors knew that this weekend was make-it-or-break-it if we wanted a shot at a profitable quarter.

Our Crewmembers

Because our crewmembers were both employees and shareholders through our stock-purchase program, they were a stakeholder group with a complex set of interests. As employees, who doesn't want a few extra days at home, especially during a winter storm? But we also had crewmembers (e.g., pilots and flight attendants) already away from home because they were operating trips on the days leading up to the storm. Those folks, in particular, really wanted us to try to operate. And of course, as stockholders, all crewmembers wanted us to make choices that would allow us to generate revenue, and subsequently, profits — profits that we would not only share with them through our JetBlue profit-sharing program, but also profits that would increase investor interest, drive up the stock price, and increase the value of company ownership overall. The forces at play had most of our crewmembers wanting us to operate.

The FAA

Our regulatory partners were not only those at the FAA — whose clear primary objective is to ensure the safety of all who travel on or operate aircraft in the United States — but we also worked with the Port Authority of New York and New Jersey, as they owned and operated JFK and all other New York airports. They had responsibility for all the terminals, gates, ramp space, and taxiways on the airport property. What were they interested in? Primarily, they wanted things to run as smoothly as possible around their airports. So, their interests would best be served by all airlines canceling everything. That way, they could plow snow and care for airport grounds without airline operations getting in the way. That said, if any airlines did intend to operate, their job would be to support them.

- - - - - - - - - - - - - - - - -

The Media

What did the media want? Ultimately, they wanted a story. And when the winter storm threatened to devastate travel plans for New York residents, they had their first story. Even if airlines canceled everything days in advance of the storm, they had a story. When it became clear that JetBlue might try to operate while all others had canceled everything, another story began to take shape. Would JetBlue become a team of heroes or a collection of overconfident fools? Either way, the media wanted to be there to watch and report upon what was sure to be an entertaining show — regardless of the outcome.

- - - - - - - - - - - - - - - - -

Our Competitors

In the airline industry, most decisions are made by corporate leaders with their own companies and customers in mind. In most cases, it doesn't really matter what the competition is doing when it comes to weather-related issues. The law is generally pretty clear on safety-related decisions. And company policies, which have evolved over years of trial and error (there are lots of both in the airline business), generally favor the more conservative option, when decisions come down to a choice between two or more possibilities. So, as JetBlue was facing our decision about whether or not to operate on Valentine's Day, competitors had already made their choices — independent of JetBlue's musings or plans. But once JetBlue decided to operate, might competitors have wondered if this just might be another unexpected feather in the cap of the upstart carrier?

There was so much to consider. JetBlue's leadership team spent nearly the entirety of the 48 hours before the storm in conference rooms and on phone bridges — working through options, considering alternatives, and playing out various scenarios. Discussions were focused almost exclusively on the intersection of conservatism, which all our competitors had fully embraced, and the *irrational sense of hope* that had been a key ingredient in JetBlue's success to date. JetBlue's stakeholder interests were pulling us in both directions. Some stakeholders wanted JetBlue to do everything it could to fly. Others wanted JetBlue to take a couple days off. Still others, like crewmembers, were torn. Stakeholder interests, even during normal operations and under the best of circumstances, typically create a tension of some sort for high-stakes leaders — in any industry and in organizations of any size. Rarely, you will find, do all your stakeholders want you to do the same thing at the same time ... to make the same decisions. If you're new to crisis planning and crisis leadership, you might be thinking that the hard part is working to resolve the crisis, but that's just the beginning. You also have to contend with groups of stakeholders who want, perhaps demand, different things. And the fallout can be noisy, painful, and long-lasting.

- -

> If you're new to crisis planning and crisis leadership, you might be thinking that the hard part is working to resolve the crisis, but that's just the beginning. You also have to contend with groups of stakeholders who want, perhaps demand, different things. And the fallout can be noisy, painful, and long-lasting.

- -

In the end, JetBlue decided to try to operate. In fact, the decision to operate was unanimous. If there was a chance to fly and we could do so safely, then we should give it our best shot. Hindsight being 20/20, it turned out to be a bad choice. Without the benefit of the stakeholder-by-stakeholder considerations that I shared with you here, you might have imagined that the decision to operate would have been a lay-up. Just cancel like everyone else and start back up when the skies clear and everyone else starts flying again. Easy-peasy, right? But it wasn't a lay-up. For so many reasons, the right choice for us was to try and operate. It was the harder choice — the riskier choice — but the best choice for our stakeholders. In the end, however, we discovered that the most valuable outcome for JetBlue was that the crisis provided a great opportunity for us to learn from our mistakes.

Ahead of the Storm:
A Deep Dive into JetBlue's Stakeholder Interests, Value Propositions, and Perspectives

The JetBlue Valentine's Day Crisis is both a cautionary tale and a success story. I am sharing it in detail in hopes of highlighting how one company (and a brand you might know and love) demonstrated the value of effective stakeholder management during and after a crisis. While some of the ideas presented here will seem quite common-sensical, the harsh reality for many company leaders is that they *will* find themselves in a crisis without having dedicated the time to truly understand their stakeholders or build relationships before the crisis strikes. When this happens, leaders at a company discover that they have no trust capital to fall back on — no previously established sense of confidence from stakeholders who are now crafting their own narrative about what they should (but probably won't) hear and see from a company in crisis. This is not where crisis leaders want to begin their recovery efforts.

Effective leaders don't *initiate* a dialogue at the onset of a crisis — they *continue* it. For any leader looking to begin their preparation efforts for a potential future crisis, there is no better place to start than with a clear understanding of each stakeholder's interests and with a solid relationship that has already been established — with a dialogue that has already commenced. I am happy to report that during those golden years leading up to our big crisis at JetBlue, we had done some great work on the relationship and communications front; when the storm hit, JetBlue leaders were able to take advantage of the work we had already done to build our capacity for resilience.

- - - - - - - - - - - - - - - - - -

JetBlue and the Customer Perspective

As a company that had been built on a commitment to exceptional customer service, JetBlue leaders always felt as though we had a good sense of customer interests. As the Valentine's Day winter storm approached, there was a great deal of concern for (and conversation about) these interests. What would customers want JetBlue to do as the storm approached? What would customers expect from JetBlue as the storm covered New York with snow, ice, and conditions that might be simply unsafe for operations? The company could cancel all its flights, just as its competitors had done, and customers would understand. But there was just something about knowing that there might be a break in the weather — enough for JetBlue to operate, and enough to deliver on the company's commitments to its customers. Our customers had come to expect that we'd always try to delight them, and that we'd never let them down if we could avoid it.

Our customers had come to expect that we'd always try to delight them, and that we'd never let them down if we could avoid it.

JetBlue had already developed an exceptional relationship with its customers before the winter of 2007. Their expectations of the airline were pretty simple:

1. **Keep me safe.** Don't do anything that might risk my safety.

2. **Don't lead me on, only to then let me down.** If you're going to cancel, then cancel. Don't make me come to the airport and then cancel my flight.

3. **Give me options.** Let me be a part of the decision process.

4. **If you can do so safely, please try to get me to my destination.** My trip matters to me, and I appreciate that it matters to you too.

Given what turned out to be an irrational sense of hope that the weather might allow JetBlue to operate, company leadership made the decision to do what it could for its customers. Sadly, the hope, while well intended, proved to be a fool's errand.

In the heat of the crisis, what did JetBlue do to care for its customers? We did everything we could.

Before flight operations began on Valentine's Day, the company tried to contact customers who had purchased tickets for the holiday weekend. Our Reservations Department called the phone numbers provided in customer records to offer travelers opportunities to reschedule their flights. Unfortunately, as this was the only holiday of the quarter and as customers had already made deposits on vacation properties, cruises, and the like, many appreciated the phone call but elected to try their luck with the weather. Hope was a powerful lure.

Once operations did begin on Valentine's Day morning, the terminal filled quickly with customers. Some of them were put on their planes and headed out to taxiways. Many, however, quickly realized that they were going to be stuck at JFK for some time. For these customers, JetBlue did its best to communicate regularly at their gates with updates and the latest projections for when they could expect to depart. Carts of snacks and drinks were wheeled out — a customer service extra that, while more commonplace during lengthy delays today, was pretty uncommon then.

Leaders from JetBlue headquarters made our way to JFK, where some of us had been since very early that morning, and positioned ourselves at gates so customers could see and talk to us about what was going on — or rather, what was *not* going on. We talked to our customers about how everyone found themselves here, and what was being done to solve this problem. Some of our leaders were there for days, handing out hundreds of business cards and looking customers in the eyes, telling them that, as executives at JetBlue, the situation was our fault, and that it would never happen again. Personally, it was really, really painful. But it was a defining moment in my career, and an opportunity for JetBlue leaders to "walk the talk."

At other JetBlue destinations (i.e., airports other than JFK), with notice that flights were not leaving or coming from New York into their airport, local gate agents did their best to communicate with customers and share everything the agents knew to help customers understand their situations. Also, it came to pass that a decision JetBlue leaders had made very early in the airline's history ended up producing an exceptional crisis mitigation instrument for station managers at locations away from JFK. During the airline's early strategic planning, executives knew that most of JetBlue's customers would be vacationers and families. With an understanding of what these customers really wanted from an airline and knowing that flight delays were inevitable, all station managers were given an annual budget for pizza, which they were to spend against whenever flights were significantly delayed. Over the President's Day weekend, JetBlue station managers spent tens of thousands of dollars on pizza for waylaid passengers. And while this did not completely resolve the ongoing crisis, it gave customer service crewmembers at JetBlue a mechanism to say "we are truly sorry" — which they had to do hundreds or thousands of times for several days while the airline tried to get its operations up and running again.

Over the President's Day weekend, JetBlue station managers spent tens of thousands of dollars on pizza for waylaid passengers.

During this time, JetBlue's Reservations Department crewmembers worked overtime to talk to customers about their options — refunds or rebookings — and they apologized profusely for something they promised would never happen again. They also had to call on hundreds of customers who had been separated from thousands of bags — helping them understand when they could expect to be reunited with their misplaced belongings.

And finally, JetBlue leadership delivered several messages to customers, designed to help the company recover their trust. David Neeleman, JetBlue's founding CEO, recorded the first-ever corporate YouTube apology (from any company, as far as historical records can determine), which got hundreds of thousands of views.

JetBlue introduced a Customer Bills of Rights to formalize what customers should expect from an airline when it fails to deliver on its commitments and to illustrate how serious the company was about accountability — a key element of establishing or reestablishing trust. Neeleman made appearances on morning and evening talk shows, from *The Today Show* to *The Late Show with David Letterman*, to personally apologize and to talk through what happened, how sorry he and the leadership team were, and the purpose of the JetBlue Airways Customer Bill of Rights.

JetBlue introduced a Customer Bills of Rights to formalize
what customers should expect from an airline when it
fails to deliver on its commitments and to illustrate how
serious the company was about accountability — a key
element of establishing or reestablishing trust.

While some claim that "any media coverage is good media coverage," it sure
didn't feel that way at the time. However, as the world continued to turn and
as we worked hard to regain confidence, six months after the Valentine's Day
Massacre, JetBlue's Brand Strength with Customers (as measured by
third-party experts) was the best it had ever been — better, even, than before
the operational meltdown.

*Why did JetBlue seem to recover so quickly and effectively after the
crisis? Because we understood the interests of our customers, owned our
mistakes as they were made, did our best to recover from the crisis as it
happened, and took steps to clearly articulate how JetBlue would not let
such a crisis happen again. I happen to believe that absolutely any organization — including your organization — can follow these principles to
rebound from a crisis.*

JetBlue and the Crewmember (a.k.a. Employee) Perspective

When JetBlue was founded, the leadership team held a strong belief that
the only way to provide great customer service was to first hire great crewmembers and create a culture where these crewmembers could thrive.
As the Valentine's Day winter storm approached, there was legitimately
as much concern for *crewmember* interests as there was for *customer*
interests. What would crewmembers want JetBlue leadership to do as the
storm approached? What would they expect when the storm was raging
at full force?

Long before the crisis, we had been dedicated to creating a culture that
would serve us well when the going got tough. We founded JetBlue with the
intention of creating a company that was a great place to work. To do so,
the company spent lots of time researching the things that crewmembers

wanted as part of *their* value proposition — compensation, benefits, work environment, culture, etc.

> Long before the crisis, we had been dedicated to creating
> a culture that would serve us well when the going got tough.

What JetBlue had *not* thought about as much during the startup phase were questions such as:

- How will the company engage crewmembers during a crisis?

- How will the company communicate plans for dealing with a particular disruption and how will crewmembers know what they can do to help?

- How will the company care for its crewmembers at least as well as it cares for its customers - in good times and in bad?

These are questions that, if you and your human resources leaders have not yet tackled, deserve your attention now — no matter what industry you work in or how unlikely you believe a crisis to be for your business.

During the Valentine's Day crisis, not having previously given these items much thought proved to be a significant missed opportunity for JetBlue. Doing so would have helped us be better prepared for the disruption.

To understand the impact of an extended crisis like the one JetBlue suffered over President's Day weekend, it is important to know where JetBlue pilots and flight attendants lived when they were not working. First, JetBlue crews — how the company referred to both its pilot and flight attendant groups — were assigned to specific bases. These bases were major operational locations for JetBlue, where combinations of flight assignments started and ended. For JetBlue pilots and flight attendants, all schedules began and finished at an assigned base. At the time of the Valentine's Day meltdown, JFK airport was the company's largest base, with approximately half of its crews based there.

What complicates the "base approach" for all airlines — and this is not unique to JetBlue — is that bases are normally located in urban centers where the cost of living can be very high. So, pilots and flight attendants often choose to live away from their base (where the cost of living is much lower) and commute to work on airplanes (rather than by car or train, like more traditional workforces typically do). While this is a great benefit for airline crewmembers, it poses a huge risk during snowstorms or other crises that impact flight operations; what happens to an airline when crewmembers cannot get from where they live to where they work? If JFK is your company's largest base of operations and almost everyone who works there flies in for their shift, what happens when all commuting options are taken away for several days? Well, what happens is that the company runs out of crews to operate the airline.

During the Valentine's Day Crisis, JetBlue crews were having a hard time getting to New York, but they were also overloading phone lines at company headquarters, expressing their strong desire to come to New York and help in any way possible. JetBlue simply did not have a good way to engage them, as our organization had not considered the possibility of a winter storm so bad that crews might not be able to get to New York for multiple days. This was frustrating for both crewmembers and company leadership. Imagine spending years building a company that was focused on creating a great place to work — where team-based problem solving and collaboration were core to your business — but then finding yourself in the midst of a crisis where employees were desperately trying to help but weren't given the tools to do so. Add to this a compensation package that included rewards for company performance — performance that depended on the company's ability to operate effectively. Accordingly, not only were crewmembers frustrated by a feeling of helplessness, but also by the performance failure of a company in which they had an ownership stake.

- -

Imagine spending years building a company that was focused
on creating a great place to work — where team-based problem
solving and collaboration were core to your business — but then
finding yourself in the midst of a crisis where employees were
desperately trying to help but weren't given the tools to do so.

- -

To further complicate the situation, JetBlue had been slow to make much-needed infrastructure investments during 2005 and 2006, as rapidly increasing fuel prices had placed a premium on cash preservation. We had not invested in the technology required to allow an expeditious reconstruction of assignments for pilots and flight attendants — something we found ourselves desperately needing so we could restart the airline after the winter storm. We also hadn't invested in the technology to quickly determine which flights were the most important and profitable to operate. If we were going to gradually reinstate flights following the storm, we certainly would have wanted to begin with the highest-priority flights. Sadly, we had no way to quickly determine which flights would be best to operate first. Our decisions to delay investments in critical infrastructure improvements unquestionably contributed to the damage done by the crisis.

Crewmember challenges during the crisis were not limited to our inability to get pilots and flight attendants to their bases and to rebuild their schedules. JetBlue's customer service crewmembers, both those who worked at airports across the route system and those who worked at the company's Reservation Center in Salt Lake City, did generally live close to the places they worked. In fact, because Reservations crewmembers (ResCrew) worked out of their own homes, they were essentially always at work — if needed. This was fortunate and has proven to be a remarkably effective crisis response resource throughout JetBlue's entire history.

For those crewmembers who worked at JFK airport, our thinking was that if customers could get to the airport, then crewmembers ought to be able to get there as well. The company had not, however, considered the need for increasing staffing levels when the operation started to break down. As it turns out, getting additional crewmembers to JFK became a problem that was never resolved during the three-day period of peak crisis.

As the storm (and the operational crisis) raged on, JetBlue's Reservations crewmembers went on overtime, which grew exponentially throughout Valentine's Day. For the next six days, every ResCrew member was scheduled for as many hours as they could accept. Shifts were long, breaks were short, and customers were angry. It was not a pretty week.

Ultimately, JetBlue learned a great deal about its crewmember stakeholders during the President's Day weekend crisis. First, JetBlue leaders learned that building a great culture and hiring crewmembers who knew and believed in the vision and mission of JetBlue was a great investment for building resilience. The leadership team was amazed by the number of crewmembers who wanted to do what they could for customers, for each other, and for any stakeholder who needed help.

JetBlue leaders also discovered that by not investing in the ability to deal more effectively with operational disruptions, we had limited our crew-members' ability to contribute. In so doing, company leadership had not only limited our company's ability to recover quickly from operational challenges, but we also sacrificed crewmember trust. Crewmembers felt that leadership had let them down — that they had been assured everything was under control but, in fact, it was not. Employee trust and confidence should never be taken for granted — and there was the appearance that leadership had done just that.

Employee trust and confidence should never be taken for granted.

To regain the trust of crewmembers, leaders took to the road just days after JetBlue relaunched a full schedule of operations. Executives from across the leadership team headed out to all JetBlue cities to deliver summaries of what happened, mistakes that had been made, and what would be done to regain their trust. The sessions were all remarkably successful. Crewleaders and crewmembers were able to connect in ways that only common experiences can facilitate, and, in this case, the common experience was the collective pain everyone felt as a result of living through the Valentine's Day Massacre.

- - - - - - - - - - - - - - - - - -

JetBlue and the Regulator Perspective

While it could be argued that customers and crewmembers were the most important stakeholders to attend to during the Valentine's Day crisis, airlines operate in a complex industry with myriad stakeholders who require attention during critical moments. Regulators were no exception.

From the very beginning at JetBlue — in fact, even before the airline had a name — JetBlue leaders knew that we would need strong partnerships with several government agencies and elected officials to be successful. In particular, we would need a great partnership with the Federation Aviation Administration (FAA).

The process of building partnerships with these stakeholder groups — and learning directly from the individuals leading these organizations what they really wanted and needed from JetBlue — helped us to deliver value. to regulators from our very first day. The rapport and trust we built with these key people and organizations also helped company leaders understand how this value might be threatened during "irregular operations" (the term used in the airline industry to describe situations when things are not running normally).

JetBlue's colleagues at the FAA were fully and transparently informed of the airline's business model, its operating philosophy, and our company goals and objectives. They knew that company leaders would want to support customers however and whenever they could. They also knew that JetBlue leaders were totally committed to safety. It was, after all, one of the company's core values — values that were discussed regularly with all company stakeholders. The FAA also knew that JetBlue leaders were keenly aware of the FAA's responsibilities in ensuring the safety of its customers.

Not surprisingly, when JetBlue leadership reached out to the FAA early on Valentine's Day morning (as we were learning that the company's attempts to operate were going to be pressured by the challenging weather), the FAA was expecting the call.

JetBlue leadership informed the FAA about what was going on and about what we were trying to do. They responded that while they were disappointed that the company had not canceled the schedule for the day — obviously the safest and easiest answer — they recognized it was a company choice (and not theirs) to make. The FAA made it clear that they were standing by to help however they could and that they were working with Air Traffic Control and the Port Authority at JFK airport to keep things moving and airspace open.

What else could a company possibly want from its regulator?

As the day got longer and JetBlue began to have greater numbers of frustrated customers in its terminals — particularly JFK's Terminal 6 — and lengthening delays, with customers and crews sequestered on airplanes stuck on various taxiways around JFK, JetBlue opened a line to the FAA and kept it open. Operational leaders gave regulators continuous updates on progress and listened to their advice and guidance on how best to manage situations that could become safety issues. While the FAA did not exist to be an operating partner, they turned out to be quite supportive when they had safety information and recommendations to share.

For JetBlue, the operational crisis lasted three days and by the end of it, JetBlue had, in fact, stranded several aircraft (with customers and crew on them) for six hours or more on JFK taxiways. The primary reason for this was an inability to physically move these planes because the taxiways were so ice-covered that they could not move under their own engine power. If that wasn't bad enough, moving the planes in an alternate fashion or even offloading people to walk away from their aircraft on foot weren't options because tow vehicles and air stairs were unable to move either. The growing coat of ice was crippling, dangerous, and literally brought all airport movement to a standstill. JetBlue leaders just had not foreseen this as a possibility. Nor, for that matter, had the FAA.

During the post-crisis debrief that was held with the FAA and facility leaders at JFK airport, all parties agreed that, while communication during the crisis had been exemplary, the outcomes were still unacceptable. Because of JetBlue's relationships with these leaders, all parties were comfortable admitting errors that had been made, moments when parties should have been more proactive, and where better choices could have been made throughout the event. We were candid about what was out of our control (i.e., the weather) but we were humble and regretful about the eventual crisis that unfolded. In the end, what happened was absolutely JetBlue's fault because the company ultimately owned the choice to try to fly. Among the three groups — JetBlue leadership, JFK facility leadership, and FAA officials — it was agreed that the outcomes could have been much less serious if all stakeholders had worked together more effectively as a team.

- -

During the post-crisis debrief that was held with the
FAA and facility leaders at JFK airport, all parties agreed
that, while communication during the crisis had been
exemplary, the outcomes were still unacceptable.

- -

In many ways, for all the pain we experienced, the Valentine's Day crisis strengthened JetBlue's relationship with its regulators. To this day, JetBlue continues to benefit from the exceptional partnership.

- - - - - - - - - - - - - - - - - -

JetBlue and the Media Perspective

A company that commences operations in the media capital of the world (New York) should recognize that great accomplishments *and* spectacular failures will be fully covered and shared with the public — and that the failures would always make the most salacious headlines.

As such, you might be wondering how JetBlue leaders viewed the interests of the media and the potential coverage of their decisions as the Valentine's Day winter storm approached. And once the storm was in full force, how did JetBlue leadership decide to engage with the media — not simply to meet their interests, but to leverage their ability to reach large audiences very quickly? It was a saga of the good, the bad, and the ugly.

JetBlue leadership knew that basing an airline in New York City would mean great performance would be rewarded with great media coverage and lots of publicity. The company also knew that if things did not go well — if performance for any reason was poor — it should expect to get more than its fair share of media coverage saying so. During the Valentine's Day Crisis, this is exactly what happened.

The local media, which quickly turned into *national* media, had a field day with JetBlue's operational meltdown. Six field days, in fact. Day after day of lead stories about our crisis.

Fortunately, in 2007, there was not the same internet-driven social media landscape that exists today. There were some early platforms but customer commentary had only a few limited avenues to become public. There were no disastrous "Twitter storms" or trending hashtags as, for the most part, print and television media were still the primary mechanisms for the delivery and consumption of news. To this day, I remain grateful for that. Thank goodness for small favors!

During the crisis, the print headlines did not miss the opportunity for some sensationalism. Local newspapers played on claims of "hostage" situations that JetBlue had created by trapping customers on airplanes for 10 or 11 hours — which were exaggerations, but for many media outlets, exaggerations were how they connected most effectively with their audiences.

One particularly brutal example of print media's treatment of the JetBlue failure was a *BusinessWeek* magazine cover[3] that was a true gut-punch. Leading up to the crisis, *BusinessWeek* had contacted JetBlue to let the company know that it was about to print a story that announced JetBlue as the #4 company in the entire United States for customer service, behind USAA, Four Seasons hotels, and Cadillac, and just ahead of Nordstrom. Pretty good company to be in! We were thrilled.

But just before the magazine went to print, as JetBlue was struggling through its winter storm crisis, *BusinessWeek* decided to update its cover story and literally scribbled out JetBlue's name and added some text next to the magazine issue's coverlines — "Customer Service Champs ... Here's the magnificent 25 ... *and one extraordinary stumble*" — to highlight JetBlue's tragic fall from grace. That was tough for all JetBlue stakeholders to see. But company leaders knew all along that the media could be your best friend or your worst enemy — and the company set out with an attitude that embraced the scrutiny — in good times and in bad. Next time, we would do better.

So, when the media is making things difficult during and after a crisis, how can a leadership team provide each outlet what it wants and, at the same time, leverage their interests to help reach key audiences? The answer is using your understanding of *their* interests to serve your own.

What does the media ultimately want? They want access — ideally exclusive access — to stories and people of interest to their audiences. During the Valentine's Day event, people wanted to hear details. What had gone wrong?

---

3   *BusinessWeek* (March 5, 2007).

How bad did things really get? Who was going to get fired? How did the CEO feel about the company's performance? What was he going to do about it? And was *he* going to get fired?

> What does the media ultimately want? They want access — ideally exclusive access — to stories and people of interest to their audiences.

All these questions circulated in one of the largest media markets in the world. People wanted details and answers. This begs two questions of leaders when engaging the media:

1. What answers *could* be given to them?
2. What answers *should* be given to them?

In every crisis, leaders are going to have to decide what information they share with various stakeholder groups. Among the many reasons to study crisis leadership is to gain an understanding of the information different stakeholders want to hear and to gain a working knowledge of the different channels that might be used to deliver that information.

This knowledge will help answer questions like: "How will we reach customers if we have *this* sort of difficult message to deliver?" Or "How will we reach investors or analysts or regulators if we have *that* sort of message to deliver?" Considering these questions before a crisis strikes can be a particularly useful exercise.

In the case of the Valentine's Day crisis at JetBlue, media outlets wanted their audiences to hear more about the tragedy — more about how decisions had been made, who made them, and why they made them, as well as more about the short- and long-term impact of the crisis and what would be different going forward. Some outlets went so far as to dig into who was going to pay for the company's "undeniable disregard" (their words, not ours) for customer safety and convenience.

The truth was that nobody at JetBlue had disregarded these things at all — in fact, they were always front of mind for us as we tried to do our best during an overwhelming situation. But the evidence did not suggest in a compelling way that company leaders had behaved responsibly. So it was easy for the media to be critical, to use superlatives in headlines and live coverage, and to make the disaster look even more disastrous than it actually was.

Given that JetBlue had an honest, transparent, and responsible message to share, and that the message made it clear that the entire crisis was, in fact, the company's fault (a product of leadership decisions that were made for the right reasons but that resulted in exceptionally poor outcomes), there was clearly a single best answer for what JetBlue should do. It was: Get company leaders in front of the cameras! JetBlue leadership had a compelling story to tell. And it was a story of ownership, accountability, and sincere repentance. The company made mistakes while trying to do the right thing for all its stakeholders. Unfortunately, the execution was poor.

JetBlue leadership had a compelling story to tell. And it was a story of ownership, accountability, and sincere repentance.

In circumstances such as this, it is best to get the story of ownership and responsibility to as broad an audience as possible. In fact, this is where social media can become an exceptionally powerful asset. Most leaders fail to consider how the media as a stakeholder can be an incredibly valuable partner in these pursuits. As with any stakeholder, if you have a clear sense of their interests and can see how your interests can align with theirs as you navigate through a significant challenge, you might just be able to satisfy everyone's interests by working together.

That said, in the spirit of increasing organizational resilience, it is worth the time for leaders to develop relationships with local media. It is also worth applying a media-worthy litmus test to the potential outcomes of challenging decisions. "If what we are about to do goes sideways," the leadership team should ask of themselves, "how will the outcome be interpreted by the media (or any stakeholder, for that matter)? Then, beyond that, how will we, as a leadership team, respond to their interpretation?"

Like having a mindset that everything you write in an email message has the potential to become public, these questions about a high-stakes leader's ultimate intentions are great ones to have in mind before clicking the send button or giving the order to execute.

JetBlue and the Investor Perspective

All businesses that require capital to operate — just about all businesses, that is — will be watched closely by those who provided the capital. This is simply a reality of business.

As the Valentine's Day winter storm approached, how did JetBlue leaders view the interests of their investors? How did these interests influence the decisions of the leadership team?

It would be easy to look at JetBlue's decision to try and operate — in very difficult conditions, while all its competitors had ceased operations for the first two days of the President's Day holiday — as a purely financial decision. This was not our sole motivation for the decisions we made but, of course, there was pressure on the JetBlue leadership team to deliver some financial returns to our investors.

For some perspective on this pressure, let me provide some context. JetBlue had delivered a total net loss of $20M in 2005, due largely to increases in fuel costs. While in 2004, the airline had paid, on average, $1.06 per gallon of jet fuel, prices in 2005 had risen to an average of $1.61 per gallon. This 52% increase in fuel prices multiplied by the 303 million gallons that JetBlue burned during the year meant that the company spent almost $167M more on fuel than it would have at the prior year's price. The airline was able to raise ticket prices moderately and find other efficiencies to offset some of the increase in fuel costs, but we were still left with a $20M loss. In 2006, JetBlue again faced increasing fuel costs. For the year, the average fuel price per gallon was $1.99, significantly higher than the prior year's average price of $1.61. This added, all in, about $145M in costs to the company's balance sheet. In an industry with typically thin margins and very little power to increase ticket prices as costs increase, it was somewhat miraculous that JetBlue was able to trim its net loss in 2006 to $1M.

> A 52% increase in fuel prices in 2005, multiplied by the
> 303 million gallons that JetBlue burned during the year
> ,meant that the company spent almost $167M more on
> fuel than it would have at the prior year's price.

The message to JetBlue's investors going into 2007 included references to how the company's operating margins for the past two years had been better than all but one of the major airlines operating in the United States — and that was Southwest Airlines. Company leaders also told investors that JetBlue's load factor (i.e., the percentage of seats filled by paying customers) was higher than all major U.S. carriers for the two prior years and that the company's flight completion factor (i.e., scheduled flights that were actually completed), incident and accident rates, denied boarding rates, and mishandled or lost baggage rates were all *the very best* of any airline operating in North America. JetBlue leaders were "talking a pretty big game" because, in performance categories other than profitability, JetBlue was objectively the best airline in the country. This is not to suggest that profitability is not important, because clearly it is. But if JetBlue's performance in virtually every category was as good as or better than its competitors and the company was still unable to make a profit, something would have to change for the entire industry to survive — and when it did, JetBlue was in a great position to benefit from it.

Thus, going into 2007, investor expectations of JetBlue were on the rise. The airline was well-positioned and performance metrics were all trending in the right direction. Two years had been spent developing new policies and procedures in all areas of the company to drive cost efficiencies. Fuel prices were still somewhat volatile, but after the past two years of significant increases, the consensus was that the forward-looking pricing curve was projected to flatten. Things were looking very promising.

Most people understand how the investor market tends to view company performance by fiscal quarter. And, yes, while today's market has more traders than ever who make investment decisions on periods much shorter than three months, financial reporting is still typically anchored to quarterly updates. So, for JetBlue, the first quarter of 2007 was going to be very important for investors. We felt a pressure and an excitement about delivering on those expectations.

As I've mentioned previously, JetBlue was very much a leisure airline. Most customers flew JetBlue for vacations, not necessarily for business. What does that say about how and when JetBlue generates most of its revenue? JetBlue typically operated with negative margins during the week (i.e., Monday through Friday), and with positive margins on weekends and holidays. The summer season was always very good for JetBlue, while the first quarter of every year was driven by how well the company performed over what are typically two separate Q1 holidays in the United States — President's Day weekend in the middle of February, and Easter, which falls toward the end of March or in very early April each year. Unfortunately for JetBlue, given investor expectations, Easter 2007 was going to fall on April 8th, which meant the entire Easter Weekend holiday was going to contribute to earnings for Q2 instead of Q1.

Why is all this so important to cover in a book about high-stakes leadership? There are two reasons. First, it serves as an illustration of how important it is for an organizational leader to understand the company's financials. If you're going to engage investors as true stakeholders (and not just stockholders), you need to understand their interests and how to communicate with them in terms of those interests. The second reason is to help you understand the financial circumstances for JetBlue leading up to the President's Day holiday weekend. Was the company's decision to fly that weekend, while its competitors had canceled everything, a financial decision? Of course it was. But it was not *exclusively* a financial decision. JetBlue leaders truly believed that other stakeholders — customers, crewmembers, and politicians who represent communities that depend on tourism, in particular — wanted JetBlue to operate if it could do so safely. And we didn't want to let those stakeholders down.

From an investor perspective, not operating — especially if the weather ultimately did not deteriorate to the point that would have precluded flying — was not in their best interests. So, JetBlue attempted to operate, and failed. As the failure was playing out, what do you suppose investors wanted to know? As JetBlue's operation deteriorated, how were investors calculating the threat to their value proposition with the airline? The answer is not rocket science. As the crisis escalated, investors first thought about lost revenue. As delays began to extend and flight cancellations became a requirement simply due to unavailable crews and equipment, investors saw short-term lost revenues.

As cancellations increased and a public relations crisis began to form, investors then started to worry not only about lost revenues, but about remuneration, regulatory penalties and fines, and, after a couple of days, they also began to question the long-term potential brand damage as seen through the eyes of customers, employees, and other investors.

As the Valentine's Day Massacre played out, JetBlue leadership could almost sense the collective gasp from their investors. In the spirit of effective crisis management, what does a company tell investors when it's in the middle of something like this? Perhaps most importantly, the company cannot relax its total focus on stopping the bleeding just to communicate with stockholders — we needed to act before we could communicate. That said, as soon as the tourniquet had been applied to our proverbial wound (and the primary crisis has been mitigated or resolved), company leaders needed to address this stakeholder group's concerns.

As the Valentine's Day Massacre played out, JetBlue leadership could almost sense the collective gasp from their investors.

In messages sent through the company's own channels — such as general and targeted emails and through various media channels — JetBlue laid out a compelling case for why investors should still have confidence in the company. JetBlue corporate communications shared timing details of when the crisis was largely resolved so that short-term losses could be calculated. Investors were accustomed to (although they did not like) the short-term impact of weather or air-traffic-related cancellations. Therefore, three days of lost revenue to "the storm of the century" was easy to explain. The other three days, however, and the long-term potential brand damage, on the other hand, were much more difficult to justify.

JetBlue leaders ultimately owned the issue, demonstrating integrity. We explained what went wrong and why it would not happen again, hopefully easing concerns about re-occurrences and impact on mid-term earnings. Also, for what it was worth, we reminded investors that Easter was a bonus holiday in the second quarter and that the airline expected Q2 earnings to be solid as long as — and this was a big question in the minds of investors — the company could restore the confidence of customers (and, to some degree, employees and politicians). This was one big reason JetBlue brought forward the first-ever Customer Bill of Rights. JetBlue's CEO had taken the concept to the U.S. Congress prior to this as an effort to raise levels of accountability among airlines for their poor customer service. But now was a chance to bring it forward again as a mechanism to restore trust in our own brand.

It seemed to work. Customers and investors alike bashed JetBlue for the meltdown, but largely applauded the company's response. Decision-making leading up to the crisis was questioned for many months afterwards, but decision-making during the airline's recovery is still, to this day, regarded as some of the very best ever seen in the sector.

Customers and investors largely applauded the company's response. Decision-making during the airline's recovery is still, to this day, regarded as some of the very best ever seen in the sector.

JetBlue and the Competitor Perspective

As we worked our way through the crisis at JetBlue, we had one more stakeholder group to consider: our competitors. How would competitors be assessing the JetBlue team's decisions as the Valentine's Day winter storm approached the New York area? Would they have any interest in these decisions at all? Or would we expect this to be an "everyone for themselves" situation, where the decisions of individual competitors don't really matter to the other players?

If you want to be a competitive force in whatever industry you decide to be a part of, you need to understand (the best that you can) why your competitors make the choices that they do. Generally, you will find that the answers are relatively intuitive. But you should still be exploring, in depth, the decision-making habits of your competitors so you can be the best competitor possible.

If you want to be a competitive force in whatever industry you decide to be a part of, you need to understand (the best that you can) why your competitors make the choices that they do.

Why were JetBlue's competitors so quick to cancel large parts of their flight schedules in and out of the New York area ahead of the predicted storm? First, they flew much smaller percentages of their operations in the New York area than JetBlue did. Canceling New York operations for Delta or American was a difficult choice, but one that did not as significantly impact their overall flight schedule or revenue plan as it would have impacted JetBlue.

Also, and perhaps more importantly, these airlines, being much more mature than JetBlue, knew that thoughtful and purposeful cancellations ahead of a weather system like this one would make it much easier to resume operations once the storm had passed. As JetBlue learned during this crisis, it is one thing to have to cancel and re-route a few flights on short notice, but it is an entirely different thing to have to completely rebuild a flight schedule that had planned to operate about 500 flights each day — even with crews and airplanes in predictable places. During the crisis, JetBlue had to recreate a 500-flight schedule with *all* its crews and airplanes in different places than they were planned to be. To make matters worse, JetBlue leadership had been slow to make investments in technology that would have allowed this to be done with what amounts to the push of a button — which is essentially what airlines have today (including JetBlue). At the time, however, on the back of two challenging years of rapidly rising costs, JetBlue just didn't have the resources to invest in updating its technology infrastructure.

As the Valentine's Day crisis played out, the reconstruction of an entire flight operations plan became a long and painful process — long enough that it required three additional days after the weather had moved on, to get things up and running again.

Initially, when JetBlue demonstrated a commitment to operating when all its competitors had canceled, the airline was clearly trying to apply some competitive pressure. If JetBlue was able to pull this off, it might create exactly the sort of message to customers that it wanted to send — that the company truly was different from the competition, and that we put customers first. So, although it can never be known for sure, there were probably a few brief moments when the competition was thinking, "Those sons of a gun. If they make this work, they'll look like heroes and we'll look like we don't care about our customers." Maybe they didn't think that, but

I can't help but imagine that they did. Ultimately, it doesn't matter what they thought. JetBlue attempted to operate and failed.

What JetBlue did accomplish, however, was to shine a spotlight on the industry. From stranding customers in terminals, which was ugly in and of itself, to stranding them in airplanes — in some cases, for hours — the airline raised regulatory concerns not just for JetBlue, but for every player in the industry. "If JetBlue could create this much pain and suffering," so the stream of consciousness went in the minds of regulators and governmental officials, "what's to stop other airlines from doing the same thing?"

This logic, driven by circumstances rather than by a complete assessment of the evidence, then morphed into regulators thinking (and some of them actually saying): "We represent our constituents, and we just can't let this happen. Those airlines are making decisions for their own benefit, not the benefit of the customers. Airlines can't be trusted to do the right things on their own, so we need more regulation across the industry. We should make a rule that imposes fines for unnecessary delays. That would force them to consider how their actions are impacting customers. Maybe we should also create a rule that requires airlines to provide opportunities for customers to deplane after sitting on a plane for an extended period." And the discussion of other "potentially helpful" regulations would play on from there. In fact, regulations like these are regular topics of discussion across the industry by airlines and regulators alike.

These types of reactions from regulators are exactly why competitors can and should be thought of as stakeholders. In some industries — and the airline industry is a good example — actions by one competitor can have an impact on all the others beyond the simple impact of what might be considered traditional competition, such as competition on price, variety, product features, or other factors.

When a company makes choices that put an entire sector at risk in some way — increased governmental oversight, decreased customer confidence, increasing costs, etc. — all competitors can be impacted in ways that create tension. Occasionally, competitive responses extend beyond typical competition and can threaten the survival of an entire industry, much like the Collateralized Debt Obligation (CDO) offering did to the banking industry during the financial crisis of 2008. For many large, established, previously successful banks, the CDO was the beginning of the end. The point here is not to argue the pros and cons of intent — as could be argued for JetBlue's decision to operate or a particular bank's decision to offer a CDO — but to highlight the potential impact a competitor could have on an entire industry. This is why considering competitors as stakeholders can provide a helpful framework for decision-making.

- -

Considering competitors as stakeholders can provide a helpful framework for decision-making.

- -

Another JetBlue decision that resulted from the events of President's Day Weekend event — one that impacted the competitive landscape of the industry — was the choice to announce its Customer Bill of Rights. While the consequences of JetBlue's attempt and failure to successfully operate seized the attention of regulators and impacted competitors in unintended and unfortunate ways, JetBlue's decision to announce its Bill of Rights was very intentional — and it was designed to impact the industry at large.

JetBlue leadership believed that a Bill of Rights would be a great way to demonstrate to customers a heightened commitment to better performance — a performance guarantee. It was designed to differentiate the airline from its competitors. Other airlines didn't have such a clearly articulated guarantee, so JetBlue could be a leader in this area. But if you further unpack our intentions, particularly if you view this action through the lens of competitors as stakeholders, why do you think competitors actually supported this bold move? If you were an executive at Delta or United at the time, how would you have viewed JetBlue's announcement?

My fellow leaders and I at JetBlue believed that executives at airlines across North America would view our Bill of Rights announcement as timely, responsible, and generally *good* for the industry. How could that be? First, airlines don't like delays any more than customers do. Delays create challenges for many different aspects of the business and they always cost more than when flights operate on time. A formalized matrix of customer compensation for delays was something all airlines either already had in place, to some degree, or had been contemplating. While JetBlue might have been a first mover in announcing something that was elegantly packaged, it was not an advantage that would last long. On top of that, JetBlue had made its announcement on the back end of a major meltdown. Bonus points for JetBlue's creativity, but it was not going to create a lasting competitive advantage.

Second, airlines were undoubtedly concerned that JetBlue's "irresponsible" decision to operate during a storm would prompt officials to impose increased regulation. Generally, if you speak to just about any business leader, they will tell you that they would prefer *less* regulation instead of more. Also, interestingly, if you speak to just about any governmental official, they will tell you that they only want to increase regulation when business decisions are not being made "in the best interests of citizens or customers." They do not generally want more regulations, but if companies are not being responsible, then regulations may be required to make them so.

JetBlue's announcement of the Bill of Rights sent the message to regulators that "we are taking steps to regulate ourselves — to be more responsible to customers, to own our mistakes, and to make things right without a regulation that requires us to do so." Viewing this action from a *competitor as stakeholder* perspective, JetBlue's competitors found it to be significantly beneficial for all.

Organizational leaders may not spend much time thinking about competitors as stakeholders. They may not *have* to, depending on the state of their industry. But in some cases, adding this perspective to the collection of stakeholders a company should be considering may provide a path to sector leadership that allows an organization to be significantly more competitive and that could increase an enterprise's ability to influence the direction of an entire industry, as JetBlue has done in so many ways.

There you have it. As JetBlue leadership worked through its operational crisis in 2007, the interests of its stakeholders were front and center. In this case, it was JetBlue's collection of primary stakeholders that drew most of our attention: customers, employees, regulators, media, investors, and competitors. Each of these groups had unique and, in many ways, competing interests.

In the end, JetBlue's ability to understand, appreciate, and address the interests of their stakeholders during and after its worst operational crisis to date allowed the company to not only survive, but to emerge from this crisis a stronger company with an even better connection to and relationship with its stakeholders. And the lessons from JetBlue, and from many other organizations who have "been there and done that" during organizational crisis or disruption, can be instructive for you and your colleagues as well. Profit from our pain, learn from our mistakes, emulate our thoughtful strategies. High-stakes leadership is an art and a science, and it *can* be learned.

- -

JetBlue's ability to understand, appreciate, and address the interests of their stakeholders during and after its worst operational crisis to date allowed the company to not only survive, but to emerge from this crisis a stronger company with an even better connection to and relationship with its stakeholders.

- -

06

BEYOND THE HEADLINES
Stakeholder Engagement During a Crisis

Once you understand that a business ultimately exists to create value for its stakeholders, it's simple to determine the value proposition of each. With your stakeholders' perspectives in mind, it is similarly simple to predict how these value propositions would be or are being threatened during a crisis. If you and your colleagues haven't taken the time to grab a notebook or huddle around a white board to thoroughly explore these exercises, now's the time. This work is the foundation for everything you can and should do when crisis strikes.

Once you know the value propositions of each of your stakeholder groups and have a sense of how stakeholder interests are threatened during a disruptive event, you have the tools necessary to develop a plan to serve and engage key stakeholders during a crisis.

Let's return for a moment to the stakeholder interests from the story of JetBlue's Valentine's Day Massacre crisis and let's develop some hypotheses about how we should be engaging stakeholders during a crisis. When we find ourselves amid a crisis, there are some questions we need to be asking ourselves.

Which stakeholders have been impacted by the situation and which have been impacted most significantly?

Exploring this question should be part of your initial steps to resolve a developing crisis, while you are seeking to limit the damage as much as possible. Identifying initial impact on stakeholders won't be an exact science, but leaders should trust themselves to assess each group and quantify the extent to which this particular situation has resulted in hardship. It's quite possible that all stakeholders will be impacted by your crisis. It's also likely that some will be impacted more than others. In this initial step, it is worth identifying both.

- -

> It's quite possible that all stakeholders will be impacted by your crisis. It's also likely that some will be impacted more than others. In this initial step, it is worth identifying both.

- -

How should each of these groups be engaged?

If you think there's time to engage them all — which is unlikely in the early stages of a crisis, but possible — then you should really try to do so in some way (at least at a high level). Why? Because when we find ourselves facing a crisis, we typically want our stakeholders to know that *we* know — that we are aware of the situation, that we recognize the need for action, and that we're hard at work to resolve the problem. At the onset of a crisis, sometimes the best way to let everyone know that you're on the case is to issue a general press release and promise additional information in the very near future. It would be even better if you set a specific date, time, and communication method for the next general update — you'll learn why shortly.

What messages do your stakeholders need to hear?

After thinking through the "who" and the "how" from the two questions above, it's time to be thinking about the precise messages you need to share with each stakeholder group. There is surely much you need to be doing to

manage the situation, but stakeholder messaging should never be an after-
thought. Consider how, when, and through what medium your stakeholders
want to hear the key messages? From what source (i.e., from your CEO, your
customer service department, the local media)? At what frequency? And, if
you can't immediately engage all stakeholders, when will you be able to do
so in a meaningful way?

These are all challenging questions and, to answer them, you will need to
draw upon the limited time and resources at your disposal during a crisis.
They will all require a great deal of thought, effort, and, unfortunately,
direct exposure to stakeholder reactions and emotions. In a crisis, we know
that our stakeholders will be looking for tangible evidence of leadership
— leaders who they can believe in. So this is when we need to step up and
lead — to put ourselves in front of our stakeholders — to make sure they see
that someone is in charge and that action is being taken. It was with this in
mind that my colleagues and I at JetBlue engaged directly with customers
in Terminal 6 at JFK during those fateful days in February 2007, and why
we produced a YouTube apology, called meetings with the FAA and JFK
Operations, talked extensively with our crewmembers, and more. If nothing
else, it was important to us that our stakeholders could literally *see* us —
stepping up, owning the crisis, and taking the heat.

**In a crisis, we know that our stakeholders will be looking for
tangible evidence of leadership — leaders who they can believe in.**

In the early stages of a crisis, leaders tend to step back to take the time to
get a clear picture of the situation and a clear sense of the facts. But you
simply won't have the time to do that — to gain enough clarity to feel good
about your understanding of the situation — or, at least, good enough to
confidently face your stakeholders. But you will still have to face them. They
want and need to hear from you. And you need to be able to engage them, as
uncomfortable and disconcerting as this may feel.

Developing the confidence, character, and capacity to do this during a crisis
requires a set of capabilities that you will need to develop over time and
with practice and experience — none of which I will be able to provide you
in sufficient quantity through this book. I will, however, do my very best to

provide a foundational set of tools that will accelerate your development of these capabilities. Ultimately, stakeholder engagement during a crisis is about preserving and re-establishing stakeholder trust. Your ability to do this effectively will be determined by your readiness to do so.

Becoming THE Source of Facts During a Crisis — The Impact of Social Media

When an organization finds itself in a crisis, each of its stakeholders will be concerned about the threat to their specific value proposition. Predictably, each will be looking for any information they can uncover to better understand the nature, extent, and potential impact of the threat. One of your many responsibilities as a high-stakes leader should be to position yourself and your team as the primary sources of this information.

Why is it so important for an individual or a small team within an organization to serve as the primary source of "the facts" during a crisis? Because not only will stakeholders look everywhere to discover information, but there is evidence that many will demonstrate a belief in just about anything that they find.

What evidence exists to support this claim? From our own experiences, we know this to be true. When was the last time that you conducted a Google search for an answer to a problem that you were trying to solve? When you searched, did you find it challenging to differentiate the good advice from the bad? Was it difficult to separate fact from fiction? If you struggled a bit in your attempts to find the "right" information, you are not alone. As we have all learned from our own experiences, sometimes the information on the internet is not particularly accurate, complete, or unbiased.

During a crisis, when stakeholders are not getting the information they want, need, or expect, where will they go to get it? When they visit the internet (particularly when they head over to Facebook or Twitter) to learn about an ongoing crisis, what might they find? How accurate is the prevailing information likely to be? How would they know the difference between good information and bad? Common sense tells us that Google may not be the best place to find accurate information about a developing crisis, but the search engine has become so integral to our lives that it is reasonable to assume that it will be used, nonetheless. For high-stakes leaders, this can become a significant liability. In fact, we all saw this play out during the COVID-19 pandemic in many ways. But before I share a pandemic-related example of this phenomenon, consider the following.

Between 2014 and 2016, researcher Jay Walker studied societal interactions during the Ebola crisis in western Africa. In an article titled "Civil Society's Role in a Public Health Crisis" published in *Issues in Science and Technology (2016)*, Walker prophetically suggested the following about a specific challenge that high-stakes leaders would someday have to face:

> "When the next major pandemic strikes, it will be accompanied by something never before seen in human history: an explosion of billions of texts, tweets, e-mails, blogs, photos, and videos rocketing across the planet's computers and mobile devices. Some of these billions of words and pictures will have useful information, but many will be filled with rumors, innuendo, misinformation, and hyper-sensational claims. Repeated tidal waves of messages and images will quickly overwhelm traditional information sources, including national governments, global news media outlets, and even on-the-ground first responders. As a result, hundreds of millions of people will receive unvetted and incorrect assertions, uncensored images, and unqualified guidance, all of which, if acted on, could endanger their own health, seriously damage their economies, and undermine the stability of their societies ..."[1]

Amidst the COVID-19 pandemic, we saw precisely these events play out before our eyes. A particularly interesting manifestation of this involved Corona Beer, a product of Grupo Modelo (a subsidiary of Anheuser-Busch InBev), which is brewed in Mexico and exported widely to the United States. While reports have suggested that Corona sales were not negatively impacted by the beer's name (which it shares with the "coronavirus," the generic term often used to refer to the SARS-CoV-2 virus that causes

---

1   Jay Walker, "Civil Society's Role in a Public Health Crisis," *Issues in Science and Technology*, 32, no. 4 (2016), https://issues.org/civil-societys-role-in-a-public-health-crisis/.

COVID-19), there is evidence to suggest that not everyone has been able to embrace the lack of relation.

In an article published by *USA Today* on January 29, 2020, a headline read "The coronavirus has nothing to do with Corona beer. But, some people seem to think so."[2] The article cited the surge in Google searches for: "corona beer," "corona beer virus," and "beer virus," suggesting that some people were presuming a correlation (or at least an entertaining irony) between the beverage and the coronavirus outbreak.

While this somewhat comical headline may result in some head scratching by most readers, there is evidence that the impact of social media's embracing of the story has, in fact, produced a behavioral result. The following photographs, taken in liquor stores in the United Kingdom, are just two of the many that were shared on social media to document the impact of the Corona/COVID-19 connection.

Image Credit: (Left) James Hurley/Twitter); (Right) Laura Kelleher/Twitter

2   Adrianna Rodriguez.,"The coronavirus has nothing to do with Corona beer. But, some people seem to think so," *USA Today* (January 29, 2020), https://www.usatoday.com/story/money/business/2020/01/29/coronavirus-corona-beer-surges-on-google-trends-as-virus-spreads/4606997002/.

While there is certainly a possibility that these photos were staged and that my references are only perpetuating an urban legend, it is important for crisis leaders to recognize the behaviors that social media can instigate. During a crisis, stakeholders will search for (and often take as fact) any information they can find in a desperate and well-meaning attempt to better understand the extent of the threat to their lives and value propositions.

What can high-stakes leaders do to diminish the likelihood of losing the attention of stakeholders to other sources of information? They can take the necessary steps to ensure stakeholders view members of the crisis management team — or other leaders at the organization — as *the* source of facts during a crisis.

What can high-stakes leaders do to diminish the likelihood of losing the attention of stakeholders to other sources of information? They can take the necessary steps to ensure stakeholders view members of the crisis management team — or other leaders at the organization — as *the* source of facts during a crisis.

The best way to accomplish this is to establish and publish a recurring schedule for the distribution of updates. Crisis managers have found that setting an expectation for the provision of updates at an established time every day and through a specific mechanism (e.g., a daily 6:00 p.m. press release or a live press conference) is very well received by stakeholders. Perhaps you watched New York Governor Andrew Cuomo or Kentucky Governor Andy Beshear during the first several months of the COVID-19 pandemic conducting their daily press conferences to update all interested stakeholders on the latest news. The commitment of these two leaders serves as an exceptional illustration of a best practice that created a means for stakeholders to receive consistent, reliable information.

The point here is that, to be recognized as *the* source of facts during a crisis, it is necessary for high-stakes leaders to be very clear about what, when, where, and how stakeholders should expect to receive regular progress updates. Then, once these expectations have been set, crisis leaders must effectively deliver on these expectations during each briefing.

"No News *Is* News" During a Crisis

One of the most challenging aspects of crisis leadership is communication with stakeholders. During a crisis, all your stakeholders will be looking for as much information as they can get. When their value propositions have been threatened, it is only natural to expect them to be desperately seeking any and all intelligence that might shed light — and hope — on their distressed expectations.

As crisis leaders, we know how important it is to share any information that becomes available with our stakeholders. We recognize that they are anxiously awaiting any news that we have to share. So, when there *is* some news to share, crisis leaders will typically find a way to share it. No rocket science there.

But what do crisis leaders communicate to stakeholders when there is no news to share?

I contend that communicating when there is "no news" is critical, and that cultural norms surrounding email communications have led leaders astray about communicating when we don't have much to say. You see, we've all become so bogged down by overflowing email inboxes that we've decided it's rude or unnecessary to "over-communicate" with our stakeholders. Perhaps your company sends a monthly newsletter now, instead of a weekly one, or has moved most of its promotional offers to social media and retains the email channel only for "important" news.

During a crisis, we are often *not* convinced that what we have learned on a given day is worth sharing, so we are tempted to hold back a communication because we aren't certain that it is "important enough" to send. We don't want to fill inboxes or mailboxes or media airwaves with messages that don't have big announcements or news of a resolution or a call to action for our stakeholders. So we sometimes go silent when we ought to be communicating most boldly, candidly, and compassionately.

The rules of engagement that you use when developing strategy for an email newsletter or normal stakeholder communications do not apply during a crisis. Remember, these are *not* normal circumstances. During a crisis, stakeholders are anxious, perhaps fearful, and they want information. You are a crisis leader, and, recognizing your stakeholder's interest in what you have to say, you need to deliver reliable, meaningful information to them.

So, what do you do when there is nothing *new* to share, when nothing much has changed from yesterday's message? Do you hold off until tomorrow for an update so as not to send something that might be viewed as lacking any substantive news? No. You must keep your communications flowing. And to help you overcome the urge to wait for *big* news to share, here's something to keep in mind: When you are leading a team through a crisis, **no news *is* news!**

> So, what do you do when there is nothing new to share, when nothing much has changed from yesterday's message? Do you hold off until tomorrow for an update so as not to send something that might be viewed as lacking any substantive news? No. You must keep your communications flowing.

Here's why. During a crisis, there are countless moving pieces. A great deal of activity is taking place and new information is becoming available all the time. As a member of the crisis management team, you're seeing much of this information first-hand. You and the team are working through it, analyzing it, and determining how it contributes to your current understanding of the situation. In many — perhaps even most — cases, you determine that, "the new information hasn't added much to your previous understanding." So, you decide that the little you have learned is not worth sharing. You might think, "Why fill someone's mailbox with something that doesn't provide any new information?" Why? Because your stakeholders are acutely interested in what you have learned. They are anxious about the threat to their value proposition, and they want to know what progress has been made, if any, to resolve things. They have been watching all the activity and perhaps they have even seen bits and pieces of news through other distribution channels. *They just know* that there is news to share — even when there isn't.

When you don't send an update in the midst of the heightened tension, you are thinking that you are sparing your stakeholders from just another useless email. Your stakeholders are not seeing it this way. *They are certain that there is news to share* — and when you fail to provide it, they decide that you're keeping it from them. They assume the worst, and they assign nefarious intent. "There's something they aren't telling us," they think (and tell their friends or colleagues). It's just the way we are wired. Knowing this, we must get out in front of such assumptions and rumors.

The point I'm trying to make is that crisis leaders should want to become *the* trusted source for information. To become this trusted source, you must establish that you and your team will communicate what you know, when you know it — even if what you know today isn't anything more than you knew yesterday. During a crisis, your stakeholders are going to assume that there is always news to share. To earn and maintain their trust, you need to share what you know at regular intervals, ideally on a programmed schedule. Then, as scheduled, you should share what you know — whether you believe it to be newsworthy or not.

Never forget that during a crisis, all news — even no news — is news.

> Never forget that during a crisis,
> all news — even no news — is news.

Stakeholder Engagement During the COVID-19 Pandemic

We have certainly seen a broad range of stakeholder engagement efforts from various sources during the COVID-19 pandemic (which is, as this book goes to press, raging on but with vaccination efforts underway). We all watched or listened to national and local government leadership, scientific and medical leaders, other community leaders, leaders of our own businesses and other businesses, family members, advocate groups, hate groups, anonymous groups ... the list goes on. Information came at us from everywhere. For many of the individuals or organizations I just listed, you were actually one of their stakeholders.

As you watched and listened to these people talk, what did you learn? Which sources provided clear, compelling, and useful information? Which did you decide that you just weren't going to trust or believe? How many did you simply switch off because they actually made you feel *more* frustrated, angry, and perhaps even fearful? How did you decide who or what you should believe? How did you sort through the noise?

Well, I'm with you; it was really challenging. It was difficult sifting through proverbial haystacks of information and listening closely to the cacophony of opinions to find the facts — and it was equally difficult to sort through the political positioning and spin. As we all experienced, when there is great complexity and limited evidence, it is really hard to find the truth.

When there is great complexity and limited evidence, it is really hard to find the truth.

I have two pieces of advice to share with you in response to what we saw during the COVID-19 pandemic. You may find this helpful as a stakeholder with a value proposition in someone else's organization, or as a crisis leader, looking to ensure your own stakeholders that what you have to offer is reliable and worth believing.

My first suggestion is to ask yourself: *What does the evidence tell me?* Are facts and data available that are compelling? Are they supported by multiple sources? Can they be validated through testing or by some other objective means? If so, then there is a strong probability that what you are hearing is true — that what you are hearing is worth believing. If not, the claims aren't automatically false, but I would tend to give them less credence, at least until more can be learned or discovered.

As a crisis leader, when presenting information, you would be wise to:

- Be very thoughtful and careful about how you present the insights you are drawing from the evidence (or lack of evidence).

- Be clear in your communications whether you are sharing facts, hypotheses, or personal/team opinions.

- Assess, before developing and delivering messages to stakeholders, whether you have drawn your conclusions from a preponderance of evidence or because you are simply doing the best you can with the information you have. If the latter, share that. Do not be afraid to be transparent. Your stakeholders will not hold it against you.

After getting clear and candid about how evidence plays into your stake-holder messaging, it's time to get comfortable with being wrong. A key characteristic of the crisis environment is that it will be almost impossible to know everything that you *want* to know during a crisis. You simply won't be able to build an airtight picture of the situation, the ideal solution, or the ultimate impact of the crisis until well after the event — if ever. Because of this, you are going to have to rely on limited, imperfect information — both when you are engaging stakeholders and when making decisions during a crisis. This means that, quite frequently, you are going to be wrong. Your insights are going to be proven faulty. Your decisions will have to be modi-fied or reversed. You'll have to admit that you were mistaken. This won't feel good, nor will it be great for your confidence. But these errors will largely be a function of the environment, not your flaws as a leader.

> You are going to have to rely on limited, imperfect information — both when you are engaging stakeholders and when making decisions during a crisis. This means that, quite frequently, you are going to be wrong. Your insights are going to be proven faulty. Your decisions will have to be modified or reversed. You'll have to admit that you were mistaken. This won't feel good, nor will it be great for your confidence.

So, knowing that you will never have a crystal-clear picture of everything during a crisis, it is OK to admit that. It is OK to tell your stakeholders that this is how you are making sense of the cloudy picture that you are working through. You will nearly always find that your stakeholders appreciate your transparency and humanity.

EXERCISE #3
Stakeholder Engagement Manifesto —
"My Commitment to Stakeholders"

The lessons from this chapter should feel immediately applicable to your work in creating and maintaining stakeholder engagement ... in good times and in bad.

Given what you have learned about stakeholders, here is your opportunity to craft a *Stakeholder Engagement Manifesto*. Don't let the curious or dramatic title be a distraction — there is a bit of tongue-in-cheek here. This manifesto is simply meant to represent a semi-formal expression of commitment to your stakeholders. You now know how important they are to your organization, so the next step is to take a few minutes to memorialize how you intend to engage them from your position as a high-stakes leader.

In the future, when you find yourself as the leader of a crisis management effort, what commitment are you willing to make in terms of your engagement with stakeholders? Document your commitment — your Stakeholder Engagement Manifesto — now. Write it in your own style and in keeping with your company's culture. If you need help getting started, use the prompts below for inspiration.

We will always ensure our stakeholders are apprised about _____

_____.

We are committed to maintaining transparency and candor with

_____ during _____ because

_____ is important to us.

Even during difficult or uncertain times, we will keep lines of

communication open because _____.

Our stakeholder engagement model is built upon a belief that

_____ and ties to our mission and vision in that

_____.

07

BACKBONE AND MUSCLE

Building Organizational Capacity for Resilience

Crisis management, as it is described in both academic and popular literature, provides a great deal of guidance about how leaders should think, behave, and lead *during* a crisis. But ultimately, business leaders simply cannot afford to think *only* about how they should deal with a raging crisis when it appears. What happens *before* a crisis is critical.

Thinking only of our duties once we find ourselves consumed by an active crisis paints an incomplete picture of our high-stakes leadership responsibilities. Yes, we need the tools and skills to guide our organization through a crisis, but we should also be taking steps to identify potential sources of future disruption and address these issues well before they manifest themselves into full-blown crises. To become effective high-stakes leaders, it is just as important that we understand how to *prevent* crises as it is to lead effectively *during* them.

To become effective high-stakes leaders, it is just
as important that we understand how to *prevent*
crises as it is to lead effectively *during* them.

Further, beyond the "before" and the "during," we have a crisis *aftermath* to deal with. After we have led our teams through an active crisis, we must move to the significant responsibilities of addressing what happens after a crisis has been effectively extinguished. Do our organizations simply return to business as usual, or are there opportunities for high-stakes leadership here as well? I will argue for the latter. Following a crisis, stakeholders will require continued attention and reassurance. Organizational processes will need review and changes will need to be made. Root causes of the crisis must be identified, examined, and addressed. There is much to be done after a crisis. For this reason, it makes sense to include these aspects of high-stakes leadership in our model as well.

Organizational resilience is the framework that I will use to encompass the full spectrum of high-stakes leadership responsibilities — from the crisis-prevention processes and actions that leaders can take ahead of any crisis-level event, to the actions leaders should be taking in the midst of a crisis, to the processes and actions leaders can take once the crisis has been largely controlled and the organization is focused on the most effective recovery possible. All three of these stages are equally important. So each deserves a good bit of our attention … in this book and in practice.

So much of *High-Stakes Leadership in Turbulent Times* is based on my own experiences, my own proprietary frameworks, and my own philosophies about what good leadership looks like. To augment my perspectives, I'd like to also borrow heavily from the work of Dr. Stephanie Duchek, the Chair of General Business Administration at Brandenburg University of Technology in Cottbus, Germany. A significant product of her research is a wonderfully complete description of the three stages we will explore. My goal in this chapter is to leverage Dr. Duchek's framework to help us not only fully understand the most important aspects of each stage, but also as a mechanism for sharing practical examples and recommended practices for each that can be immediately put into action at your organization.

High-stakes leadership is about much more than being able to step up and lead when a crisis appears. Yes, this is often the most visible aspect of high-stakes leadership — and it is vitally important to our organizations that we have the knowledge, skills, and abilities to navigate this incredibly challenging environment. But high-stakes leaders must also be able to provide tangible evidence of leadership well before, and well after, a crisis. Because of this, we will speak of resilience not simply as the ability to pick oneself up, wipe away the dust, and get back to business after we stumble. No, resilience is a much broader concept.

A Model for Understanding Organizational Resilience

In April 2020, a wonderful research paper titled "Organizational Resilience: A Capability-Based Conceptualization" by Stephanie Duchek was published by Springer Open Access, allowing me to share her insights with you here. This article will serve as the foundational platform upon which we will build an understanding of resilience.

Here is an excerpt from the abstract that Dr. Duchek uses to describe her work:

> "In highly volatile and uncertain times, organizations need to develop a resilience capacity which enables them to cope effectively with unexpected events, bounce back from crises, and even foster future success. Although academic interest in organizational resilience has steadily grown in recent years, there is little consensus about what resilience actually means and how it is composed ... We conceptualize resilience as a meta-capability and decompose the construct into its individual parts. Inspired by process-based studies, we suggest three successive resilience stages (anticipation, coping, and adaptation) and give an overview of underlying capabilities that together form organizational resilience. Based on this outline, we discuss relationships and interactions of the different resilience stages as well as main antecedents and drivers."[1]

---

1   Stephanie Duchek, "Organizational Resilience: A Capability-based Conceptualization," *Business Research*, 13, no. 1 (2019), doi:10.1007/s40685-019-0085-7.

Dr. Duchek believes, as I do, that organizations need to develop the capacity for resilience ... particularly now, in our VUCA (e.g., volatile, uncertain, complex, ambiguous) world. We will all deal with significant events, major disruptions, and crises. And when we do, we must have the ability to bounce back, to recover, and to be resilient. I suspect that one reason for the increase in academic interest in organizational resilience has been an increase in cases where resilience was either a primary contributor to a successful recovery or a root cause of significant difficulties while attempting to recover. We can't afford not to build resiliency — in ourselves as individual high-stakes leaders and in our organizations.

Interestingly, while most practitioners view resilience as simply the ability to bounce back from adversity, Dr. Duchek proposes three resilience stages: anticipation, coping, and adaptation. We will explore all three of these stages to help you understand what it means to be resilient, and how best to develop resilient practices. These practices will help you and your organization develop a greater capacity for resilience. Here, however, it is enough to recognize that resilience is described as a collection of stages, each of which presents challenges and obstacles, and that an understanding of each can help an organization become much better prepared for the inevitable.

Dr. Duchek's summary suggests a collection of relationships and interactions between and among these three stages. The most important and meaningful common thread running through all three stages is the potential for stakeholders to be incredibly helpful in all aspects of organizational resilience — to serve as your greatest assets, in good times and in bad.

The Conceptualization Model

Look at the graphic in Figure 1, which is an illustration of the Duchek model. The model, once fully unpacked, helps us see why the most resilient organizations are better able to manage both potential and actual crisis situations.

As you reviewed the model, I hope that a few high-level key features immediately became clear. First, it should have been easy to identify the three resilience stages. On the left of the illustration is the pre-crisis stage, or what Duchek calls the Anticipation stage. In the middle is the Coping stage — during which actual crisis leadership is needed and hopefully taking place; when we're in the thick of the drama, we're "coping." On the right side of

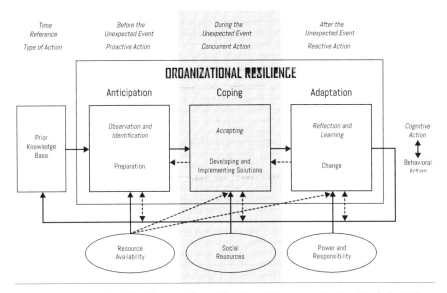

Figure 1: Organizational Resilience: A Capability-Based Conceptualization, Duchek, 2020

the illustration is the post-crisis stage, or what Duchek calls the Adaptation stage. This is where all post-crisis recovery takes place.

Duchek adds to her model some broad categories of what should, ideally, be taking place in terms of cognitive processing (i.e., how leaders should be thinking) and behavioral processing (i.e., what leaders should be doing) during each stage.

In the Anticipation stage, members of an organization should be thinking about scanning their environment for signs of potential trouble and, when signs are spotted, identifying them as such. Behaviorally during this stage, with the support of high-stakes leaders, organizations should be taking specific actions to prepare for a potential future crisis, while, of course, they are also doing what they can to resolve troubling issues before they become full-blown crises.

During the Coping stage, when organizations are in the middle of a crisis, the first cognitive steps that leaders must take are recognizing and accepting that they are, in fact, in a crisis. Denial is not an option if you want optimal outcomes, but it's not uncommon for organizational leaders to look the other way when they see things that they don't like or that make them uncomfortable. Consider how long it took the United States government to accept that COVID-19 was, in fact, a national crisis. An earlier acceptance of the COVID-19 situation as a crisis that required a coordinated, nation-wide emergency response would have almost certainly reduced the number of cases and fatalities resulting from the pandemic. Once we acknowledge the crisis, we need to start tackling it. During the Coping stage, crisis management teams and their leaders need to be developing and implementing solutions to resolve issues and respond to their consequences.

Throughout the post-crisis Adaptation stage — once the major disruption has been resolved to a manageable level — organizations should be cognitively focused on reflection and learning. Behaviorally, this is the time for high-stakes leaders to be implementing change initiatives. These should be designed not only to prevent similar future crises, but to apply lessons learned from the entire crisis management process, and to further develop the organization's capacity for resilience.

As I think about my own experiences with organizational crisis, it's easy to place my thinking and behaviors into these three phases of before (anticipation), during (coping), and after (adaptation). Having read in Chapter 5 about the JetBlue Valentine's Day crisis, you can probably think of that crisis in these terms as well.

We will return to this model a bit later. For now, it's important to recognize that resilience is not simply the ability to deal with adversity when it appears. Improving your organization's capacity for resilience can help you prevent crises, deal more effectively with them when they do appear, and then optimize your learning from them once they have been resolved. To build an organization that can thrive even in these turbulent times, high-stakes leaders must develop enterprise capacity for resilience across all three of these stages.

Resilience is not simply the ability to deal with adversity when it appears. Improving your organization's capacity for resilience can help you prevent crises, deal more effectively with them when they do appear, and then optimize your learning from them once they have been resolved.

Organizational Resilience Capabilities Are Good for Business

A great deal of research has been conducted on the challenges associated with the management of major, sometimes catastrophic events. As we know from our own experiences, these events are not as rare as we would hope. But while the topic of crisis *management* has been studied in detail, the notion of organizational resilience has not. I am, however, seeing a developing appreciation for the idea that crisis leadership is not only a matter of managing crises when they arise, but also before and after they occur.

Researchers are also beginning to call out a very interesting connection between the capacity for resilience and the capacity for what they refer to as *operational agility*. Operational agility, a capability that became particularly important as organizations responded to the impact of COVID-19 on their businesses, is essentially an enterprise's ability to assess the environment, make sense of it, and then quickly mobilize resources — such as people and other assets — to take advantage of the opportunities they have encountered. In today's business environment, agility is necessary for organizations to be able to effectively adapt to their constantly changing, VUCA world. Could these same capacities help companies become more resilient? It certainly seems so.

In the research conducted for *Mastering Turbulence*, a book by Joseph McCann and John Selsky, four necessary capabilities were identified as elements of organizational agility. McCann and Selsky suggested that, to be operationally agile, an organization must have the capacity for:

1. **Sense-making:** Scanning and analyzing tremendous amounts of diverse information, and then quickly forming hypotheses and mental models about what the organization is experiencing

2. **Transforming knowledge**: Efficiently and quickly acquiring, building, sharing, and applying valuable knowledge to clearly defined, critical priorities

3. **Acting decisively:** Cultivating a strong but informed action bias throughout the organization, and

4. **Aligning and realigning resources:** Quickly deploying and then redeploying sufficient resources, talent, and skills to support effective execution.[2]

Considering these four capabilities, it's easy to see similarities between the knowledge, skills, and abilities necessary to be agile in the context of normal business, *and* those necessary to be resilient — to have the ability to identify potential threats, to deploy resources accordingly when action is necessary to ensure the survival of the business, and to evolve over time, applying the lessons that only experience can offer. The moral of this story? Developing the capacity for resilience is worth our time not only because it will help us deal more effectively with potential or actual crises, but also because these same capabilities will simply help us run a better business. As you struggle with questions about where you should be making investments in your business, be on the lookout for opportunities to invest where the benefits are multi-dimensional in this way.

Developing the capacity for resilience is worth our time not only because it will help us deal more effectively with potential or actual crises, but also because these same capabilities will simply help us run a better business.

In related research on the connection between resilience and agility, authors Cynthia Lengnick-Hall and Tammy Beck offer meaningful insights in their working paper titled "Resilience Capacity and Strategic Agility: Prerequisites for Thriving in a Dynamic Environment." In the article's introduction, they write:

> "An organization's resilience capacity captures its ability to take situation-specific, robust, and transformative actions when confronted with unexpected and powerful events that have the potential to jeopardize an organization's long-term survival. Strategic agility ... can take multiple forms, but

---

2   Joseph E. McCann and John W. Selsky, *Mastering Turbulence: The Essential Capabilities of Agile and Resilient Individuals, Teams, and Organizations* (San Francisco, CA: Jossey-Bass, 2012).

describes an organization's ability to develop and quickly apply flexible, nimble, and dynamic capabilities.

"Together, agility and resilience capacity enable firms to prepare for changing conditions, to restore their vitality after traumatic jolts, and to become even more proficient as a result of the experience."[3]

This connection between resilience and agility is fascinating to me and it's not just conceptual. I found during my years as a military leader and as an executive at JetBlue that organizations — and teams within those organizations — were always much better prepared to both compete and to respond effectively to disruptions if they had been built to be nimble and adaptive to changing environmental conditions. As a high-states leader myself, I have always emphasized and looked to improve my team's ability to recognize and adapt to changing conditions. If you make this a priority for your team, you will find that it will become much more agile, resilient, and competitive.

The Anticipation Stage: Exploring What Happens Before Crisis

Let's dig just a little bit further into Dr. Duchek's model of organizational resilience and then start applying the "Anticipation/Coping/Adaptation" stages to the real world of business. The first stage of the model, as you might recall, is Anticipation. As you think about the anticipation of crisis or disruption in your organization, ask yourself these two questions:

1. Why is early warning and prevention critical to organizational resilience?

2. How can we leverage our understanding of and relationships with stakeholders to identify potential issues that could eventually become crisis-level events?

---

3   C. Lengnick-Hall and T. Beck, "Resilience Capacity and Strategic Agility: Prerequisites for Thriving in a Dynamic Environment," *Resilience Engineering Perspectives* (2016), doi:10.1201/9781315244389-4).

In the context of this book's subtitle — *Why Stakeholders Are Your Greatest Assets in Good Times and In Bad* — these two questions will help us home in on the "in good times" part of the equation.

In her "Organizational Resilience" article, Dr. Duchek explains that the anticipation stage "comprises three specific capabilities: the ability to observe internal and external developments, the ability to identify critical developments and potential threats, and — as far as possible — to prepare for unexpected events."[4]

So how can high-stakes leaders deploy and develop these capabilities to increase organizational resilience? Here's my take ...

- - - - - - - - - - - - - - - - -

Observing Developments and Identifying Threats

There are many ways to think about conducting internal and external observations for the purposes of identifying potential threats to an enterprise. Regardless of how you go about making your observations, the way to get there is pretty simple — you need to embrace your stakeholders, first establishing the optimum culture for internal stakeholders and their focus on internal observations, and then establishing exceptional relationships with external stakeholders for external observations. Relationships and culture are the keys to finding out (i.e., to seeing and truly understanding) what you need to know before a crisis occurs.

Internal Observations

Which of our primary stakeholder groups is in the best position to conduct internal observations for indications of possible organizational trouble? The employee group, of course. If your goal as a high-stakes leader is to create the ideal environment for motivating employees to be on the lookout for developments that require attention, what would you do? First, if you want your employees to serve in an observational capacity (i.e., if you want them to be on the lookout for areas of opportunity for improvement), then you

---

4   Stephanie Duchek, "Organizational Resilience: A Capability-based Conceptualization," *Business Research*, 13, no. 1 (2019), doi:10.1007/s40685-019-0085-7.

need to make sure they understand what that means and what you expect them to do. Just by taking this step, you will be increasing your organization's resilience. When you share this expectation with your colleagues and direct reports, you will receive lots of questions, such as:

- *What should I be looking for?*
- *How should I report what I find?*
- *What happens after I report something?*
- *Will my identity be shared, or will observations be anonymous?*

These are all great questions, and you'll have to develop responses that fit your unique circumstances. However you proceed, just know that if you want your employees to support the organization in this capacity, then you'll need to be clear about your expectations and be ready to respond to questions in a way that inspires them to take on the responsibility.

Second, you will need to tell your employees what to look for. At organizations that do this most effectively, employees are educated on the sorts of threats they are likely to see and how they are expected to deal with them. Earlier in this book, you read about a collection of crises that took place at United Airlines, Samsung, Starbucks, and Boeing. As you think about these crises, do you suppose that employees of those companies had observed indications that a significant problem might arise if something was not done to address the underlying issue(s)? The answer is probably a resounding yes, which begs questions about why these problems weren't reported (if they weren't) or why they weren't acted upon by leaders (if they *were* reported). It is rare that an internally generated crisis doesn't offer early warning signals — signals that employees are likely to see. Therefore, to improve resilience and the capacity for identifying potential organizational threats that may start small and grow rapidly, employees must be taught how to search for and respond to them.

> It is rare that an internally generated crisis doesn't offer early warning signals — signals that employees are likely to see.

Third, with employee expectations set and a sense of clarity around the types of things that are targets for observation and subsequent reporting, the organization needs a process for passing the information from an observer to someone (or some team) who can address the issue(s). The process must include specifics for dealing with all the questions I mentioned earlier — questions about reporting processes, communication channels, anonymity, consequences, reputational safety, and the like. These will all take time and effort to define and communicate; but done effectively and with a genuine commitment to employee engagement in the identification of organizational threats and opportunities for improvement, a culture can be created that wonderfully supports a capacity for resilience.

Done effectively and with a genuine commitment to employee engagement in the identification of organizational threats and opportunities for improvement, a culture can be created that wonderfully supports a capacity for resilience.

External Observations

Relationships with external stakeholders are quite a bit different from relationships with internal stakeholders. This is not breaking news. All the steps shared in the previous section are made possible by the unique nature and value proposition of the employer-employee relationship. How does an organization engage *external* stakeholders, then, to serve as observers for potential threats to the enterprise? It does so exactly as we have already learned in this book — by taking the time to understand the interests of each stakeholder group and building relationships with them.

Consider how your organization gets feedback from your customers about your products and services. How do you learn about what customers are buying, what they like best about your offerings, what they like least, and what they would change if they could? These are the types of questions being asked of customers today in just about every sector. Customer feedback has become a primary source for product development and innovation. Online reviews everywhere — from Amazon to Yelp to Google to individual corporate websites — are driving the way customers interact with brands and are determining the future for those companies. But those reviews often come too late or don't tell you enough. Asking your customers directly to tell you about their experiences can be game-changing, and establishing an ongoing feedback loop with customers can help you collect information on threats to your organization too.

Customers in just about every business sector on the planet have demonstrated a willingness to share their thoughts and feedback in any number of forums, often with remarkable honesty and specificity. They will respond to surveys, post comments and reviews on websites, and many are happy to participate in focus groups or on discussion panels. As a high-stakes leader, your threat detection efforts might benefit considerably from leveraging these connections to get feedback not only on product features and future innovations, but also on customer concerns and minor incidents involving your products. You can learn about whether your customers' price sensitivity has changed (and if they think your price tags are too high or too low), whether their tastes or aesthetics have shifted in a way that might drive you to offer your product in new varieties (e.g., colors, sizes, designs), and whether they have any unmet needs you can address in ways that would delight them (and generate revenue for you). While all these types of feedback might sound positive, they belie threats. If you fail to address the fact that customers want your product in purple and not just in black, they might flee to a competitor that offers the color they want. If your product or service is deemed too fussy, the user instructions too confusing, the price tag just a tiny bit too high, or the quality not quite up to expectations, you only have a small window of time to address these concerns before they become threats. Smart companies "live and die by their customer insights." Second only to your employees in their willingness to help your company succeed, customers can be an exceptional resource in your threat identification efforts.

- -

Customers in just about every business sector on the planet have demonstrated a willingness to share their thoughts and feedback in any number of forums, often with remarkable honesty and specificity.

- -

Can your other external stakeholders also support your external observation and threat detection efforts? They certainly can. As with your customers, strong relationships with everyone from regulators to the media to the customers of your competitors can create opportunities to both formally and informally solicit observations and receive feedback that can be useful to your organization. Consider what you could be doing with your external stakeholders to more effectively engage them in conversations that will help you learn how to make your company better and how to identify potential issues (sooner rather than later) that could grow into full-blown crises but that you can start mitigating right now. While the collection of stakeholder feedback may seem a bit disconnected from the notion of crisis anticipation, what do you think leaders at Blockbuster were hearing from their customers as Netflix began to provide home-delivered, digital content? Blockbuster's customers were doing their best to warn company leadership of the pending crisis that would eventually shutter the company.

Preparing for Unexpected Events

In Chapter 12, we'll go deep into the topic of preparing for a crisis. That preparation actually begins in what Dr. Duchek called the Anticipation Phase. She argues:

> "Being prepared means that a firm or agency is equipped to deal with unforeseen adversity and it is ready to capitalize on unexpected opportunities. This means that preparation capabilities help to develop resources that are necessary in times of crisis (e.g., suitable recovery plans, effective relationships, and mutual understanding) ... However, it is not solely the developed plans and formal procedures that prepare organizations for the great variety of unexpected events. Such events often do not correspond with planning assumptions and require intuitive acting and ad hoc decisions. The most important benefit of preparing the plan is the growing of effective relationships and mutual understanding among those involved in the plan preparation process. Thus, preparation does not mean planning for the unexpected — this is impossible. Rather, it means that organizations prepare without knowing if, when, or where an unexpected event will occur in the future."[5]

---

5   Stephanie Duchek, "Organizational Resilience: A Capability-based Conceptualization," *Business Research*, 13, no. 1 (2019), doi:10.1007/s40685-019-0085-7.

Two important processes take place in the Anticipation stage of the resilience model. First, observations and threat detection efforts can increase organizational resilience by helping organizations identify and address potentially threatening issues before they can reach crisis-level. Secondly, organizations must create mechanisms and build relationships to deal with crises when they do appear, as threat detection efforts will not create an impenetrable barrier against them.

What can you and your organization do to improve the effectiveness of your Anticipation efforts?

Organizational Resilience Goal #1: Anticipating Crisis Through Stakeholder Engagement

Let's think about how we might apply these concepts in our own organizations. Looking back on our earlier examination of stakeholders, we acknowledged the importance of establishing relationships with each of our stakeholder groups to better understand their interests — so we could enhance our ability to create value for them. The logic here is simple. Learn what stakeholders want from your business, and you will be in a better position to deliver in a way that delights them.

Another benefit of deep, healthy relationships with stakeholders is that, over time, these relationships begin to feel more like partnerships. In a partnership, all parties tend to develop a sense of teamwork such that everyone is on the lookout for anything that might threaten the partnership. Perhaps you have experienced this yourself. Do you have a favorite coffee shop or dry cleaner or grocery store? When you visit these places, do you find yourself paying more attention to your surroundings? If you see something that needs to be fixed or straightened or refilled, are you more likely at these places to say something to an employee or even make the repair or adjustment yourself? Are you more likely to tell others about these places?

These behaviors are typical of stakeholders who have assumed some responsibility for the quality of the partnership. Customers who are truly "fans" have a kind of loyalty and ownership of the brand, and are willing and eager to be part of your proverbial family. Maybe you have experienced this yourself as a customer or an employee. These are the two stakeholder groups that are most easily engaged as partners. But these same partnership characteristics can develop among other stakeholders as well.

I am reminded of my earliest days at JetBlue. I was the head of training at JetBlue when the company was launched, and it was in my best interests to have a very healthy relationship with the FAA — particularly with the Principal Operations Inspector (POI) who was responsible for, among other things, the company's compliance with training regulations.

Early in the formation of JetBlue, the leadership team made the decision to become the first airline in the world with a completely electronic training records system. I know that is almost hard to believe today. But in 1999, when we made the decision, almost all training records for every airline on the planet were kept in paper files at the company's headquarters or training center. At JetBlue, we thought that it would be better to manage them electronically. It actually took some work to convince the FAA that electronic recordkeeping could even be done in a reliable way — and frankly, before the turn of the century, that wasn't necessarily a baseless concern. But we were able to convince our regulatory authority that it could and should be done.

What really created some noise in our industry — and by that I mean we received dozens of calls from other airline training and operations leaders — was when I informed the FAA that one benefit of electronic training records was the ability to securely allow real-time access to anyone's record at any time — and that I wanted to provide members of the FAA 24/7 access to our training records. Why the ripple through the industry? Because the general perception of the FAA through the eyes of a typical airline was that the FAA was there to spot mistakes — to catch airlines trying to bend the rules — and to fine them when those infractions were discovered. What was our perception of the FAA at JetBlue? They were our safety partners. They were there to help us create the best company in the industry. We didn't think of them as "big brother" or a disciplinarian. Yes, they were a key stakeholder with safety oversight responsibility — but we knew they didn't want to catch us being unsafe. We knew they wanted to help us *be* more safe. It was this nuanced difference in philosophy that I believe allowed JetBlue to become one of the most successful airlines in history.

What was our perception of the FAA at JetBlue? They were our safety partners. They were there to help us create the best company in the industry. We didn't think of them as "big brother" or a disciplinarian. Yes, they were a key stakeholder with safety oversight responsibility — but we knew they didn't want to catch us being unsafe. We knew they wanted to help us *be* more safe.

How did our provision of training records access to our regulators ultimately play out? They loved it. They felt like an honorary member of our team; they felt trusted, and they were the best partner we could have possibly had. And to put a fine point on the FAA as our partner — not simply our regulator — every now and then I would receive a message from a member of the FAA who had been looking through our training records. The message would say something like: "Hi Mike. I was going through your ground operations records this afternoon, and I saw that Jane Smith will be needing her safety training refresher by the end of this week. Don't forget to make sure that she gets it. Thanks." In the eyes of other airlines, they would have expected the FAA not to say anything, hope we would miss the training requirement, and pay a visit to company headquarters to fine the company for a training failure. In our case, because we treated the FAA like a partner, they returned the sentiment and helped us become safer — and more resilient.

The Coping Stage: Building Organizational Resilience by Surviving the Crisis Itself

The second stage of resilience in Dr. Duchek's model is called the Coping stage. During this stage, high-stakes leaders must be able to accept that they are, in fact, in a crisis — and then they must be able to develop and implement solutions to resolve the crisis. The Coping stage is where the proverbial rubber meets the road.

- - - - - - - - - - - - - - - - -

Accepting

In their *Harvard Business Review* article "The Quest for Resilience," authors Gary Hamel and Liisa Vaelikangas suggest that to be resilient, organizations must be able to overcome what they describe as "the cognitive challenge." This challenge is presented as the need for an enterprise to be able to "become entirely free of denial, nostalgia, and arrogance," which are common states of mind among leadership teams, which slow or prevent situational awareness. This argument for the importance of being able to overcome the cognitive challenge is an acknowledgment that our increasingly complex and turbulent business environment (VUCA, you'll recall) should actually elevate an organization's interest in looking for signs of trouble. Alas, a great deal of research suggests that this heightened sense of awareness is not widely adopted.

The article goes on to say: "To be resilient, an organization must dramatically reduce the time it takes to go from 'that can't be true' to 'we must face the world as it is.'" This defines the challenge facing high-stakes leaders: How can we help our organizations embrace the idea that crises are no longer a question of "if," but "when?"[6]

- -
How can we help our organizations embrace the idea that crises are no longer a question of "if," but "when?"
- -

Why is it so hard for some leaders to face the world as it is? One explanation for our discomfort with complex topics stems from our discomfort with the notion that the more we know about them, the greater our awareness of how much we truly *don't* know. As John Meacham explains in an article titled "Wisdom and the Context of Knowledge:"

> "Each new domain of knowledge appears simple from the distance of ignorance. The more we learn about a particular domain, the greater the number of uncertainties, doubts,

---

6   G. Hamel and L. Välikangas, "The Quest for Resilience," *Harvard Business Review* (September 2003), https://hbr.org/2003/09/the-quest-for-resilience.

questions and complexities. Each bit of knowledge serves as the thesis from which additional questions or antithesis arise."[7]

Karl Weick, a researcher and author on the topic of sensemaking, followed up on this premise in an article titled "The Collapse of Sensemaking in Organizations" with this conclusion, framed in the context of what he describes as *wisdom*:

> "In a fluid world, wise people know that they don't fully understand what is happening right now, because they have never seen precisely this event before. Extreme confidence and extreme caution both can destroy what organizations most need in changing times, namely, curiosity, openness, and complex sensing. The overconfident shun curiosity because they feel they know most of what there is to know. The overcautious shun curiosity for fear it will only deepen their uncertainties. Both the cautious and the confident are closed-minded, which means neither makes good judgments. It is this sense in which wisdom, which avoids extremes, improves adaptability."[8]

I will not, in this book, attempt to present an elegant solution to the cognitive challenge of some leaders' inability or unwillingness to accept that a crisis is taking place. I believe, however, that as you are now much more aware of the ubiquity of this significant leadership challenge, you are better positioned to identify it — in yourself and in the leaders around you — when it occurs. When it does, you may find it helpful to gather your leadership team and conduct a thought experiment where the team discusses possible scenarios should the potential crisis play out. "If this escalates further," you might ask the team, "how might this situation impact our company, our stakeholders, our operations, and our future?" Perhaps a discussion of these questions can help high-stakes leaders work through their own version of the cognitive challenge.

---

7   J. A. Meacham, "Wisdom and the Context of Knowledge: Knowing That One Doesn't Know," *On the Development of Developmental Psychology*, 8 (July 13, 1983), https://www.researchgate.net/publication/240419729_Wisdom_and_the_context_of_knowledge_Knowing_that_one_doesn't_know.

8   Karl E. Weick, "The Collapse of Sensemaking in Organizations: The Mann Gulch Disaster," *Administrative Science Quarterly*, 38, no. 4 (1993), doi:10.2307/2393339.

Developing and Implementing Solutions

When an organization finds itself in a crisis (and accepts this fact and begins to face it), steps must be taken to resolve the threat. What are these steps? Where do these steps come from? Because no two crises are the same, and their appearance is almost impossible to predict, is it reasonable to assume that organizations should not waste their time on preparation? No, it is not. This is precisely why the resilience model we have been exploring includes some degree of crisis preparedness in all three of its stages. Solution planning can be accomplished in the Anticipation stage, as organizations should be able to predict the types of crises most likely to appear at their organization. In fact, an entire chapter in this book is dedicated to crisis typologies to serve just this purpose (see Chapter 9) — to help organizations determine what types of crisis to look for and what types to be ready to address should they appear.

Naturally, crisis planning that takes place in the Anticipation stage will be generic. Pre-planning will not be able to predict specific details of a future crisis. These details will need to be incorporated into previously developed plans or those created in the midst of a crisis — during the Coping stage. In either case, these solutions will be specific to the crisis at hand. Who creates these plans? How are they created? How are they formalized and communicated out to those expected to execute them? Who does, in fact, execute them? There is much to consider as we anticipate the crises that await us, and the time to start doing this work is now (while you're *not* in the middle of a crisis!).

Organizational Resilience Goal #2:
Coping with Crisis Through Stakeholder Involvement

Imagine that you are a high-stakes leader in the middle of a crisis situation. All hell is breaking loose around you right now. How might you involve your stakeholders in the Coping stage of the resilience model? Have you ever thought about how your stakeholders might be a great resource *during* a crisis? If not, now would be a great time to pause to consider the value of your stakeholders when the going gets tough.

Consider the COVID-19 pandemic and how leaders around the world processed the evidence they were facing. As you watched the pandemic develop, what did you see from these leaders? Yes, let's acknowledge that sometimes it is difficult to predict how situations will evolve. It is always easy to look back and judge the performance of crisis leaders once the facts have become clear and the impact of the crisis can be measured more accurately. But as the COVID-19 pandemic began to present a global threat, we saw many world leaders in full denial of the fact that the situation would become an actual crisis. Denial will almost certainly lead to a greater degree of crisis. We all watched this notion become a reality.

- -

Denial will almost certainly lead to a greater degree of crisis.

- -

In the context of our resilience model, what could these leaders have done to help themselves embrace the pending crisis and begin to more effectively deal with it? They could have engaged their stakeholders — their experts, those who were analyzing the situation (like public health officials, infectious disease experts, doctors and scientists) — and given more credence to their input. From the COVID-19 pandemic, there is a great lesson in the value of engaging stakeholders to help us recognize when we are, in fact, facing or about to face a crisis. I am not suggesting that we won't have to sift through *interpretations* of the facts, or expert *intuition* rather than certainty — because we will. But we saw far too many cases of leaders completely ignoring the experts — or dismissing their assessments — during the COVID-19 crisis not to recognize the deep flaw in that approach.

Why do some leaders feel that *their* intuition is more accurate than that of experts who have spent an entire lifetime studying a very narrow slice of science? The psychologists can and have had a heyday with this very topic. But even without an understanding of the human psyche or the group sociology of arrogance and denial, we all understand it enough. Having watched the COVID-19 pandemic play out, we all know that it happens — that some decision makers will repeatedly downplay a crisis as it looms ... or even as it burns down the house. And, sadly, we now know that it happens a lot. As high-stakes leaders, we must check our hubris at the door and invite our experts into the conversation. Then — and perhaps this is the hard part for some — *we need to listen to them!*

As high-stakes leaders, we must check our hubris at the door
and invite our experts into the conversation. Then — and perhaps
this is the hard part for some — *we need to listen to them!*

The second stage of the resilience model (Coping) involves taking action — developing and implementing solutions. How might a crisis leader engage stakeholders to play an active role in the Coping phase of our model? There are a couple of ways that I would like you to consider.

First, as you are developing solutions, you can ask your stakeholders for input. Now, in the midst of a full-blown crisis situation, you may not have time to ask stakeholders for their ideas. But you may have time — if your relationships with stakeholders are solid and you have established a partnership with a number of these groups — to ask stakeholders to help you identify the root cause of an issue, to help you formulate solutions, or to identify a preferred option from a small set of potential solutions. You could also (and I really like this option) ask your stakeholders to take actions that would allow them to help themselves. Does that sound a bit radical for you? Then let's explore what such a solution might look like.

As a former airline executive, I must say that I have been impressed with Delta Airlines' commitment to technology and providing a sense of control to their customers through their various web-based and mobile-friendly digital tools. Imagine that Delta has found itself in the middle of a significant system disruption — perhaps a major operational crisis caused by large weather system (like a once-in-a-century ice storm in NY? ?) or an air traffic control issue. Now imagine that this disruption has impacted *your* flight with the airline. As a customer, what are your expectations of Delta in this situation? What level of control would you want to reduce or eliminate the impact that the crisis is having on *you*?

Delta has created a mechanism for customers to help themselves in these types of situations. They allow their customers to use their mobile devices to rebook their own flights — to find solutions that are best suited to each individual customer. Historically, the rebooking process has been a long and frustrating experience for customers. It has also placed a tremendous strain on the company's resources when hundreds or thousands of customers have needed the help of human customer service agents. Not anymore. Now, when Delta finds itself facing an operational crisis, it is able to offload some of its crisis management tasks onto customers who, interestingly, are very happy to accept the responsibility — because it is clearly in their best interests. We live in a world in which customers appreciate convenience and control, and sometimes ceding that control to the customer has a win-win effect for company and customer alike.

This is an example a company leveraging their relationship with a key stakeholder group to develop and implement a solution during a crisis — to more effectively cope with the situation — to increase their capacity for resilience. This is also a wonderful illustration of how important it is for high-stakes leaders to proactively develop solutions for what we will call "predictable crises" and have them ready to implement when they are needed.

As you look to increase your capacity for resilience, keep these lessons in mind. Stakeholders aren't just a liability when an organization is working through a crisis situation. Sometimes, they can actually provide a significant contribution to the solution.

The Adaptation Stage: Becoming Stronger in the Aftermath of Crisis

Once an organization has moved beyond the Coping stage (i.e., once it has largely resolved the cause(s) of the crisis and moved the enterprise past the peak danger zone into a prolonged but much less stressful period of recovery), it transitions to a period of Adaptation. This is the third stage of the resilience model we've adopted for our purposes from Dr. Duchek. In the Adaptation stage, two types of capabilities become important for an enterprise:

1.   Reflection and Learning, and

2.   Organizational Change

Let's take a look at how each are vital to an organization's capacity for resilience.

Reflection and Learning

Two important cognitive actions (i.e., thought-based activities) that must take place during the Adaptation stage of crisis are Reflection and Learning. These are implied, to some extent, by the use of the term Adaptation to describe the stage. For an organization to become more resilient, it must find ways to help employees grow and develop from their experiences. According to DR. Duchek:

> "To use failure experience for own purposes, both cognition and behavior are essential. On the one hand, organizations must be able to reflect on the crisis situation and to incorporate the gained insight into the existing knowledge base. On the other hand, they must be able to act on this knowledge and produce change."[9]

These recommendations suggest a few process questions if organizations are to optimize the value of both reflection and learning following a crisis.

- What is meant by reflection and learning?
- What should I be doing to make the most of these practices?
- How will these be facilitated?
- Who will perform the facilitation?
- What should be the focus: Observations? Root causes? Insights? Formalized lessons?
- How will these be shared once they have been captured?
- How will they be incorporated into new or revised processes to help the enterprise become more capable — more resilient?

These are all great questions — and they are questions that must be solved in unique ways for each organization. To be optimally effective for organizations looking to become more resilient, however, they *must* be solved, sooner rather than later.

---

9   Stephanie Duchek, "Organizational Resilience: A Capability-based Conceptualization," *Business Research*, 13, no. 1 (2019), doi:10.1007/s40685-019-0085-7.

Reflection

Reflection can be an incredibly powerful process. It is a process, in fact, that plays an important role in our ability to learn. To provide some background on the notion of reflection and learning, here are some thoughts shared by Marilyn Daudelin in an article titled "Learning from Experience Through Reflection":

> "... the day-to-day experiences of managers as they confront challenges and problems on the job are rich sources of learning. But managers need support in their efforts to make sense out of their developmental experiences. While reflection is a natural and familiar process that could help managers learn most effectively from their experience, organizations have been slow to embrace formal reflective practices as a way to encourage learning. Henry Mintzburg once wrote in the *HBR* "study after study has shown that managers work at an unrelenting pace, that their activities are characterized by brevity, variety, and discontinuity, and that they are strongly oriented to action and dislike reflective activities." More recently, Rosabeth Moss Kanter identified short-term managerial incentives and demands as forces working against managers' ability to pause and reflect. But recent progress in companies seem to be acknowledging the need to provide time, space, and tools to help their employees reflect more effectively and learn from these reflections."

Are you giving yourself and your team enough time to decompress, to reflect, and to learn? Daudelin goes on to describe the process of reflection in this way:

> "Reflection is often stimulated by the nagging, unresolved problems or challenges that are a normal part of any manager's job. Reflection then progresses through four distinct stages: (a) articulation of a problem, (b) analysis of that problem, (c)

formulation and testing of a tentative theory to explain the problem, and (d) action (or deciding whether to act)."[10]

Following a crisis, this framework can be particularly useful for high-stakes leaders who want to help employees reflect on their recent experiences. Leaders may also choose to create a mechanism for using these reflections in group settings, as fodder for discussion, and as a starting point for the identification of areas of opportunity for improvement. The process of reflection can be immensely valuable and can transform your culture and your company.

Learning

Unfortunately, very little research has been conducted on the various ways that people within organizations have or have not learned from their experiences following a crisis. Case research has been conducted on companies that appear to have learned from experience and on those who have not, with limited insights on why learning did or did not take place. It is generally agreed, however, that learning can take place through both formal and informal processes. Rich reflection, as mentioned previously, can be a source of exceptional individual learning. But this process appears to rarely provide broader benefits without some sort of facilitated sharing and group discussion. Some researchers have found that learning from failures is enhanced considerably by interaction and collaboration among employees and that knowledge sharing between teams and units is a meaningful predictor of perceived ability to learn from failure. While post-crisis learning may not, necessarily, suggest a necessity to "learn from failure," it would be logical to assume sufficient similarities that like practices would produce similar outcomes.

It may be useful, at this point, to share a personal story about how flight instructors at the US Navy's TOPGUN school approach learning as a way to highlight the importance of individual and team reflection. The TOPGUN training course is essentially a 10-week program of successive, increasingly complex crises. Training flights involve simulated missions, designed to represent potential real-world combat scenarios, where the opposition is

---

10   M. Daudelin, "Learning from Experience Through Reflection," *Strategic Learning in a Knowledge Economy* (2000), doi:10.1016/b978-0-7506-7223-8.50016-2.

expertly provided by highly trained TOPGUN instructors. Student pilots plan for each specific scenario and then head out to the flight range to conduct their simulated — intense and very realistic — training events. These events are designed such that if students perform flawlessly, then they have the potential to achieve what you might describe as a mission victory. Unfortunately, as a product of the sheer complexity and dynamics of each training "crisis" (that's how these training events feel), students are unable to perform flawlessly, resulting in some exceptional lessons in terms of "what should have happened, what actually happened, and what impacted or impeded performance." Not that mission success wouldn't provide some great lessons, but there is even greater learning to be gained by examining that which didn't quite go according to plan. Imagine being put through 10 weeks of high-stress, high-risk training sessions like these at your organization. What might you learn about yourself, your team, and your organization? Perhaps more importantly, what would you do to optimize your learning?

At TOPGUN, learning is an exhaustive and deeply reflective practice. What the staff at the school has learned over 52 years of teaching excellence is that very little quality learning takes place simply as a result of flying the training events. While experience is vitally important to the learning process, that experience, by itself, does not automatically produce learning. In fact, due to the complex nature of each event and the nearly impossible task for students of having a crystal-clear picture of the events as they played out (does this sound like the crisis environment we have been talking about?), it is difficult for students to know what actually took place, much less to be able to identify key lessons. This is why *all* training events at TOPGUN are debriefed (i.e., examined and discussed) in teams of students and instructors for several hours after the fact. The students reflect on, present, and discuss their performance — what they expected, what they *believe* happened, what they did well, and what could have been improved — while instructors facilitate by providing clarity about the objectives of the scenario, what *actually* happened, and what should (sometimes must) be improved for the students going forward.

In my three years as a member of the TOPGUN instructor staff, my single most significant takeaway about the learning process following a complex experience — like a TOPGUN training event or an organizational crisis — is that learning cannot take place to a significant degree simply as a result of experience. Complex events require deep reflection, facilitated discussion, and input from as many different perspectives as possible to truly learn and improve. What does this mean to you? That learning from complex experiences should *not* be left to individuals to realize. Learning should be thought of as a team sport and it should *not* be taken for granted.

Learning cannot take place to a significant degree simply as a result of experience. Complex events require deep reflection, facilitated discussion, and input from as many different perspectives as possible to truly learn and improve.

It's also important for high-stakes leaders to understand that just because an experience (like a crisis or disruption) produces lessons and insights does not necessarily translate into *sustained* organizational learning. Ultimately, learning matters little if the lessons aren't translated into improved practices and behaviors that last. Once again, this is where facilitation can become an important factor in the ability of an organization to learn from its experience. Facilitated workshops and working sessions can be exceptional tools in a high-stakes leader's toolkit to help an organization learn from experience and translate those lessons into improved and more resilient practices.

Organizational Change

The process of translating lessons into improved practices fits neatly under the umbrella of organizational change. Change leadership and the process of optimizing organizational change is an incredibly broad and complex topic that I will only touch upon briefly. Indeed, organizational change is remarkably challenging and will require an incredible amount of time and energy. Keep the following in mind regarding the contribution of organizational change to your personal and organizational capacity for resilience. Again, I borrow from Dr. Duchek:

> "To produce organizational change, it is particularly important to actually act on previously generated knowledge. Organizations must be able to exploit a newly developed solution and transfer it to their individual parts. To achieve that,

change management capabilities are needed. For example, it could be shown that an organization's change management process is fundamental to organizational resilience. Other scholars point to the importance of a robust strategic planning process with an entrepreneurial focus. In this context, organizations must also be aware that putting new knowledge into practice can create new problems or necessitate further changes. Hence, how change is managed is critical to resilience. As with every other organizational change initiative, change in response to unexpected events may result in different types of resistance. Thus, adaptation involves not only making important changes but also overcoming resistance to change. Resistance to change may be rooted in the individual, team, or organizational levels. To overcome the specific manifestations of resistance, various change management practices can be applied. Soft managerial practices such as effective communication and relationships within the organization seem to be particularly important to enhancing an organization's resilience. Furthermore, the ability to change can find expression in the successful use of so-called 'change agents,' which accompany the change and implementation process and, if necessary, have intervention methods and options."[11]

There are volumes of useful materials available to high-stakes leaders looking to implement a change initiative within their organization. If you are considering building some change management capability, just a bit of research will provide several great approaches and tools. As someone who has taught university courses on change management, I can tell you that one of the primary barriers to change is the lack of a compelling reason to change *now*, and not wait for "a better time." Everyone will tell you that people are too busy or times are too uncertain to introduce a big change right now. Personally, I never quite bought that argument. Will there really *ever* be a better time? No, there probably won't. That said, however, one key benefit that crisis leaders will have when attempting to lead a change initiative following a recent crisis will be that the pain, frustration, and fear will

---

11   Stephanie Duchek, "Organizational Resilience: A Capability-based Conceptualization," *Business Research*, 13, no. 1 (2019), doi:10.1007/s40685-019-0085-7.

still be fresh in everyone's minds, making the case for change relatively easy to demonstrate.

- -

One key benefit that crisis leaders will have when attempting to lead a change initiative following a recent crisis will be that the pain, frustration, and fear will still be fresh in everyone's minds, making the case for change relatively easy to demonstrate.

- -

The Adaptation stage — the days, weeks, months, and even years after a crisis — is critical for translating the lessons from a recent crisis into improvements that will allow an enterprise to evolve and benefit from their experience. The lessons produced during this stage will also contribute to improvements in an organization's Anticipation practices (i.e., the way it listens, observes, prepares, and plans before crisis). In almost every case, an effective post-crisis exploration of opportunities for improvement will uncover ways that the enterprise could have or should have "seen this crisis coming." The next time you have an opportunity to lead your team through a process that explores lessons to be learned from a mistake (or a failure or a crisis), don't stop at "what did we learn?" Make sure you pursue potential lessons that would allow you to prevent a similar situation in the future. If you can do so, you have contributed demonstrably to improving your organization's capacity for resilience.

- -

In almost every case, an effective post-crisis exploration of opportunities for improvement will uncover ways that the enterprise could have or should have "seen this crisis coming."

- -

Organizational Resilience Goal #3: Developing Stronger Relationships with Stakeholders After a Crisis

Once we have faced a crisis, what can we do to reduce the chances that it could happen again? What can we do to learn from the experience? To improve our practices and processes? To examine what we did *not* do, what we did poorly — and what we did well — that led to the situation that played out? Winston Churchill famously said: "Never let a good crisis go to waste." His point was ultimately that, when tensions are high and those around you recognize the need for action   for something to happen to produce a more promising path forward — then you have the best possible environment for meaningful, positive change. This is the opportunity we all have after a crisis. What can we do to leverage it?

As you reflect on a recent crisis, I urge you to ask yourself: "How might we think of engaging stakeholders right now, learn from their input and from the experiences of being vulnerable with them, and ultimately create a stronger organization going forward?" To do so effectively, there are a few things that we must get right.

Once the peak of the crisis is clearly behind you — and your organization begins its recovery efforts — stakeholder engagement becomes vital to the future of the business. These stakeholders have been impacted, at least to some degree, by the crisis. Their value proposition was threatened; their trust in your enterprise, and the team leading it, has been diminished — perhaps entirely; and they are now forced to reconsider the value of their partnership with you. Looking back on what we learned about stakeholders and the importance of understanding their interests, we dare not lose sight of the fact that, once a crisis has passed, we must re-engage these groups to restore their pre-crisis assessment of their value propositions (to the extent that we can). We need to engage them in a way that rebuilds the trust capital that was lost or diminished during the critical sequence of events. And we must help each of these groups — perhaps even specific individuals within these groups — find reasons to stick with us, as we learn from the past, to create a better future.

- -

Stakeholders have been impacted, at least to some degree, by the crisis. Their value proposition was threatened; their trust in your enterprise, and the team leading it, has been diminished — perhaps entirely; and they are now forced to reconsider the value of their partnership with you.

- -

For many business leaders, as they look to right the ship after having weathered a storm, they think first and foremost about their customers. It is *this* stakeholder group, after all, that most likely fuels the business's revenue engine. But while it is, in fact, critical to engage customers as much as you can during and after a crisis, particularly if they were a group that was significantly impacted by the crisis, it is just as important — sometimes even more so — during the Adaptation or post-crisis stage, to engage *all* your stakeholder groups. Why? Because more than likely, all of them have, to some degree, been impacted by the event. They are *all* wondering what happened, what led to the issue, what damage was done, what changes will be made, and what the answers to these questions mean to *their* value propositions going forward.

At this point, perhaps you are thinking, "What do you mean when you suggest that we engage our stakeholders in ways that restore their trust in our enterprise? What options do we have?" Well, there are a number of different ways that you can engage stakeholders after a crisis to make your company more resilient going forward. Here are a couple of tangible suggestions.

The first engagement approach is simply to welcome stakeholders into a dialogue — and I am using the term dialogue intentionally. Yes, your stakeholders want to hear from you — they want to know that you care for and empathize with them. But they also want to *speak* to you. They want (and deserve) to be heard. Many members within these groups will want the chance to tell you how this whole experience has felt to them — about how it impacted them and, perhaps most helpfully to you, how they think you can prevent a recurrence or at least make changes for the better going forward. Find a way to set up a dialogue with your stakeholders. Such interactions can be exceptionally helpful and, by drawing key people in to be part of a solution, they may actually feel a sense of ownership in your future success.

Another way to engage stakeholders, beyond simply communicating, is to formally invite them into the change process. I recall a great example of this from my time at JetBlue. It followed our Valentine's Day Massacre crisis in 2007. Once we had worked our way through the crisis, we were faced with the challenge of addressing the many root causes that contributed to it. One way we chose to engage a key stakeholder group was to create a large,

cross-functional team of our crewmembers to help us identify and propose
solutions to the problems that led to the crisis. In the end, we recruited
assistance from 120 crewmembers, from all parts and levels of our operation, for several months to be a part of this major project — a project we
called IROP Integrity, or Irregular Operations Integrity. These crewmembers
would eventually identify the need to complete dozens of significant projects. The senior leadership team at JetBlue made sure they received the time
and resources to complete all of them.

It was an incredible experience to be a part of, and JetBlue has been a much
better company ever since, on many levels. Perhaps most importantly
— and germane to our learning here — our crewmembers felt as though
their input was both welcome and necessary to help JetBlue adapt to its
post-crisis way of doing business. These employees also felt a renewed
sense of ownership and commitment to the company. Every member of
the IROP Integrity team felt as though JetBlue could be more resilient in the
face of potential future crises because they had played a role in helping it
learn from this one. We were never accused of sweeping problems under
the rug because we put a bright spotlight on the problems and invited our
employees to help us fix them.

If you are looking for a way to "win back" the loyalty and commitment of
your employees — or *any* stakeholder group — following a particularly
challenging situation, a great way to do so is to include them in the process
of implementing solutions. You may just find that not only are the final
solutions better than they would have been if you had created them in
a vacuum, but that your stakeholders will find them more compelling and
effective (and will therefore more passionately support those changes). And
as a welcome, added bonus, your relationships with these stakeholders will
never quite be the same — in a very, very good way.

- -

If you are looking for a way to "win back" the loyalty and
commitment of your employees — or *any* stakeholder group —
following a particularly challenging situation, a great way to do
so is to include them in the process of implementing solutions.

- -

Applying the Resilience Model to the COVID-19 Pandemic

Let's take a moment to consider how an understanding of and commitment to the Anticipation/Coping/Adaptation resilience model could have helped business and community leaders navigate the early days and weeks of the COVID-19 pandemic. And let's do so by looking individually (and very briefly, I promise!) at the three stages of our model.

In the Anticipation stage, how do you think our business and community leaders (in whatever country or region in which you live) could have employed some of the lessons you have learned about observation, identification, and preparation? I can think of several, but let me share a really important lesson that you must keep in mind if you truly want to create a resilient organization.

The model we have explored in this chapter suggests that we can create greater capacity for organizational resilience when we embrace our lessons from the past. In the context of global pandemics, the truth is that we actually have a great deal of experience to draw from, not necessarily from COVID-19 specifically, but from other similar, globally relevant virus scenarios. While many comparisons have been made to the Spanish Flu of 1918, I have found that it can be very difficult for some leaders to embrace the lessons of events from the distant past — regardless of their relevance. Much more instructive to the COVID-19 pandemic, in my view, are the lessons that we should have learned from the SARS-CoV-1 pandemic the world experienced between 2002 and 2004, the H1N1 Swine Flu pandemic that we saw in 2009, and the deadly Ebola virus that spread across West Africa between 2014 and 2016.

Each of these outbreaks helped healthcare officials around the world learn how to recognize, treat, and prevent the emergence of similar outbreaks in the future. Given the lessons that business and community leaders should have learned from history, I find it difficult to understand why so many were completely and utterly unprepared for COVID-19. An important lesson here is that, consistent with our definition of resilience — which emphasizes the importance of anticipation and preparedness for potential crises — we must find a way to depend on the knowledge gained from previous events to make our observation and identification efforts more effective, and to help us prepare for future, similar situations. I know this doesn't sound like rocket science. Yet, as we all watched the events of COVID-19 sweep across the world, we had the opportunity to see how many — or how few — of the lessons available from experience were brought to bear on the current crisis.

In terms of coping with the COVID-19 pandemic, how do you think our business and community leaders could have employed some of the lessons you have learned about accepting the realities and potential consequences of a situation and then developing and implementing solutions to deal with them? Like you, I can think of many things that I believe should have been managed differently. (In some cases, quite a bit differently.)

We could spend a good bit of time on this topic, and I am certain that thousands of researchers and pundits will study not only the healthcare lessons of the COVID-19 outbreak, but also the leadership lessons to be learned as a result. We saw quite a spectrum of leadership performances during the pandemic. I encourage you to reflect on what you witnessed, and to draw some lessons of your own. If you are a leader who has made a commitment to continuous growth, as I have, you will find it best to spend very little time dwelling on the apparent incompetence of some business and community leaders and instead to spend your time looking for nuggets of wisdom — looking for practices that resonated with you as a member of a specific stakeholder group — and incorporating them in your crisis leadership toolkit, with a little personalization to make them truly yours. Yes, we saw many examples of how *not* to lead during a crisis. But we also saw many examples of exceptional leadership. Find examples of the latter — and learn from the experience.

A leader who has made a commitment to continuous growth will find it best to spend very little time dwelling on the apparent incompetence of some business and community leaders, and instead to spend their time looking for nuggets of wisdom and incorporating them in their crisis leadership toolkit.

The future is still unclear as to how business and community leaders will reflect on their performance during the pandemic, learn from their experiences, and implement changes to help their organizations become more resilient. I think we can all agree that the potential lessons will be plentiful. Let's not "waste the crisis."

Demonstrating Commitment to Our Stakeholders Before, During, and After a Crisis: A Resilience Building Effort

I am hopeful that this chapter didn't feel overly academic to you, despite the degree to which I drew upon the research and theories of others. I believe the concept of resilience is vitally important for all high-stakes leaders to understand, particularly because it presents a clear illustration of the intersection between crisis prevention and crisis management.

At the beginning of this chapter, I suggested that business leaders cannot afford to think only about how they should deal with a raging crisis once it appears. The "before" and "after" are equally important as the "during." I have tried to make a case for the importance of identifying potential sources of crisis and addressing them well before they manifest themselves into full-blown crises. To become an effective high-stakes leader, I have argued, it is just as important that we understand how to *prevent* crises as it is to lead effectively *during* them.

I have also tried to make the case that, following a crisis, stakeholders will require continued attention and reassurance as organizational processes are reviewed and changes are made to build a better, stronger, more resilient organization for the future. One particularly effective way of engaging stakeholders following a crisis is to formally invite them to play an active role in the post-crisis change process. When you can do this, you will find that your change initiatives will not only be better aligned with stakeholder interests, but they can actually serve as mechanisms to improve stakeholder relationships and brand loyalty. I can speak from my experience as a leader at JetBlue for many years that you will be pleasantly surprised by your stakeholders' willingness to help *you* to help *them*.

As we bring this chapter to a close, I want to share a final shout-out to Dr. Stephanie Duchek and her work on organizational resilience. I really do believe that she has provided an exceptionally useful framework for our exploration of the topic — from crisis-prevention processes and actions that leaders can take ahead of any crisis-level event, to the actions leaders should be taking in the midst of a crisis, to the processes and actions that leaders can take once the crisis has been largely controlled and the organization is focused on the most effective recovery possible. All three of these stages are essential for high-stakes leaders to keep in mind during their proactive crisis planning, and will provide plentiful opportunities for both individual and organizational learning.

High-stakes leadership is about much more than being able to step up and lead when a crisis appears. Yes, this is often the most visible aspect of high-stakes leadership — and it is vitally important to our organizations that we have the knowledge, skills, and abilities to navigate this incredibly challenging environment. But high-stakes leaders must also be able to provide tangible evidence of leadership well before and well after a crisis.

> **High-stakes leadership is about much more than being able to step up and lead when a crisis appears. High-stakes leaders must also be able to provide tangible evidence of leadership well before and well after a crisis.**

Because of this, we should think of resilience as a much broader concept than simply as the ability to pick oneself up after a stumble and get back to business. As you go forward as a high-stakes leader, I hope that you will find these lessons to be incredibly valuable and wonderfully practical.

Exercise #4
Three Actions to Improve Our
Capacity for Resilience

You have learned a great deal about organizational resilience in this chapter. What three actions can you take, starting immediately, to make your team, your unit, and/or your organization more resilient?

In your responses (one paragraph per action), include brief descriptions of:

- Why these actions are important

- What these actions will help to solve

- How you will know the actions have been impactful

Action 1: _____

_____

_____

_____

Action 2: _____

_____

_____

_____

Action 3: _____

_____

_____

_____

08

PREDICTING THE FALLOUT
Anticipating Stakeholder Reactions to a Crisis

It has been said that you never know how someone might react when the going gets tough. And that's true, to an extent. But, as we have explored together in this book, understanding stakeholder value propositions can go a long way toward informing leaders about how certain people will react in times of crisis. In this chapter, we'll explore the reactions themselves — what to expect that your organization's stakeholders might think, feel, say, and do … during and after a crisis.

First, let's review what we know to be true.

The Three Incontrovertible Truths About Crisis Leadership and Stakeholder Concerns

1. **Not if, but when.** We all live and work in a volatile, uncertain, complex, and ambiguous (VUCA) world and no matter how you cut it, we'll all eventually find ourselves in a crisis situation — in some way, shape, or form. When it comes to organizational crisis, it's really not an "if" anymore, it's a "when." And because our odds of having to provide

leadership during a crisis are pretty much 1 in 1, it makes sense for each of us to build some crisis leadership capability.

2. **Stakeholder engagement is the key to short-term survival.** One of the most important aspects of crisis leadership is the ability to effectively engage stakeholders. Your organization will have many different stakeholders, each of whom will draw value from their relationship with your firm. It is these value propositions that are threatened during a crisis, so the most effective way to engage stakeholders is with these value propositions in mind.

3. **Stakeholders stand at the center of long-term organizational resilience.** The most resilient organizations leverage their intimate knowledge of stakeholder interests and the relationships that have been established between the organization and those stakeholders. It is through these relationships that businesses can identify potential sources of crisis (i.e., future threats) and address them before they become critical. Also, as a product of these relationships, our stakeholders can become valuable assets during and after a crisis, helping organizations recover as quickly as possible and move forward with improved processes, the benefit of experience, and stronger bonds with their stakeholders than ever before.

We now know that crisis is inevitable and that how we think about, engage, and treat our stakeholders (before, during, and after a crisis) is at the heart of successful high-stakes leadership. So let's explore more deeply *how* we should be engaging our stakeholders during a crisis.

Let's imagine that crisis has struck and we're in the middle of the disaster at this very moment. We know that our stakeholders might have been able to help us prevent this crisis but, for whatever reason, that didn't happen. So here we are, amid the crisis and we know that we must engage our stakeholders as one of our many crisis leadership responsibilities. But there's much to consider:

- What is the best way to engage them?
- What information do we think they want to hear?
- How should we package the information that we want to share?

- What goals should we have as we plan and evaluate the effectiveness of our engagement efforts?

An interesting aspect of stakeholder engagement is the science behind how humans process information during a crisis. Some fascinating research has been done in this area. We know, for example, how we process crises physiologically — that when we experience or observe a crisis, our perceptions stimulate brain function that can invoke a fight-or-flight response. Psychologically, we know from research that negative events activate our brains more than positive ones. We have a negative bias such that we automatically give more attention to a negative event and negative information than we do to positive information or positive events. As high-stakes leaders, it's useful to know that there are natural, human forces working against us in a crisis. Basic human physiology and psychology will provoke your stakeholders (and others) to watch intently as the events of a crisis unfold. Just as we all rubberneck to see a car accident when we're driving on the highway, stakeholders want to see and know what's happening, especially when it looks to be tragic, scandalous, or salacious. This natural human inclination to fixate on the negative is *the* key consideration for how stakeholders perceive threats to their value propositions during a crisis.

- -

As high-stakes leaders, it's useful to know that there are natural, human forces working against us in a crisis. Basic human physiology and psychology will provoke your stakeholders (and others) to watch intently as the events of a crisis unfold.

- -

Have you ever thought about how *you* process a situation where your value proposition is being threatened? It turns out that researchers have spent time studying this very question. In the section that follows, you will learn a simple but powerful model that will help you better understand how stakeholders react to crisis situations. This model will not only be useful for understanding stakeholder reactions during a crisis but, perhaps just as importantly, it can help us predict how stakeholders *are likely to react* to a given scenario. And the more we can predict, the better we can prepare.

A Model for Predicting Stakeholder Reactions to Crisis

Within an extraordinarily rich publication titled *The Handbook of Crisis Communication* (2010), an entire chapter is dedicated to the topic of stakeholder reactions during a crisis. Chapter 31, "Exploring Crisis from a Receiver Perspective: Understanding Stakeholder Reactions During Crisis Events," was written by Drs. Tomasz Fediuk, W. Timothy Coombs, and Isabel Botero. In the introduction to the chapter, the authors suggest the following:

> "In day-to-day operations, organizations are susceptible to a variety of events that can create a crisis situation. Such crises can damage the reputation of the organization and can induce negative responses from angry stakeholders. Stakeholder responses can range from minor annoyance to active disruptions of organizational objectives through protests and boycotts, to challenging an organization's legitimacy to exist. Thus, understanding crises, how organizations manage them, and the way stakeholders assess and respond to them is important for managers handling crisis events.
>
> The messages communicated by an organization in crisis play a vital role in the alleviation of a crisis situation. More specifically, communication assists in reducing the damage incurred by the impacted organizations due to the crisis event. Therefore, understanding how individuals perceive and cognitively process crisis events and post-crisis messages is crucial to the crisis manager."[1]

With this guidance in mind, let's explore a compelling model that will help you better understand how stakeholders react to crisis situations. If you can predict how stakeholders are likely to react to a particular situation — particularly if that situation has some degree of likelihood — then spending time working through a few of these scenarios would help high-stakes leaders in numerous ways:

---

1   T. A. Fediuk, PhD, W. T. Coombs, PhD, and I. C. Botero, PhD, "Exploring Crisis from a Receiver Perspective: Understanding Stakeholder Reactions during Crisis Events," *The Handbook of Crisis Communication*, ed. W. T. Coombs, PhD, and S. J. Holladay, PhD (Hoboken, NJ: Wiley-Blackwell, January 2012), doi:10.1002/9781444314885.

- They could begin to build generic/templated/standardized response plans for certain types of situations.

- They could identify gaps in crisis response capabilities.

- They could begin to prioritize the types of crises for which it would be most important to prepare.

The model introduced by Fediuk, Coombs, and Botero is illustrated in Figure 2 and, according to the authors, it "presents a framework for understanding how stakeholders process crisis events." While this framework was created primarily for what the authors call "transgression-based events or crises that are believed to be due to intentional organization misconduct," it is useful for our purposes to view *any* sort of crisis that threatens a stakeholder's value proposition as a case in which that stakeholder is likely to, at least initially, consider the organization to be a primary contributor to the threat. (In short, no matter whose fault it is, stakeholders will most likely blame you.) Therefore, we will consider this model as being applicable to any type of crisis.

The model is divided into four simple parts: a trigger event, an evaluation of the event, the affective reactions generated by the evaluation process, and outcomes. Let's take a brief look at each of the parts.

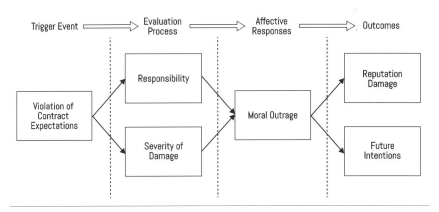

Figure 2. Exploring Crisis from a Receiver Perspective: Understanding Stakeholder Reactions During Crisis Events, Fediuk, Coombs, and Botero, 2010.

- - - - - - - - - - - - - - - - - -

Trigger Event

At the onset of a crisis, something happens to threaten the value proposition stakeholders have with an organization. This "something" will be referred to in our model as a "trigger event." As a trigger event takes place, stakeholders are likely to view the situation as one in which the organization will ultimately fail to fully deliver on its commitment to provide value. In other words, when a crisis appears and value propositions are threatened, stakeholders will sense what the authors of this model call a potential "violation of contract expectations." As the crisis plays out and value propositions are impacted in some negative way, the potential violation of expectations will begin to appear as an actual violation. ("See? I knew this would happen!" stakeholders will think or say.) This perception will lead stakeholders to sense that an injustice has been committed against them. Not surprisingly, they will react in some way to this injustice. According to Fediuk et al, this reaction will lead to an "evaluation process," which is the second part of the model.

- - - - - - - - - - - - - - - - - -

Evaluation Process

When a violation of expectations has been perceived by a stakeholder, an evaluation process will follow. The first process that takes place is a determination of whether the violation is good or bad for them. For our purposes, we'll assume that this assessment is negative, which is most often the case. Next, stakeholders will evaluate the situation in two ways: 1) to what extent is the organization responsible, and 2) how severe is the impact likely to be for me?

The determination of responsibility will be made using multiple inputs (e.g., Who did or didn't take action to create this situation? Should this have been prevented? Is this part of a long history of errors?), but there's a very high likelihood that at least some responsibility is going to be assigned to the organization. As humans, we want to know why things are happening to us and we want to find a way to assign blame or responsibility. In the early stages of a crisis, little will be known about the event. Therefore, it's reasonable to assume that stakeholders will tend to believe that some — or all — of the fault lies with the organization.

Severity of damage determinations will be based on perceptions of how significantly the crisis *might* impact a specific stakeholder (in the early stages of a crisis) or *has already* impacted that stakeholder (typically later in a crisis). Pretty straight forward here. The greater the amount of perceived or actual damage, the more extreme the severity evaluation.

Once these initial evaluations have been completed, "affective responses" will follow. These responses represent the third stage in the model. High-stakes leaders should keep in mind that as crises evolve, stakeholders are likely to revisit their initial evaluation of responsibility and severity of damage. As more is learned — as more information becomes available — stakeholders will re-evaluate both areas (i.e., the degree to which they assign blame to the company and the degree to which they believe the issue impacts them personally) and are likely to modify their evaluations accordingly.

- - - - - - - - - - - - - - - - -

Affective Responses

According to Fediuk et al, "crisis incidents are not only inconvenient times for organizations, but also are important psychological events experienced by individuals. Often, these events are emotion-laden experiences. Specific emotions experienced after a contract violation event are determined by the significance and meaning a stakeholder assigns to the specific event and different appraisals lead to different emotions and action tendencies. *Affect* is a term that is often used interchangeably with emotions."

Once a stakeholder has made an evaluation regarding responsibility and severity of damage, an "affective response" (i.e., an emotional response) will lead to some degree of what is often called "moral outrage." Moral outrage is used in the model to describe the anger and resentment a stakeholder feels when they believe they or someone else has been wrongfully harmed. Naturally, the extent of this outrage will be a direct result of the degree to which the stakeholder has perceived the severity of the contract violation and the organization's responsibility for the situation. The extent of the outrage will also be strongly correlated with the resultant "outcomes," which represent stage four in the model.

- - - - - - - - - - - - - - - - - -

Outcomes

The outcomes in our stakeholder-reactions model will manifest themselves in two ways that matter to high-stakes leaders. First, stakeholders will update their confidence in the brand of the organization (for better or for worse). Second, their evaluations and subsequent level of moral outrage will inform a stakeholder's future intentions. For the sake of simplicity, we won't explore the myriad outcomes that stakeholders could pursue in the wake of the crisis, but high-stakes leaders should recognize the potential for a broad spectrum of potential reactions — from stakeholders who dismiss the situation entirely on one end of the spectrum, to stakeholders who resort to confrontation, retaliation, or revenge on the other. What is most important here is that stakeholders' reactions to a crisis will produce outcomes of *some* sort. These outcomes will impact how stakeholders will perceive the organization's brand going forward and their future intentions to interact with the company.[2]

- -

High-stakes leaders should recognize the potential for a broad spectrum of potential reactions — from stakeholders who dismiss the situation entirely on one end of the spectrum, to stakeholders who resort to confrontation, retaliation, or revenge on the other.

- -

Why is this model of stakeholder reactions to a crisis useful to high-stakes leaders? Because it can help us think through potential crisis scenarios and imagine how different stakeholders are likely to respond in each case. As I suggested earlier, these likely response predictions can support efforts to proactively:

- Build generic response plans for certain types of situations
- Identify gaps in crisis response capabilities

---

2   T. A. Fediuk, PhD, W. T. Coombs, PhD, and I. C. Botero, PhD, "Exploring Crisis from a Receiver Perspective: Understanding Stakeholder Reactions during Crisis Events," *The Handbook of Crisis Communication*, ed. W. T. Coombs, PhD, and S. J. Holladay, PhD (Hoboken, NJ: Wiley-Blackwell, January 2012), doi:10.1002/9781444314885.

- Prioritize the types of crises that would be most important to be prepared for.

Trigger Events and the Precipitation of Crisis

To thoroughly understand the nature and impact of a trigger event, we need to think about the perception of each stakeholder group and the extent to which a crisis is impacting their value proposition with the organization — keeping in mind that, for a given crisis scenario, each of our stakeholders will be viewing the trigger event in a unique way.

This trigger event, according to researchers, produces what is perceived as a violation of contract expectations. What does this mean? For our purposes here, as we are considering how our stakeholders will "perceive" a threat to their value proposition, let's think of the relationship between stakeholders and an organization as a "psychological contract." Yes, in many cases, there will be written or formal contracts between stakeholders and an enterprise. In cases where the terms of formal contracts appear to have been violated, there are legal remedies to address these claims. That's not what we are talking about here. What we're talking about are stakeholder *expectations* — like when a person expects to be notified by their child's school if the children were placed into lockdown today due to a bomb threat, or when an employer closes a factory or a retail outlet without giving ample notice to employees who are left feeling betrayed. "Perceived violations" are all about how stakeholders *feel* in the midst or wake of a crisis, and how those feelings are directed at *you* as a leader of the team or organization that caused the perceived harm.

In our model (i.e., Trigger Event ⟶ Evaluation Process ⟶ Affective Responses ⟶ Outcomes), we are dealing with cases in which there are no formal written contracts. And even if there *are* formal terms on some level (such as the "contract of carriage" that you agree to when you purchase an airline ticket), these are typically not thought of by stakeholders as formal contracts. As high-stakes leaders, it's most useful to think of our partnerships with stakeholders as if we have entered into psychological contracts with them — informal agreements that represent the perceptions of two parties and their mutual obligations toward each other. By definition, these obligations are typically informal and imprecise, and they may be inferred from statements, implications, advertisements, or other sources. And while I recognize that consumer protection laws exist to ensure the fair treatment of customers, these laws are not generally well understood, nor do they tend to influence a stakeholder's perceptions when they feel that a company has broken its promise to them. The important idea here is that once stakeholders have communicated their intentions to do business with a company, they perceive that they have entered into a psychological contract — that you owe them something and that failure to deliver what is owed in a manner that satisfies constitutes a betrayal of sorts.

As high-stakes leaders, it's most useful to think of our partnerships with stakeholders as if we have entered into psychological contracts with them — informal agreements that represent the perceptions of two parties and their mutual obligations toward each other.

A crisis — our trigger event — presents a potential violation of stakeholder value expectations. In other words, the crisis creates a situation in which the terms of our psychological contract are being threatened. Why is it useful to think of a crisis this way? It reminds us, as business leaders, that a crisis doesn't just put the future of our *business* at risk, but that it makes our stakeholders feel threatened too.

I know that you have had experiences in the past where your expectations were not met by a business or the provider of a product or service. How did you feel when you learned that you were about to be disappointed? To be let down? To not receive something that you really expected, or wanted, or needed? Similarly — and this is a vitally important lesson for business leaders — how do you think your stakeholders are feeling when an emerging crisis begins to suggest a threat to *their* value proposition with your business? How might the uncertainty and anxiety of this growing threat manifest itself in worry, frustration, expressions of anger, or demands for alternatives from some (or all) of your stakeholders?

This is the context to remember when you begin to think about the early stages of a crisis. You will have much to do for your company and your team. But never forget that, beyond your immediate concerns, you have a broad collection of stakeholders who need support, attention, and as much of your consideration as you can afford to give them.

Never forget that, beyond your immediate concerns, you have
a broad collection of stakeholders who need support, attention,
and as much of your consideration as you can afford to give them.

All organizational stakeholders — your employees, customers, communities, investors, regulators, the media, and even your competitors — have a literal stake in your ability to manage a crisis that threatens the value they hold with your enterprise. When a crisis is looming — when a trigger event presents a tangible threat to your stakeholders' implied contract or expectations with your organization — the effectiveness of your efforts to engage these stakeholders and acknowledge and address this threat will go a long way to preserving their confidence, trust, and loyalty in you, your leadership team, and your enterprise.

A Crisis Is Rarely Rooted in a Single, Spontaneous Cause

Researchers have determined that most organizational crises are *not* the product of an instantaneous, unpredictable eruption of bad fortune. Yes, events of this nature do happen, but they happen rarely. Crises are typically the result of choices made by organizational leaders. When poor choices lead to poor outcomes, those responsible will be held to a higher standard of accountability. This should certainly seem reasonable. But what about the case where the leadership choices involve decisions to *not* act on issues that, in some stakeholders' eyes, require attention and should be resolved immediately?

Most organizational crises are *not* the product of an
instantaneous, unpredictable eruption of bad fortune.

Earlier in this book, as you explored the importance of stakeholder relationships and their contribution to organizational resilience, it was argued that both internal and external stakeholders were critical to the anticipation

stage of resilience. It was also argued that both internal and external stakeholders could serve as observers for signs of trouble. What happens when
these observers identify signs of trouble, report them to organizational
leaders, and the reports are ignored or the actions taken by leadership are
insufficient to address the raised issues? When stakeholders try to report
an issue and the effort is largely ignored or not given some reasonable
amount of attention, a couple of very powerful messages are sent back to
these stakeholders: First, that leaders don't really value the feedback (while
this may not be true, it is the perception that many stakeholders will have);
and second, that leaders don't believe the issue to be important enough to
resolve. This could be perceived as either: "Thank you, but this isn't really
a big deal" or "Thank you, but we've got much bigger issues to deal with." In
either case, what stakeholders will perceive is a lack of attention to something they believe should be addressed. They will feel dismissed, conde-
scended to, or even victimized by leadership arrogance.

Now let's connect the dots between stakeholder contribution to pre-crisis
resilience and stakeholder evaluation of in-crisis responsibility. Some organizations do a wonderful job of engaging stakeholders when they identify
an opportunity for improvement. They offer employees recognition and
other rewards for their awareness and commitment to making the company
better — more efficient, more effective, more profitable, and more safe or
secure. They also find ways to recognize other stakeholders for their contributions through discounted or free merchandise, special recognition events,
and other tangible benefits — both to thank them for their commitment
to making the company better and also to inspire similar future behavior.
High-stakes leaders want their stakeholders to be on the lookout for threats
... and opportunities.

Interestingly, and this is where organizations suffer a "triple whammy" of
sorts, when stakeholders aren't recognized or rewarded for their efforts,
three things will happen. First, these stakeholders will no longer make the
effort to help the company get better — or, perhaps more importantly for
our purposes, they will no longer be willing to serve as trusted pre-crisis
observers for signs of trouble. Second, the organization misses a great
opportunity to reinforce stakeholder loyalty when they fail to reward them
for their "extraordinary and chivalrous" efforts. By not formally recognizing
praiseworthy acts of loyalty, the company also misses the opportunity to
inspire similar actions from other loyal customers who might like to receive

some recognition for supporting a company they like being associated with. Third, and particularly germane to the way stakeholders evaluate responsibility during a crisis, if stakeholders have been trying to tell a company that something is broken and needs to be fixed, and then that something grows into a crisis, these stakeholders will almost certainly assign a much greater degree of responsibility to organizational leaders. You don't ever want your stakeholders, during times of painful crisis for your business, to be looking at you smugly and thinking (or actually saying): "We told you so."

Crises are frequently the result of insufficient attention to early indications of trouble. It's time to pay better attention and to listen to the warning signals sounded by our stakeholders. If we don't listen and respond appropriately and then the issues grow into a major disruption, stakeholder evaluations of the company will be harsh and their affective responses are more likely to be emotionally charged to a much greater extent. Avoiding customer outrage on social media or costly and damaging employee walkouts (or any other sort of secondary crisis spurred by a leadership team's failure to prevent disaster) starts by listening to people when they first tell you that something requires your immediate attention.

Stakeholder Evaluation of Trigger Events

We have established that crises, whether they are just beginning to show themselves or are fully developed, create situations in which stakeholders' contract expectations — their perceptions of typically undocumented, but implied and assumed, commitments from an organization — are being threated or have been violated. In either case, high-stakes leaders must consider how to best engage these stakeholders, to minimize the potential impact of the situation on their value propositions, and to ensure that stakeholders can and will pursue a healthy, long-term, future relationship with the organization.

According to our simple model for understanding stakeholder reactions during a crisis, once there has been a perceived violation of expectations, stakeholders will begin to evaluate their own personal situation. They are thinking, naturally, about "what this means for me." Think about how this is consistent with your own personal experiences. Something is happening that tells us we are about to be disappointed — or worse — and we begin to form judgments, to harbor worries, to make contingency plans, and to voice our concerns (sometimes loudly and publicly). The same thing happens to your organization's stakeholders. Once they have determined whether a situation is good or bad for them, they evaluate the situation through two primary lenses: 1) an evaluation of the responsibility for the crisis, and 2) an assessment of the severity of the situation. Let's take a moment to look at both perspectives.

Responsibility

The idea of evaluating responsibility and assigning blame during or immediately following a crisis is a feature of human society long observed by historians. Mary Douglas, an anthropologist and researcher of societal culture, has expertise in the areas of risk and blame and she has spent much of her career studying these topics. She has written extensively on how societies respond to a crisis by demanding a degree of certainty about consequences and action in cases where none had been clearly defined. Faced with uncertainty, she suggested, societies respond with a collective call for the placement of blame on someone. Historically, from medieval witch-trials blaming women for disease outbreaks and community misfortune, to the much more recent suggestion that COVID-19 was synthesized as a biological weapon in China, the response to extreme risk and uncertainty has always led to the assignment of blame.

- -

> Societies respond to a crisis by demanding a degree of certainty
> about consequences and action in cases where none had been
> clearly defined. Faced with uncertainty, societies respond with
> a collective call for the placement of blame on someone.

- -

Why is this idea important to crisis leaders? It should not come as any surprise that when our stakeholders believe that we have failed to honor our commitments — irrespective of cause or circumstances — they will look to determine responsibility and try to assign blame. Knowing this, we should be able to predict the disposition of our stakeholders when we begin to engage them. They will likely have already considered the question of responsibility and will probably already have some sense of who they would like to blame. Given this reality, how should crisis leaders craft

their early communications with stakeholders? I would suggest that, at
a minimum, leaders recognize that their stakeholders are not likely to be
oblivious bystanders awaiting an introduction to "the harsh realities of
business." Rather, even without a clear picture of the facts, the mere perception by stakeholders that there might be a threat to their value propositions
has already inspired an estimate of impact, an evaluation of responsibility,
and an assignment of blame. When we begin our engagement efforts with
an assumption of the latter, the tone, content, and intentionality of our
messaging changes dramatically.

Let me say one more thing about responsibility. With some background on
the propensity of stakeholders to assess responsibility and assign blame,
leaders should regularly revisit the framing of their engagement with
stakeholders throughout the lifespan of a crisis. Over time, we (leaders and
stakeholders alike) can see a clearer picture of crisis causes and impact. As
a natural course and as time passes, stakeholders will continuously learn
more about what happened, why, and how an organization is responding
to it. These stakeholders will just as continuously re-evaluate responsibility
and adjust their assignments of blame. The flames of discontent might be
fanned, or the fury might be quelled; a crisis is an evolving and dynamic
event. As such, during a crisis, as more is learned, your efforts to engage your
stakeholders must also evolve with the most current information available.

Severity of Damage

In addition to assessing who they think is responsible during a crisis, stakeholders will evaluate the severity of the damage. Damage assessments may
include criteria such as the number of individuals harmed or killed by the
incident, the amount of property damage, the impact on the community
and the environment, the financial impact of the incident, or simply a purely
subjective appraisal of severity. As we are dealing with perception here,
crisis leaders should assume that there may be a surprisingly broad range
of severity estimates. What is considered an "outrage" to one stakeholder
might be "not a huge deal" to another.

Because of this, a key takeaway for leaders is not to underestimate the
assessments of severity and impact, as stakeholders have a great deal of
freedom to assign whatever values they see fit (and then voice and share
those assessments widely, on social media and elsewhere). As we formulate

our engagement strategies, it is generally best to assume that stakeholders have assigned greater levels of severity and impact than the organization has — that while you're taking the crisis seriously, your stakeholders might be demanding an even higher level of accountability and even remorse from you. Remember that "moral outrage" sometimes looks and feels just like it sounds. Keep in mind the importance of demonstrating care and empathy in your communications. In many ways, when it comes to stakeholder engagement, the facts telling the story may matter less than the perceptions of impact and the feelings others have about your approach to rectifying damage or making things right.

Based on the evaluation of responsibility and the assessment of severity, stakeholders will formulate a response to the situation, which will be reflected in their post-evaluation actions.

Stakeholder Responses to Crises and the Outcomes They Produce

Once stakeholders have evaluated the impact of some trigger event — specifically, according to our model, once they have considered the extent to which a person or organization is responsible and the degree of hardship created by the situation — stakeholders will draw some conclusions about an appropriate response. The response will manifest itself in two ways: their assessment of the organizational brand, and their future intentions for the conduct of business with that organization.

Once stakeholders have evaluated the impact of some trigger event, they will draw conclusions about an appropriate response.

We know that our stakeholders' evaluation process will lead to an "affective" (i.e., emotional) response of some sort. As we have learned, the incident can prime feelings of many different emotions, including anger, hostility, shame, frustration, disappointment, sadness, or guilt — and these feelings can be particularly intense if the stakeholder believes an injustice was done. When a crisis has been deemed by stakeholders as "clearly our fault," and the damage assessment is significant, stakeholder responses will likely be extreme.

In our model, "moral outrage" is used to describe the extent of negative emotions (such as anger and resentment) that stakeholders feel when they or others have been wrongfully treated or harmed. Estimating stakeholders' levels of outrage can help us predict their behaviors during a crisis. Specifically, when we can predict that stakeholders will project outward-facing negative emotions, we can assume that they might also feel the need to correct the wrong or engage in retaliatory behaviors.

When we can predict that stakeholders will project outward-facing negative emotions, we can assume that they might also feel the need to correct the wrong or engage in retaliatory behaviors.

Clearly, a primary objective for high-stakes leaders is to reduce the impact of negative stakeholder sentiments. In our model, the two outcomes we are most interested in are:

- The reputation damage perceived by a given stakeholder, and
- Any future intensions that are not in the best interests of the firm.

We will not go into great detail here on the brand impact of a crisis. Nor will we pay nearly enough attention to the different ways stakeholders might perceive a company and its leadership after a crisis, or the extent to which they will change the way they engage with the business. Suffice it to say that crises, unless they are managed very effectively, will put pressure on the reputation or brand value perceived by stakeholders and will likely result in future stakeholder behaviors that are not consistent with the best interests of the firm.

How does this realization help us? The point of understanding this entire model is to have at our disposal a model for predicting the likely stakeholder responses to certain crisis scenarios. If we are in the middle of a crisis, it's already too late to start predicting how our stakeholders might respond because the responses will be coming —fast and furious. (I can assure you that stakeholders will be letting us know what's on their minds!) Having a model and a mechanism for predicting likely stakeholder responses is crucial to our crisis preparedness and planning. This is true for two reasons.

First, during a crisis, you will have limited time and resources to engage stakeholders as effectively as you would like. A model like this will help you develop a predictive instrument for identifying priority stakeholders for different types of crises. How? By spending time thinking through crises that your company is most likely to face and then using this model to predict which stakeholder groups are most likely to be impacted, you'll be able to ascertain who is most likely to respond most fervently or loudly. While it may be nearly impossible to predict the exact circumstances of your next crisis, you should be able to identify categories of crisis that are most likely to produce a disruption.

While it may be nearly impossible to predict the exact circumstances of your next crisis, you should be able to identify categories of crisis that are most likely to produce a disruption.

Second, a model such as this will help crisis leaders at your firm develop a general communication plan for certain types of crises based on how different stakeholder groups are likely to react in each scenario. A crisis is a little less painful if you enter it with a template in place for who will communicate to which stakeholders, in what priority order, through which channels (e.g., email, phone calls, press conference, social media), and adhering to what principles or key messages.

As high-stakes leaders, we can benefit greatly from thinking through the ways our stakeholders are likely to react because of different crisis scenarios. Having a sense of these likely reactions, we will be able to prepare stakeholder engagement plans that can address the concerns of employees, customers, media, competitors, partners/suppliers, and others as they: 1) evaluate responsibility and the severity of the damage of the event, 2) affectively/emotionally respond, and 3) make choices about the extent to which we are trustworthy and worth their partnership going forward.

Predicting Stakeholder Reactions Can Help Us Craft Communication Plans

Taking the time to predict how stakeholders are likely to react during a crisis can be extremely helpful to our crisis-planning efforts. If we have a sense of how a particular scenario is likely to be perceived and processed by our stakeholders, we will gain insights in several ways.

First, working through a variety of crisis scenarios will give us a great sense of how those events are likely to impact our stakeholders and, therefore, should help us see why it is worth making investments in preventive measures. Perhaps the most obvious example of this is the justification for airline safety programs. Airlines invest in safety because, well, it's the law. But the law doesn't state how much or in which ways to invest. Of course, safety is critically important to airlines — not just because it is the law or because it is the right thing to do. It is also prudent because of the ways different stakeholder groups will react to a safety crisis and the actions they will take as a result. Take a minute to think about why this logic does or doesn't quite work for you. I believe that you will find some value in the thought exercise.

Second, working through different crisis scenarios will illustrate steps that can be taken to influence stakeholder reactions at various points in the model. We now know that stakeholder reactions begin with an expectation of a commitment from an organization — what we referred to earlier as a psychological contract. Can we imagine ways of providing a greater degree of clarity around expectations or goods and services to be rendered? Taking time to educate stakeholders — in an effort to clearly set expectations and, if they exist, limitations on your ability to meet those expectations — may be well worth your time. When organizations teach their stakeholders what to expect from them (through marketing efforts, clear "terms of service," written contracts that are accessible and avoid legalese, and through cultural practices like a customer 'bill of rights'), those organizations go a long way toward ensuring that all parties agree on the "contract" (literal or psychological) … long before a crisis might occur and bring a glaring light of scrutiny upon those expectations.

We also know that when our stakeholders experience a perceived violation of contract expectations, they will judge our level of responsibility and the severity of the situation. Working through scenarios proactively — and creating ways to mitigate stakeholder judgment — will provide your organization with a ready set of tools to effectively engage stakeholders when emotions are running high. This leads me to one of the most useful collections of tools that a company can have at its disposal in times of crisis — and that is a set of communication plans.

One of the most useful collections of tools that a company can have at its disposal in times of crisis is a set of communication plans.

For certain types of crises, once we have used our model to predict likely stakeholder reactions, we can create a collection of stakeholder communications that can be prepared and set aside for use if and when they could be helpful. We've established the critical importance of stakeholder engagement throughout a crisis and, in this chapter, we've learned of a mechanism that can help us predict how these stakeholders are likely to respond. If we combine these two lessons — and amplify them by acknowledging that we will have very little time *during* a crisis to craft all of the communications that we would want — then taking time to pre-plan communication templates for different scenarios should make perfect sense.

Why do I use the term "templates?" The fact is that you will not be able to predict the full set of details surrounding a future crisis. (If you can, then go fix things *now*, because you know an awful lot about a crisis that hasn't happened yet.) Even though you won't be able to predict all the details of a future crisis, you can predict a few of the most probable types of crises within your organization or industry sector, and how these crises will likely be perceived by your stakeholders. With this information, you can prepare a generic, templatized collection of communications — ready to be tailored to the specifics of your situation and just minutes away from being ready to deliver.

The organizations best prepared for crises and major disruptions have a crisis communication binder or folder (digital and physical) with general messages for many of their most-likely crisis types, and for the majority of their primary stakeholders, ready to go at a moment's notice. This practice has proven immensely valuable on countless occasions for these organizations and may be one of the most useful tools you could ever have in your high-stakes leadership toolkit,

The Proactive Development of Stakeholder Engagement Plans

At some point in your organization's crisis-preparation process, you and other leaders from your organization will want to consider a number of different crisis types and use the stakeholder reaction model to help you predict not only how stakeholders will react to each scenario, but also how your communications can help these stakeholders understand why you are making certain choices, that you recognize the hardship they are feeling, and that you have their interests in mind as you do your best to resolve the crisis as quickly and painlessly as possible.

Your communications can help stakeholders understand why you are making certain choices, that you recognize the hardship they are feeling, and that you have their interests in mind as you do your best to resolve the crisis as quickly and painlessly as possible.

The real benefit of developing crisis-communication plans — what some might describe as stakeholder-engagement plans — is that doing so will allow you to rapidly adapt to any scenario and begin, as quickly as possible, to help your stakeholders understand your key messages. If you wait to begin this process until you are knee-deep in a full-blown crisis, time limitations and other critical responsibilities will make it difficult to engage stakeholders as quickly as you would like. High-stakes leaders know that having these plans on the shelf, ready to tailor, provides the best possible opportunity to preserve stakeholder trust.

To help you think through the purpose and process of having these plans at the ready, consider the following. Keep these things in mind as you bring your leadership team together to work on a collection of these plans.

Some incredibly useful guidance that will help your proactive development of stakeholder engagement plans comes from the book *Ongoing Crisis Communication: Planning, Managing, and Responding* (2019) by researcher and crisis management expert W. Timothy Coombs (emphasis mine).

"If an organization has done any crisis preparation, it is usually the drafting of the crisis communication plan (CCP). While important, a CCP is not a magic insurance policy that protects an organization from a crisis. Nor is it a step-by-step set of instructions for what to do when a crisis hits. It must contain the information needed to manage a crisis but should not be overly long and cumbersome. Long CCPs look nice on shelves as they collect dust but are not practical when a crisis hits. Smart crisis managers know a CCP does not tell them exactly what to do to handle a crisis. Crises create uncertainty, and no CCP could anticipate all the subtle twists and turns in a crisis. The value of the CCP is as a reference tool. **Crisis management is the art of emergent strategy.** The crisis team must react to the crisis events; the strategy emerges from understanding the nature of the crisis situation.

Crises are time-pressured events during which quick responses are essential. During a crisis, time should not be wasted finding needed background information, deciding who will do what, and trying to determine the sequence of events. A CCP helps to reduce response time by gathering these elements together beforehand. In addition to speed, the CCP helps create an organized and efficient response. A CCP creates a system that can save lives, reduce an organization's exposure to risks, and permit remedial actions without embarrassment and scrutiny. The CCP is, at its roots, a communication document and involves identifying who to contact and how. Contact information is provided for team members and additional experts that might be useful to the team. A crisis communication plan covers such information as how to reach various stakeholders and the creation of pre-crisis messages. It can include reminders, in checklist form, of key actions that typically are taken during a crisis."[3]

Remember this acronym — CCP — as you embark on the development of a proactive stakeholder-engagement plan. If you haven't recently led your team through a CCP development exercise, might now be the ideal time?

Do not discount the value of starting with someone else's draft plan as a starting point for you to customize. Do a little research to find publicly available CCP examples that resonate with you — even a quick search will yield a great deal of proverbial food for thought. And beyond the thinking it will spur, having a sample plan can help you begin the actual work. Indeed, starting with a framework developed by someone else is always less intimidating than starting from a blank page. Perhaps check out the outline from the Ready Campaign (https://www.ready.gov/crisis-communications-plan) and build something customized to your organization and its operations, its stakeholders, and its values.

> **QUICK TIP:**
>
> **Do not attempt to perform a CCP development exercise while you are reading this book.** Complete the book in its entirety first, then come back to this section when you and your leadership team are ready to take on the task of creating a crisis communication plan of your own. Make note of this location so it will be easy to find at a later date.

Eight Guidelines for Developing a Crisis-Communications Plan

The creation of a Crisis-Communication Plan requires a great deal of organizational specificity. It is, after all, a guide that requires total customization for its users. These eight guidelines are instructive to the development of a custom CCP.

---

3   W. Timothy. Coombs, *Ongoing Crisis Communication: Planning, Managing, and Responding* (Thousand Oaks, CA: SAGE Publications, 2019).

1. *Identify the goal of the plan.* Before you begin, your team should determine what the objective of the plan is. It can be as simple as: "This plan creates a structure for communicating with internal and external stakeholders in the event of a crisis that affects the reputation or normal business functions of the organization." Then ensure that every aspect of your plan aligns with this common goal.

2. *Identify stakeholders.* When writing the plan, it is important to know who the plan is designed for. Outline a list of all stakeholders you would want to keep informed about the crisis. This list probably includes employees, customers and users, partners, investors, media outlets, the government and/or regulators, and the general public. The latter likely includes social media followers or people located nearby in the event of a location-based crisis. You should also add all necessary contact information for each of these groups in your plan.

3. *Create a hierarchy for sharing information on the crisis.* The person or team that reports a crisis doesn't always handle crisis communications. So, a part of the plan should be dedicated to forming a hierarchy that outlines how information should be shared within the company. That way, no matter who notices the crisis emerging, they will know who to contact first. This order depends on the structure of your team. The first step may be to notify the CEO or president of the organization, followed by the head of communications or public relations. The plan should also clarify what information should immediately be disclosed to these parties. This might include known details about the crisis, the source of the incident, and any existing backlash.

4. *Assign people to create "fact sheets."* Your plan should detail which people on the team oversee the creation of fact sheets about the crisis. Fact sheets are lists of known facts pertaining to the crisis. They prevent rumors or misinterpretations from spreading to media outlets or across social media platforms via user-generated content. Additionally, you should set a deadline for when these fact sheets will be prepared. Depending on the crisis, you may need them within 24 hours, six hours, or even 30 minutes.

5. *Identify and assess example crisis scenarios.* When a crisis does happen, you will likely feel overwhelmed. Your mind will race, and you will feel

pressured to respond to phone calls, social media mentions, and media inquiries. Therefore, it is best to outline common scenarios in advance. In Chapter 9, we will explore the identification of specific crisis types that your organization may encounter.

6. *Identify and answer common questions.* During any crisis — no matter how big or small — people are going to ask questions. Whether they are customer advocates or reporters, the public will want to uncover the truth. After all, in most cases, companies are considered guilty until proven innocent (remember our previous discussion about how stakeholders quickly assess crisis severity and assign blame). Crisis-communication plans can help you identify and answer questions that you can expect to be asked during your crisis scenarios.

7. *Identify potential risks.* No matter how well thought-out your crisis-communication plan is, there are always going to be pros and cons of your default practices. Naturally, you will stick with the plan that maximizes benefits while minimizing costs. However, the costs are still important to consider. Under each plan, you should document the potential risks you will face. That way, if the plan does backfire, you won't be caught off guard. You will have prepared yourself and laid out steps for recuperating from these additional losses. Consider having a "risk register" of sorts in the plan, which outlines "If X happens, what's the worst outcome? How will we react? What's the best outcome? How will we react? What's the most likely outcome? How will we react?"

8. *Create guidelines specific to social media.* Proactive communication is essential during a crisis. To offer as much transparency as possible, teams should focus on preparing press materials and sharing information about the crisis. The more information you withhold, the more the public will want to know what you're hiding. Reactive communication is just as important. It is vital that team members are focused on social-media monitoring during a time of crisis. Any negative social-media mentions should be dealt with immediately and with consistency, and should be handled in a manner that is consistent with the brand and culture you want to project. It's far too easy to destroy your own reputation by going too far when reacting to stakeholders online — to be too defensive, to be seen as "censoring" unpopular perspectives, or to be perceived as ignoring online comments that

deserve a response. There should be sections of your plan dedicated solely to social-media crisis management.[4]

Summarizing the Value of Predicting Stakeholder Reactions to Crises

Let's do a quick review of the concepts that we have covered in this chapter.

As we began, I asked you a few questions about how you have previously thought about engaging stakeholders during a crisis:

- What is the best way to engage them?
- What information do we think they want to hear?
- How should we package the information that we want to share?
- What goals should we have as we plan and evaluate the effectiveness of our engagement efforts?

I think that we have made a pretty compelling case for the importance of giving due attention to a deep consideration of how stakeholders are likely to react when facing a crisis, and for the development of some tools as a product of our consideration.

In this chapter, we have examined a simple but powerful model that can be used by leaders at your organization to help you better understand how stakeholders are likely to behave in a crisis. This model, I suggested, would not only be useful for understanding stakeholder reactions *during* a crisis, but perhaps *more* importantly, it could help us predict how stakeholders *are likely to react* in each scenario. If we could predict how stakeholders are likely to react to a particular situation, I offered, then spending time working through a few of these scenarios would help us in a number of ways.

I said that, first, we could use the model to help us begin to prioritize the types of crises that would be most important to prepare for. We considered this notion throughout the chapter and determined that by considering

---

4   Swetha Amaresan, "Six Crisis Communication Plan Examples and How to Write Your Own [Template]," HubSpot.com (April 2020, accessed July 11, 2020), https://blog.hubspot.com/service/crisis-communication-plan.

those crises that some stakeholders might react to in the most extreme or severe ways, we would benefit from first preventing then preparing to manage these specific crises. Our stakeholder response model can help us sort through potential risk scenarios to identify our priority types

Second, I suggested that our model could also be used to help us identify gaps in our current crisis response capabilities. If we can identify the sorts of things we must do well to mitigate the severity of stakeholder evaluation outcomes, then we should be able to determine how well we actually do those things. In other words, if we need to do a better job of defining expectations with stakeholders or educating them on the factors beyond our control (which impact our ability to consistently meet those expectations), then we should evaluate our current capabilities in these areas and make improvements where necessary.

And finally, I suggested that our model could help us begin to craft generic response plans for certain types of situations. All the concepts we explored in this chapter are critically important for high-stakes leaders to understand and practice. They provide key building blocks that can help an organization increase its capacity for resilience, as they help us create mechanisms to anticipate crises and cope more effectively with them when they appear.

Exercise #5
Three Key Opportunities to Better
Understand Likely Stakeholder Reactions

You have learned a great deal about stakeholder reactions in this chapter. What three actions can you take, starting immediately, to help your team, your unit, and/or your organization improve their ability to understand and predict stakeholder reactions during a future crisis?

In your responses (one paragraph per action), include brief descriptions of:

- Why these actions are important
- What these actions will help to solve
- How you will know the actions have been impactful.

Action 1: _____

_____

_____

_____

Action 2: _____

_____

_____

_____

Action 3: _____

_____

_____

_____

09

TYPES OF TROUBLE
Mastering Your Management
of Different Kinds of Crises

No two crises are exactly alike, but most crises fall into general categories or "types." As such, I'd like to spend some time with you as we explore common crisis typologies. What is a "typology?" It is simply an organizing framework that will help us learn about different types of crises based on categories of characteristics. Practitioners and researchers have spent quite a bit of time categorically organizing different types of crises to facilitate both their research efforts and their ability to describe what they have learned. Unfortunately, as you will see, no one has been able to develop a single typological framework that effectively illustrates the unique features of all crisis types. So, in this chapter, we will explore several different typologies that have been proposed for different purposes and for different users. By the end of this chapter, you'll have a good sense of the typology that would work best for *your* organization.

Why Craft a Typology?

Why consider different typologies? I can think of three reasons why such a pursuit might be helpful as we try to improve our high-stakes leadership effectiveness. First, if we are willing to accept that there are different varieties of crisis — and one of our goals in this chapter is to make a case for the validity of this assumption — then understanding the differences in various crisis situations should help us more effectively develop and execute an optimum, customized response for each scenario.

Second, having a working knowledge of different types of crises — and some key characteristics of each — will help us more effectively understand how crises could impact the interests of each of our stakeholder groups. Armed with this knowledge, we will be well-positioned to develop effective communication strategies for each of these groups that we can use at every stage — before, during, and after a crisis event.

And third, with this understanding of how specific crisis types could impact various stakeholders (and how we should be communicating with these stakeholders), we can more effectively focus our relationship-building efforts on: 1) Establishing sensing mechanisms for crisis-predicting — a key component of resilience, and 2) Setting expectations and developing channels for crisis-management feedback.

So let's explore a number of different perspectives and crisis typology outputs, from categorical lists to multivariable matrices, each designed to make it easier for you, the crisis leader, to not only more accurately define the crisis you are working to prevent or manage, but also to quickly identify key characteristics that can be addressed through pre-planned crisis responses. By the end of this chapter, you will understand and appreciate the benefits of having the ability to categorize different types of crisis. And, as I mentioned previously, you will also be able to determine the most useful organizing framework for your current and (when the need arises) future leadership responsibilities.

Categorical Lists of Crisis Types

The easiest and most common way to identify and organize different varieties of crisis is to produce a simple list of the different types. During the production of such a list, the author, leader, or organizer will use some sort of differentiation criteria to facilitate the distinction of one item on the list from another. In most cases, the first criterion for their list is simply: "This item is different enough from the others that it will need to be managed differently." At a deeper level, the purpose of having different crisis types on a list is that the different items on the list will have different implications for different stakeholder groups. Following this logic, having a list of unique crisis types can help a great deal in the development of a stakeholder centric approach to crisis management.

**Having a list of unique crisis types can help
a great deal in the development of a stakeholder-centric
approach to crisis management.**

The general idea here is the creation of a tool that will help us identify, understand, and respond more effectively to a given situation. "If we find ourselves in *this* type of crisis," we might think as we use our crisis typology tool, "then *these* stakeholder value propositions are threatened. Therefore, we should be doing *these* sorts of things, and engaging *these* stakeholder groups with *this* sort of information."

I am about to present you with four examples of categorical crisis typology lists. These lists are not exhaustive but should be useful in helping you see how different experts have organized their frameworks. As you will see, each of these lists was created with a slightly different objective — and perspective — in mind.

At the end of this chapter, after we have explored several different sample typologies, I'll ask you to craft a high-level, not particularly detailed, crisis typology of your own. Therefore, as you are reading through the lists that follow, be on the lookout for specific items that might be worth adding to your own list. Even though you will see many common elements and overlapping concepts across the four lists, you will almost certainly be able to identify some unique crisis varieties worth noting for your own typology.

Nine Types of Business Crisis

The first categorical list of crisis types comes from Gerald Meyers, who founded the "High-Stakes Leadership" course taught at the University of Michigan's Ross School of Business. He spent a great deal of time as a senior leader in the automotive industry and led teams through many crises. His experience had a great influence on the list he ultimately created. You can find this list in his book, which he co-authored with John Holusha, titled *When It Hits the Fan: Managing the Nine Crises of Business.* The book was published in 1986 and the categories have stood the test of time. Meyers' nine categories are listed below, with my commentary:

1. *Public Perception.* While almost all categories of crisis have some impact on public perception, some crises are driven almost entirely by changes in public perception. In these cases, trust is at risk and must be restored. When United Airlines dragged Dr. David Dao off a plane, a PR crisis (i.e., a "public perception" crisis) erupted.

2. *Product Failure.* When a product fails to deliver on its value promise, or worse, threatens the safety of its consumers, a crisis can develop. In these cases, confidence must be restored in the product (and perhaps the company as a whole). The Samsung Galaxy Note 7 crisis we examined earlier is a perfect illustration of this type of crisis.

3. *Market Shift.* Crises can arise from major changes in a market. These changes can take place over a long period of time or can happen fairly quickly. Blockbuster Video offers a great example of a company that failed to recover from a market-shift crisis when consumers started clamoring for ways to get their hands on movies and video games without having to leave their homes. Netflix, on the other hand, leveraged the opportunity to pivot in response to the same crisis, which was stimulated by the shift in customer demand to digital media access.

4. *Cash Shortage.* Businesses require capital (i.e., money) to operate. When access to cash becomes limited, a crisis will almost certainly follow. During the 2008 mortgage banking crisis in the United States, investment banks Bear Stearns and Lehman Brothers ultimately failed because bad investments led to their insolvency. A cash crisis can easily devastate a small or mid-sized business, as smaller companies often find it difficult to secure additional investment or financing when times get tough. As we teach in business schools, "cash is king."

5. *Management Change.* While a change in senior management may not sound like a big deal to some, there are many examples of an institution's change in management causing major anxiety (internally

and externally) and a lack of confidence as a result. Perhaps one of the best-known examples is the replacement of Steve Jobs by Tim Cook at Apple. When it was announced that Jobs would be stepping down, many stakeholders expressed great concern — sufficiently, it could be argued, to create a confidence crisis. These types of crises can also happen when professional sports teams name a new head coach or when municipalities welcome a new mayor, alderman, or village president.

6. *Merger/Hostile Takeover.* When two companies come together, the outcomes are rarely exceptional for everyone involved. A common benefit of mergers is the economy produced by merging two sets of administrative and leadership support into one. This reorganization, on its own, this does not produce economic benefit. But when duplicative work is subsequently eliminated (usually through the release of redundant employees), economic benefit is the product of lost jobs. When jobs are at stake, especially when lots of jobs may be at stake, a crisis may result. Telecommunications (telecom) companies Sprint and T-Mobile made multiple attempts to merge before they were finally able to do so. With each attempt — as well as after the merger was completed — many stakeholders for both organizations felt crisis-level uncertainty about the future.

7. *Regulation/De-regulation.* When the rules and regulations change, businesses must comply ... and this often has significant consequences. When the consequences are significant enough, a crisis may develop. As regulators consider different mechanisms for the improvement of services to their constituents, rule changes may create critical situations for companies. Healthcare and aviation security regulation changes over the past several years have created crisis-level challenges for organizations within those sectors.

8. *Human Capital.* When relations between management and labor become strained, it becomes difficult for the enterprise to function effectively. In some cases, it becomes impossible. When either management or labor take extreme measures to underscore their demands, crises develop. Over the decades of automotive production around the world, human capital crises have threatened the solvency of corporate entities, and teacher strikes have caused K-12 schools to close for weeks

or months at a time. But "labor" isn't just an issue for industries or companies that have unionized employees or contractors. Any organization that relies upon the availability or interest of a uniquely qualified (and/or scarce) group of workers can find itself in a human capital crisis. Think about the nursing shortages in recent decades, the demand for doctoral-trained pharmacists in the US, or the scramble to educate and employ STEM experts like cybersecurity professionals.

9. *International Events.* When the global business climate changes for any number of reasons, the interests of organizations that depend on international trade are threatened. Sometimes the climate changes because of an event, such as the Brexit vote or an international war. Sometimes they change because of a strained relationship or policy decision, such as the U.S. decision to increase trade tariffs with China. In either of these or any other similar case, international events can create crisis-level economic hardships for some stakeholders ... and international events can trickle down to impact public and private organizations in nearly any sector and of any size.[1]

Now that you have read through Gerald Meyers' list of categorical crisis types, you should return to the top of the list and read through it again. This time, as you consider each of the nine categories, you should make note of those you believe could create a significant threat for your organization. Are you vulnerable to a regulatory crisis? A leadership change crisis? A crisis related to a cash shortage or public perception? If a number of these crisis types seem plausible at your company, make note of them and commit to exploring them in future exercises (here in this book and later with your leadership team).

PwC's Crisis Categories

Now let's look at a second list of crises, which will not be presented in as much detail as the first set. This particular list was developed not long ago by PwC (formerly known as PricewaterhouseCoopers) as part of their annual

---

1   Gerald C. Meyers and John Holusha, *When It Hits the Fan: Managing the Nine Crises of Business* (London: Unwin Hyman, 1987).

CEO Pulse Check, where they interviewed hundreds of CEOs from organizations around the world to get a sense of their interests, pursuits, and concerns for the year ahead. Recently, PwC summarized the responses to their questions about crisis triggers — or, as you will see, different types of crises that respondents had faced in the "recent past."

Note: Do not be surprised to see some overlap with the previous list of crisis types. You will notice, however, that there are some new and different items. Pay particular attention to these.

PwC's crisis typology list includes these seven categories:

1. *Financial.* Over 80% of the CEOs indicated that they had "recently" experienced a financial crisis. Subcategories within this type are bankruptcies, insolvencies, and significant asset devaluations. At the time that this book is headed to press, companies across the world are facing financial crises related to the impact of the COVID-19 pandemic. You'd be hard-pressed in 2021 to find a business owner or business leader without a horror story about financial losses, major and unexpected expenses, or the scramble for emergency funding.

2. *Legal.* What these CEOs typically described as crises driven by compliance failures or sanctions fell into the legal category. Many organizations find their operations disrupted or sidelined by lawsuits, OSHA citations, or other legal complications and crises.

3. *Technological.* It's not unusual for technological crises to be brought about by cybersecurity breaches, technology failures (like an insurance company's website crashing during open enrollment), or R & D failures (such as the battery flaw that led to the Galaxy Note 7 failure for Samsung).

4. *Operational.* PwC described "operational crises" as infrastructure or product failures. 50% of CEOs indicated that they had suffered an operational crisis in the past year. The 2007 JetBlue winter storm crisis was, as you will recall, an operational crisis. Amazon's abandoned Fire Phone project, which led to a $170M write-down for the company back in 2014, could also be considered an operational crisis — the technology didn't fail, but the product wasn't operationally successful.

5. *Humanitarian.* This category of crisis is described as including catastrophe caused by terrorism or natural disaster. Think about businesses impacted by fires, hurricanes, floods, or tornadoes, or those victimized by rioting, looting, arson, workplace shootings, or other tragedies.

6. *Reputational.* These crises on the PwC list tended to be described as losses in market position or an adverse association with the company brand. Think of a cruise line after a norovirus outbreak, a company when a key leader is accused of misconduct, or laundry detergent brands after the "Tide Pods Challenge" in 2017-2018. It doesn't take much for reputation and brand value to take a nose-dive, and it can happen in an instant.

7. *Human Capital.* These crises were categorized by PwC as periods of high staff turnover, low retention, or a labor strike. Even companies that are large and powerful (like Amazon and Nike) can be disrupted by staffing crises.

As you did with Meyers' list of categorical crisis types, you should return to the top of this new PwC list and read through it again. As you consider each of the seven categories, you should make note of those you believe could create a significant threat for your organization. If a number of these crisis types seem plausible at your company, make note of them.

A Public Relations Perspective on Crisis Categories

A third list of crisis types can be drawn from the public relations (PR) world. Author and researcher Gerry McCusker, in his book *Public Relations Disasters*, shares this typology for categorizing different varieties of crisis. You will find this list to be noticeably different from the first two that you reviewed. One lesson to take away regarding categorical lists of crisis types is that *perspective* should be an important consideration. Each of these lists is generated by viewing different varieties of crisis from a specific perspective. The first two lists were generated from the perspective of an organization's senior leadership team. In this case, the perspective is that of a public relations expert. McCusker suggests that there are seven key types of PR crisis:

1. *Acts of God.* When the crisis is a result of a natural disaster.

2. *Business Operations.* Where corporate activity adversely impacts one or more stakeholder groups.

3. *Corporate Moves.* This is how McCusker describes the events associated with a major corporate restructuring and/or change initiative.

4. *Legalities.* When contentious issues make their way to the courtroom and the proceedings allow the media to follow the story.

5. *Rumors.* When a story takes on a life of its own, particularly when the facts are not allowed to get in the way of a good story.

6. *Staff.* When employees behave badly, and the company's brand is placed at risk.

7. *Scandal.* When the extremely poor behavior of one or more members of an organization draws media attention.[2]

As you think through this particular list, did you identify any types of crises that you would like to add to your list? Your first thought may be, "Wow, this list really is quite a bit different from the first two." Your second thought might be, "That said, I could see any of these happening at my company." A useful question as you consider adding one or more of these items to your list is this: "Could some or all of these simply represent examples of a PR crisis, as defined on Meyers' list, or a reputational crisis, as defined on PwC's list?" If and when you decide to create a categorical list of your own, you will want to try and keep your perspective consistent across all the items on your list. So, you may choose to have a list that defines some very specific scenarios in a particular area, as this list does from a PR perspective, or you may want a much broader set of alternatives, such as in the first two lists. Choose the approach that makes it easiest for you and your team to consider how you would respond to the crisis types you identify.

---

2   Gerry McCusker, *Talespin: Public Relations Disasters — Inside Stories & Lessons Learnt* (London: Kogan Page, 2008).

Ten Categories of Political Risk

A final categorical list of crisis types comes from the book *Political Risk: How Businesses and Organizations Can Anticipate Global Insecurity* by Condoleezza Rice and Amy Zegart. This book was specifically written to facilitate learning from political challenges, in both national and international environments. Once again, you will find this list to be quite different from the first three. The perspective is unique and the items on the list have been curated for leaders with some degree of involvement with (and exposure from) international relationships and influencers. The final list is as follows:

1. *Geopolitics.* This category includes cross-border crises such as interstate wars, great power shifts, multilateral economic sanctions, and interventions.

2. *Internal Conflict.* Defined as domestic crises, such as social unrest, ethnic violence, migration, nationalism, separatism, federalism, civil wars, coups, and revolutions.

3. *Laws, Regulations, Policies.* Which can be thought of as changes in foreign ownership rules, taxation, environmental regulations, and/or national laws.

4. *Breaches of Contract.* Where governments renege on contracts, including expropriations (i.e., the seizure of property) and politically motivated credit defaults.

5. *Corruption.* Via mechanisms such as discriminatory taxation or systemic bribery.

6. *Extraterritorial Reach.* Which is the cross-territorial legal (or policy) reach of powerful states into the affairs of others in such cases as unilateral sanctions, criminal investigations, and prosecutions.

7. *Natural Resource Manipulation.* Such as politically motivated changes in supply of energy or rare earth minerals.

8. *Social Activism.* Not always a threat, but these polarizing events or opinions become crises when significant social responses are generated in the wake of "viral" events.

9. *Terrorism.* Which are politically motivated threats or the use of violence against persons or property.

10. *Cyber Threats.* Specifically, the theft or destruction of intellectual property, espionage, extortion, massive disruption of companies, industries, governments, or societies.[3]

What did you think about *this* list? Were there any items that seemed particularly well-suited to your list? If so, add the item or items to the list you have been crafting for yourself.

Summarizing the Benefits of a Categorical List

You have just completed a review of four categorical lists of crises that should serve as a useful launch of your own exploration into the many ways a crisis leader might craft a crisis-type system of organization. What struck you about these lists as you reviewed them? Did you find any one objective or perspective to be particularly useful? If you're like most people, you found the first list to be the most accessible and the others helpful in adding important nuances or deepening your overall thinking.

The first list, if you recall, was Gerald Meyers' Nine Types of Business Crises. As the title of this list suggests, all the items on it would resonate with senior business leaders. While the other lists may have inspired you to think of crisis types that were not on Meyers' list, most of the items you saw here could serve as a solid foundation for your list. Depending on the maturity of your business and the sector in which you operate, some number of these crises are solid candidates to start your own typology. That said, if you are not a senior leader at your company, it is possible that several of these items may not seem as useful to you in your current role, which raises another point about these lists.

---

3   Condoleezza Rice and Amy B. Zegart, *Political Risk: How Businesses and Organizations Can Anticipate Global Insecurity* (New York, NY: Twelve, Hachette Book Group, 2019).

When it comes to crisis readiness, this book focuses primarily on risks of the strategic variety. This was illustrated clearly by the items on Meyers' list. Market Shift? Cash Shortage? International events? Maybe these are items that don't fall within your immediate scope of work. At some point in your career, they will. Until then, perhaps these items can serve as a representative distribution of crisis types that you might create at a level appropriate for your responsibilities. OK, so your team is not responsible for an enterprise cash shortage. But maybe your team will find itself on a path to far exceed/outspend your annual budget. While that might not qualify as an organizational crisis, it may feel to your team like the end of days. In any case, this first list of types should help get you pointed in the right direction to craft a typology of your own.

> Market Shift? Cash Shortage? International events? Maybe these are items that don't fall within your immediate scope of work. At some point in your career, they will.

The second list, created by the research team at PwC, offers a slightly different look at crisis types. Like the first list, the listed categories represent large, strategic challenges. In fact, there is a good bit of overlap between the two lists. There are also a couple of new items. Perhaps this slightly different perspective gave you an idea or two for your list that the first set did not.

The third list was crafted entirely from the perspective of a public relations professional. While experts make the argument that almost all crises have some element of public relations impact to them, the items on list three were all intended to guide stakeholder communication efforts. Were there any items on this list that fit nicely into your own?

The fourth list that you scanned was created to illustrate a set of potential political risks that a company may encounter. Once again, it is possible that most of the items on this list are concerns for more senior leaders in your organization, or for organizations that operate in a different environment from your current organization. That's OK. Someday you may need to worry about these things. What is particularly useful about this list is how it differs from the others. The book from which this list is borrowed, by the way, is a fascinating and informative read — especially if your company conducts a significant amount of international business.

Ultimately, my objective in sharing these lists with you is to get you thinking about different types of crises that your team, your unit, or your organization may encounter in the future. Spending some time identifying crises that may become issues for you is a first step in the development of a crisis response plan. You will find that building your plans, with specific crisis types in mind, will help you to introduce and activate plans that are more tangible, more realistic, and better suited to thoughtful planning.

COVID-19: Where Might the Pandemic Appear on a Categorical List?

When you think about your organization's management of the COVID-19 pandemic, did you get the impression that policies or practices existed that could help your leadership team navigate this global healthcare crisis? One way to think about this is on a micro scale. Let's think small. Did your company have policies and practices to manage people issues — such as working remotely, freedom to express discomfort in coming to work, provisions for lapses in daycare support, policies for extended health issues, etc.? Alternatively, did your company have macro policies and practices in place, such as: extended loss of access to your main business locations, periods of extended medical leave, and so on? You may not have developed practices that were directly tied to a mass pandemic, but a focus on potential crisis types and the development (frankly, *any* development) of policies and practices to deal with major disruptions, would probably be applicable in such a crisis as the world is dealing with post-2020.

The SARS-CoV-2 global pandemic illustrates one major benefit of having a crisis typology. We can all generally accept the notion that no two crises will be identical. In fact, when I teach crisis leadership at the University of Michigan's Ross School of Business, I like to use a snowflake analogy. No two crises will be the same. But there will be some common characteristics of crises that fit within one or more categories of crisis. Ultimately, it is these characteristics — with their unique causes and outcomes — that provide a basis for preparation. For example, in a crisis caused by natural disaster, a common characteristic of the situation is the inability for some (or all) of your employees to have access to the main business location. In preparing for a natural disaster, your company may have crafted some policies and procedures for allowing employees to work remotely or to access necessary information from outside the local network firewall. While the COVID-19 pandemic may not fit neatly within a natural disaster crisis-type category — although some might argue that it does — the fact that there are some common characteristics can be helpful to crisis leaders. The moral of this story is that when crisis leaders are preparing for different types of crises, they are actually preparing for the best ways to deal with the characteristics of a particular type.

So, let's review our example typologies in the context of the COVID-19 crisis. Is there an intersection between the items on a crisis-type list that a company — perhaps your company — might have created to prepare itself for a future crisis and the crisis-type that might be illustrated by a global pandemic, such as COVID-19?

Borrowing from the first list of Nine Crisis Types, I could see how elements of a Market Shift, Cash Shortage, Regulation, Human Capital, or International Events crisis could be helpful in the production of a response to the COVID-19 pandemic.[4] No, the list as it stands does not have a "Global Pandemic" category, but the consequences of pandemic-related shifts fall into several of these categories. Would your organization have been better prepared for COVID-19 if it had a basic plan for dealing with a crisis that had similar characteristics to a global pandemic? I'm certain that it would have.

Reviewing the PwC list, we might consider the benefits of having prepared ourselves for a crisis that has elements of a Financial, Operational, Humanitarian, and/or Human Capital crisis.

From Gerry McCusker's list of public-relations crises, we can see how a response to the pandemic might benefit from earlier preparations for the characteristics of a crisis in the categories described as: Acts of God, Business Operations, Corporate Moves, Rumors, and Staff.[5]

---

4   Gerald C. Meyers and John Holusha, *When It Hits the Fan: Managing the Nine Crises of Business* (London: Unwin Hyman, 1987).

5   Gerry McCusker, *Talespin: Public Relations Disasters — Inside Stories & Lessons Learnt* (London: Kogan Page, 2008).

Finally, from Condoleezza Rice and Amy Zegart's list, we might find support for dealing with the COVID crisis in our plans for navigating crises in: Geopolitics, Internal Conflict, Laws/Regulations/Policies, Extraterritorial Reach, and Social Activism.[6]

Suffice it to say that if your company had plans to deal with a potential pandemic, then not only were you better prepared than most of the world, your organization also has a rare but exemplary predictive capacity. If your organization did not have a pandemic response plan, it may still find great benefit in the crises that it had prepared for. Perhaps a silver lining of COVID-19 is our realization that some of us were better prepared than others, and perhaps some have seized the moment to further enhance their crisis planning. If your organization was not among those that were prepared, then COVID offers an invitation to take the necessary steps to join those that were. If you're reading this book in the midst of or the recent aftermath of the SARS-CoV-2 pandemic, don't waste *this* crisis. Pay attention to the lessons, and put them to use.

Exercise #6
Crafting Your Own List of Crisis Types

As directed in the previous activities, it is now time to craft your own categorical typology.

Don't worry about creating the perfect typology for your company. This exercise is merely a first step in getting you to think about different types of crises that your team, your unit, or your organization might encounter in the future. At some point, when you set about to build or refine your actual crisis *plans*, you'll find that your rough-draft typology allowed you to have specific crisis types in

6   Condoleezza Rice and Amy B. Zegart, *Political Risk: How Businesses and Organizations Can Anticipate Global Insecurity* (New York, NY: Twelve, Hachette Book Group, 2019).

mind, making your future work more tangible, more realistic, and better suited to thoughtful and realistic planning.

Now, please take some time to review the categorical lists that were just presented to you and identify a collection of types, no larger than 10, that illustrate the set of crises that may very well expose your company to some level of threat in the future. You should have already been taking notes to identify crisis types that seemed appropriate for your own typology, so, hopefully, this is a relatively simple exercise.

What categorical crisis types should be included in the typology for your organization?

1. _____   6. _____

2. _____   7. _____

3. _____   8. _____

4. _____   9. _____

5. _____   10. _____

Incorporating Additional Dimensions into Your Crisis Typology

So far in our exploration of crisis typologies, we have examined the potential benefits of having a list of different types to allow us to more easily differentiate the typical characteristics of these different scenarios. We've also established that having a list of "could happen" types of crises can help us develop some basic response plans for each, and will at least help us identify key stakeholder groups that are likely to be impacted by each crisis type (as well as some early actions that we should be taking in each case).

In the previous exercise, in fact, you crafted your own list of crisis types that you believe are likely candidates to assail your organization. Regardless of the length of your list, if you have identified even a few different types, you have taken a significant step forward in launching a crisis readiness campaign. Well done.

Now I would like to help you think about different ways to build upon your categorical typology.

Over the next few pages, I am going to introduce you to some researchers who have discovered that a simple list of crisis types is not sufficient to facilitate planning for an adequately broad spectrum of likely scenarios. In their research, they have determined that it can be helpful to organize the distinguishing characteristics of different crises into several dimensions or subcategories, where each dimension offers a continuum of potential outcomes. These additional dimensions, the researchers argue, can help us more effectively define and subsequently differentiate between crisis scenarios. Let me illustrate how the addition of a dimension or two might be helpful to your crisis planning efforts.

Let's say that one of the entries on your categorical typology is Product Failure. Most companies that I have worked with have a plan for dealing with a Product Failure-related crisis. When considering the potential impact of a product failure, one planning step is to estimate the impact such a failure might have on different stakeholder groups. Generally, and this is fairly commonsensical, product failures have a significant impact on your customer group. As you consider how the product failure will impact and be perceived by the customer group, you will discover that these outcomes will be influenced greatly by the nature of the failure and by the severity of the outcome. Clearly a product failure that causes a significant injury or death will be perceived differently than a failure that produces no injury. A faulty electrical outlet has a different impact from a faulty artificial hip, just as a faulty baseball cap has a different impact from a faulty coffee cup. And even within those products, a "failure" can cause varying degrees of catastrophe (e.g., the same faulty coffee cup might cause severe burns to one customer but might only inconvenience other customers when the cups shatter onto the floor).

As such, crisis leaders may opt to incorporate a Version A and Version B to their Product Failure planning. Version A might be a product failure that causes personal injury or death, and Version B might produce a much less severe outcome.

As you can see, there can be significant value to the task of adding additional characteristics to categorical lists for crises. These more robust lists provide greater specificity, which allows for more precise planning (and, hopefully, a quicker recovery and overall better outcomes for your organization and its stakeholders).

A Different Model of Crisis Typology

Now I'm going to introduce you to a different way to think about organizing unique types of crises. Many leaders I have worked with agree that a categorical list of crisis types is perfectly suited to their readiness efforts. Others, however, felt it was easier and more intuitive to use a completely different, multi-dimensional approach to crisis-type organization. For these leaders, the utility of a simple, two-by-two matrix allowed them to visualize four quadrants of potential crisis scenarios that helped them formulate basic response plans for situations that could be described by the characteristics of each quadrant.

The argument for this approach, as you will see in the section that follows, is that there are so many different potential crisis types that it would simply be easier to imagine four possible crisis scenarios — one for each quadrant of a four-quadrant framework — where plans could be prepared for each of the four general scenarios. Sound confusing? It won't in a bit. In my experience, this argument has some merit. Personally, I like the idea of having a list of types in my crisis plan. But I also like the idea of adding a dimension or two, as I described earlier, to help me image the scenarios that I might have to face.

As you work through the following section of this chapter, decide for yourself what makes the most sense to you. A simple list of crisis types? A two-by-two or three-by-three matrix of dimensions, or some sort of hybrid/combination of the approaches? At the end of this chapter, you will be asked to decide which you prefer and you'll have the opportunity, should you choose to accept it, to craft a more complex and nuanced typology than what you created in the previous exercise. But before we go there, let's examine a few two-dimensional and multi-dimensional typologies. I think you'll find these approaches interesting and informative.

Examples of Multi-Dimensional Typologies

For some, the process of differentiating crisis types with simple lists doesn't meet their specific needs. They suggest that there would simply be too many different items on a categorical list for that list to be useful. They also suggest that it would be more useful to think of crisis types in terms of their *characteristics*, not their category. The logic for this approach is summarized by researcher and author Stephan Gundel in his article "Towards a New Typology of Crises." He suggests:

> "Classifying crises is 'the first step to keep them under control.' A useful classification system allows for analysis and planning of crisis management actions. Four conditions must be met to produce a useful typology: 1) The classes used in a typology should be mutually exclusive; 2) The typology should be exhaustive, thus covering all possible crises both now and in the future; 3) The typology should be practically applicable, suggesting both measures of prevention and actions for resolution; and 4) the typology should be pragmatic, thus manageable."[7]

Using these criteria as a guide, you will now be introduced to three typologies that are presented as two-by-two (or "four-area") matrices.[8] Each will attempt to illustrate how four combinations of two different characteristics can be used to meet the objectives set forth above. As you read through the following, consider the effectiveness of this method of typology creation. You may find this method more intuitive than the categorical list approach, or you may find these more limiting or difficult to use. Ultimately, all we are attempting to create is a way for high-stakes leaders at your organization to differentiate between different types of crises so you can embark on planning efforts focused on prevention and management of such crises.

---

7   Stephan Gundel, "Towards a New Typology of Crises," *Journal of Contingencies and Crisis Management,* 13, no. 3 (2005): doi:10.1111/j.1468-5973.2005.00465.x.

8   If you're still curious about four-area matrices after finishing this chapter, you might enjoy consulting Albena Björck's 2016 research article in the *Central European Business Review,* "Crisis Typologies Revisited: An Interdisciplinary Approach," which inspired the examples shared in the next pages. https://www.ceeol.com/search/article-detail?id=673133.

- - - - - - - - - - - - - - - -

Example 1: Predictability-Influence Matrix

The first typology presented here was created by Stephan Gundel. His four-area matrix is based on two variables: Predictability and Influence. He defines "predictability" as the extent to which a particular variety of crisis can be predicted based on an organization's previous experiences. He defines "Influence" as a dimension that considers known and executable actions that could be taken to address the causes of a crisis and prevent occurrence or reoccurrence. Why would Gundel choose these two variables? Because his research on organizational crises suggested that every crisis he examined could be described (and differentiated) by the extent to which it could have been predicted and the degree to which steps could have been taken to prevent or, the term he uses, influence it. When Gundel plotted the crises he had studied on a two-axis graph with predictability on one axis and influenceability on the other, the crises formed four clusters. These four clusters became the four quadrants in his two-by-two matrix.

Let's unpack this first example to get comfortable with the mechanization and utility of a two-by-two matrix as a way to help crisis leaders think about and plan for different varieties of organizational crisis.

As a product of Gundel's four unique situational clusters, he created a matrix that helped him illustrate four different categories of crisis. The resulting typology produced a matrix that looks like Figure 3. For our purposes, let's assume that these quadrants have been numbered simply as a matter of convenience.

PREDICTABILITY

Hard	**Quadrant 2** Hard to Predict, Easy to Influence	**Quadrant 4** Hard to Predict, Hard to Influence
Easy	**Quadrant 1** Easy to Predict, Easy to Influence	**Quadrant 3** Easy to Predict, Hard to Influence
	Easy	Hard **INFLUENCEABLE**

Figure 3

Gundel determined that it would be instructive to create a descriptive label for each of the four quadrants as represented in this Figure 4. These labels would make it easier for crisis leaders to easily identify and distinguish the four different general scenarios.

PREDICTABILITY

	Easy	Hard	
Hard	Unexpected Crises (Q2) Hard to Predict, Easy to Influence	Fundamental Crises (Q4) Hard to Predict, Hard to Influence	
Easy	Conventional Crises (Q1) Easy to Predict, Easy to Influence	Intractable Crises (Q3) Easy to Predict, Hard to Influence	
	Easy	**Hard**	**INFLUENCEABLE**

Figure 4

Gundel went on to describe the unique nature of the crises that appeared in each quadrant. His aim was to help crisis leaders better understand the characteristics of different types of crisis so they could proactively develop prevention practices and, should they be needed, mechanisms for dealing most effectively with crises if they materialized. You will notice that a benefit of this approach, when compared to the categorical list approach, is that each quadrant in the two-by-two matrix represents a set of general characteristics, allowing us to plan for broad categories of crisis rather than specific cases. In fact, if you were so inclined, you could actually plot the items of a categorical list into the quadrants of Gundel's matrix. Ultimately, this is simply another method of differentiating crisis varieties in a way that facilitates preparation and planning.

What did Gundel actually have to say about the crises that clustered in each of his four quadrants? Here are his summaries.

For "Conventional Crises," like mishaps in a production facility or a transportation sector accident, a crisis management team could easily predict the conditions under which a crisis could occur. Organizational leaders should be able to identify the steps necessary to influence the likelihood of an occurrence of this type of crisis. Therefore, potential crises in this quadrant should be relatively easy to prevent with proper quality controls and planning.

"Unexpected Crises" in this model are manageable but they are difficult to predict. Winter and summer storms for airlines are difficult to predict, but the procedures necessary to manage them are relatively easy to implement. Consider JetBlue's Valentine's Day operational crisis. Had JetBlue followed a more conventional contingency plan for bad weather, the outcome would not have reached crisis level. The lesson about crises in this quadrant is that just because they will be hard to predict — and may be somewhat rare — they are relatively easy to manage with the proper prior planning.

An "Intractable Crisis," according to Gundel, can be easily anticipated, but "interference is almost impossible due to the attributes of the systems concerned." Gundel's example of an intractable crisis was the Chernobyl nuclear disaster — a disaster that could surely have been foreseen, particularly as the conditions of the facility deteriorated over time, but one for which a simple solution doesn't exist. A more recent example of an intractable crisis was the COVID-19 pandemic; scientists, clinicians, and public health experts had been predicting a global outbreak of a respiratory virus for many years, but when it struck, the ability to stop the pandemic in its tracks eluded everyone.

"Fundamental Crises" are unpredictable and difficult to influence. These situations are clearly the most dangerous type and they are the most challenging to prevent or prepare for. We don't see them coming and we don't know how to respond. The tragic events of 9/11/2001 in the United States is an example of this type of crisis.[9]

Given the descriptions of these four quadrants, a crisis leader might find it useful to make one final addition to the four-quadrant matrix, further adding to its utility. By adding a very brief summary of the measures to be taken to prevent, to the extent possible, these potential crisis scenarios, or to deal most effectively with them when they appear, the resultant table could be quite informative as illustrated in Figure 5.

---

9   Stephan Gundel, "Towards a New Typology of Crises," *Journal of Contingencies and Crisis Management,* 13, no. 3 (2005): doi:10.1111/j.1468-5973.2005.00465.x.

PREDICTABILITY

	Easy	Hard	
Hard	Unexpected Crises (Q2) Measures: Activate the Emergency Response Plan	Fundamental Crises (Q4) Measures: No formal preparation possible; develop a general crisis response capability	
Easy	Conventional Crises (Q1) Measures: Improve quality control processes; proactively develop crisis response plans	Intractable Crises (Q3) Measures: Reduce complexity and conflicts of interest; proactively develop crisis response plans	
	Easy	Hard	INFLUENCEABLE

Figure 5

Now that you have seen an example of a "four-area" matrix of crisis types, what do you think? Do you find this approach easier or more challenging than a categorical list of crisis types to create and implement? As there is ultimately no best answer to the question of an optimal approach, you can feel free to use the approach that best suits your needs.

- - - - - - - - - - - - - - - - - -

Example 2: Probability-Impact-Matrix

The second typology presented here was created by Nassim Taleb and was explored in detail in the 2007 book *The Black Swan: The Impact of the Highly Improbable*. In Taleb's four-area matrix, he uses the two variables:

1. Predictability (probability of occurrence)
2. Payoff or impact[10]

According to an interpretation of Taleb's work by researcher and author Albena Björck, here is why this four-quadrant matrix can be useful:

> "In the context of the last financial crisis, risk assessment received a new interpretation and meaning through the work of Nassim Taleb. His analysis of risk events questioned the overreliance on statistics and addressed the illusion that

---

10   Nassim Nicholas Taleb, *The Black Swan: The Impact of the Highly Improbable* (London: Taylor and Francis, 2017).

complex models can predict the future. According to Taleb, the human mind suffers from three limitations when it comes to interpretation of past experiences: 1) 'the illusion of understanding, how people think they know what is going on in a more complex and random world than they realize,' 2) 'the retrospective distortion, or history seems clearer in a history book than in an empirical reality,' and 3) 'the overvaluation of factual information, or the handicap of authoritative and learned people.'

People regularly dismiss improbable events as they seek arguments to justify their own prognoses than to falsify them. They prefer to concentrate on familiar information sources and a few known scenarios. When the unexpected and unthinkable happens, they try to rationalize ex-post. These unexpected and unthinkable events happen more often than we realize — Taleb calls them 'black swans.'"[11]

How does this background information help describe the matrix offered by Taleb? It provides context for how an organization might organize its efforts to prevent a crisis and then, if necessary, manage it. On the horizontal axis, Taleb suggests differentiating events by the extent of their impact. (Of note here, Taleb uses this same matrix to describe financial modeling, which is why "payoff" is used along with "impact." For our purposes, we are more interested in the impact perspective.) On the vertical axis, Taleb uses the idea of predictability or the probability of occurrence and differentiates between high and low.

What is particularly interesting about Taleb's model — which we could examine in much greater detail, but I'll leave that deep exploration to you — is how this approach helps crisis leaders appreciate that challenges associated with situations where statistical data aren't useful for predicting the scale of a crisis. As I present an example for each of the four quadrants in Taleb's model, you will get a sense of both the complexity of our VUCA world — which will dramatically appear in the model — and the importance

---

11   Albena Björck, "Crisis Typologies Revisited: An Interdisciplinary Approach," *Central European Business Review,* no. 3 (May 2016), https://www.ceeol.com/search/article-detail?id=673133.

of preparation, even when predictive statistics suggest an extremely low probability of occurrence.

IMPACT/PAYOFF

	High/Known (Normal)	Low/Unknown (Random)
Not Affordable (Complex Outome Set)	Predictable and Complex (Case 2)	Not Predictable (Case 4) "Black Swan"
Affordable (Simple Outcome Set)	Predictable and Simple (Case 1)	Predictablo ond Extreme (Case 3)
	High/Known (Normal)	Low/Unknown (Random)	**PREDICTABILITY**

Figure 6

For Case 1, in the lower-left quadrant of the matrix, crises are highly predictable and have relatively low stakes (i.e., low impact). Like those in the first matrix we reviewed, these cases should be relatively easy to prevent or manage when they do appear. A good example is the effectiveness of a production process where the binary outcome of the process is either: a) the produced item works or b) the item doesn't. When leaders consider ways to manage this type of potential crisis, they should explore the costs and merits of improving process quality (i.e., reducing the number of flawed outcomes) and they should develop plans for dealing with the impact of flawed item production on the enterprise (i.e., how these events and their implications will be remediated.)

For Case 2, in the upper-left quadrant of the matrix, events are less likely than in the lower-left quadrant, but they can be predicted through the use of mathematical models. In this quadrant, however, events are highly impactful when they do happen. A good example is a commercial airline accident. We can predict, based on historical statistics, the likelihood of a crash. We cannot, however, effectively predict a precise time for the event, nor can we predict with any degree of accuracy the cost or impact of a future event. Crisis examples in this quadrant support the argument for investment in safety processes and procedures despite the low probability of occurrence — the argument being that even one such crisis is not acceptable or affordable.

Taleb's breakthrough analysis becomes apparent when we consider Cases 3 and 4. Again, without getting into excruciating detail, Taleb introduces the idea that population distributions can be either of Mediocristan or Extremistan, two notional geographic provinces that he uses to describe different shapes of population distributions. The nature of a population's distribution (Mediocristan or Extremistan), he argues, determines our ability to predict the size and impact of a single outcome from a population of potential outcomes. In Mediocristan distributions (bear with me, this is worth knowing, and offers a great conversation starter for social gatherings), statistical modeling can help us predict both the likelihood and the impact of a specific outcome. I suggested this earlier for Cases 1 and 2 in Taleb's model. In both my quality control example (Case 1) and my aviation accident example (Case 2), we can see that statistical modeling allows us to predict the likelihood of occurrence and the extent of any single outcome in the population because these distributions can be described as generally normal. Are you still with me? In Cases 1 and 2, we can use math to help us prevent and plan for crises.

In Extremistan distributions, statistical modeling is much less useful to us because there are data points within the population that are wildly different from other members of the set. Taleb offers a wonderful example in *The Black Swan* to illustrate the differences between these two distributions.

> In Mediocristan: "Assume you round up a thousand people randomly selected from the general population and have them stand next to each other in a stadium. Imagine the heaviest person you can think of and add him to that sample. Assuming he weighs three times the average, between four hundred and five hundred pounds, he will rarely represent more than a very small fraction of the weight of the entire population (in this case, about a half a percent.) You can get even more aggressive. If you picked the heaviest biologically possible human on the planet (who yet can still be called a human), he would not represent more than, say, 0.6 percent of the total, a very negligible increase. And if you had 10,000 persons, his contribution would be vanishingly small." In Mediocristan, *"when your*

sample is large, no single instance will significantly change the aggregate or the total."

In Extremistan: "Consider by comparison the net worth of the thousand people you lined up in the stadium. Add to them the wealthiest person to be found on the planet — say Bill Gates, the founder of Microsoft. Assume his net worth to be close to $80 billion — with the total capital of the others around a few million. How much of the total wealth would he represent? 99.9 percent? For someone's weight to represent such a share, he would need to weigh fifty million pounds! *In Extremistan, inequalities are such that one single observation can disproportionately impact the aggregate, or the total."*

The point of this distinction is to illustrate for crisis leaders (and financial decision-makers) that when possible samples (or outcomes) within a distribution of outcomes are so extreme as to be not representative of the remainder of the population, then statistical models aren't very helpful for predicting the extent or impact of a single event.

For Case 3, in the lower-right quadrant, the set of potential outcomes is small and generally easy to understand, but the potential impact of events in the quadrant can be very difficult to predict. A clear and timely example of a crisis in this quadrant is the COVID-19 pandemic. A pandemic is ultimately a function of how many people contract the virus. At the simplest level, the option set for a person being infected by the virus is either a) Yes or b) No. This binary option set is what makes this example fit into Case 3. Where this scenario gets messy, however, is what happens once people start to get infected. As we saw with the COVID-19 pandemic, it became very difficult to predict the extent to which the virus would spread. This is the challenge with a Case 3 crisis.

To manage potential and realized Case 3 crises, leaders must recognize that it may be difficult to rely on statistical models to predict the eventual severity of a crisis of this type. Prevention and response methods will have to include considerations for worst-case scenarios (such as we've seen with the recent pandemic) and the appropriate steps to aggressively respond to the earliest indications of trouble.

Finally, in Case 4, situated in the upper-right quadrant of Taleb's model, we are dealing with another Extremistan distribution where the stakes are very high, the events are unpredictable, and there is a much more complex set of potential outcomes than in Case 3. This is Taleb's so-called "fourth quadrant" and the location within which his now famously named Black Swan events are captured. These are the most challenging to manage and an organization is not likely to have a pre-planned response for crises in this category. But organizations *can* make commitments to general crisis readiness to give themselves the best possible chance of surviving these highly impactful events.[12] Some examples of crises that fit within this Case 4 quadrant are the 2008 financial crisis, the terrorist attacks of 9/11/2001, the dot-com crash in 2000, and the Fukushima nuclear powerplant accident of 2011 (three partial reactor meltdowns caused by a tsunami). While none of these events were predictable using statistical models, all included early indications of potential peril that could have been addressed had high-stakes leaders been paying sufficient attention.

- -

Black Swan events are the most challenging to manage, and
an organization is not likely to have a pre-planned response for
crises in this category. But organizations can make commitments
to general crisis readiness to give themselves the best
possible chance of surviving these highly impactful events.

- -

The utility of Taleb's model is that it offers crisis leaders a way to organize potential crisis types into categories that account for differences in both complexity and scale. Perhaps you and your organization would benefit from thinking about prospective crises in this way.

---

12   Nassim Nicholas Taleb, *The Black Swan: The Impact of the Highly Improbable* (London: Taylor and Francis, 2017).

Example 3: Locus-Controllability Matrix and the Responsibility Continuum

The third and final example of a matrix for organizational crises is based on how the organizational crisis response influences the perception of stakeholders. Given our focus on stakeholders, you might find this a useful framework for organizing your company's potential crisis types. This model incorporates a concept developed by Bernard Weiner known as Attribution Theory, which attempts to explain how people make sense of events.[13]

Attribution Theory holds that people will make judgments about the causes of events, especially unexpected events with negative outcomes. Attributions, according to Weiner and colleagues, are "perceptions of the causality or the perceived reasons for a particular event's occurrence." "People" (and let's consider groups of these people as "stakeholders" for our purposes) will attribute the cause of an event to an individual involved in the event (i.e., "personal causality") or to some outside force (i.e., "external causality"). Attributions essentially indicate the extent to which a person believes that the cause of an event was controllable by the people involved. And the research has shown that greater attributions of responsibility lead to stronger feelings of anger and more negative views of people and organizations. This interpretation provides the variable that is placed on the horizontal axis of the four-area matrix. The two alternatives for this variable are presented as under control (of the organization) and not under control (of the organization). The other variable is called locus of cause, which is a technical way of differentiating between events that were caused by actions occurring outside the company and those caused by internal actions.

Research has shown that greater attributions of responsibility lead to stronger feelings of anger and more negative views of people and organizations.

---

13   Bernard Weiner, *Handbook of Theories of Social Psychology, Vol. 1*, ed. Paul A. M. Van Lange, Arie W. Kruglanski, and E. Tory Higgins (London: Sage Publishing, 2011), Ch. 7.

LOCUS OF CAUSE

Figure 7

This matrix may be a little more challenging to use for crisis prevention purposes than the others. It will, however, serve as an exceptional guide for the framing of stakeholder communications.

For Case 1, in the lower-left quadrant of the matrix, crises are caused by a source outside of the organization and are not controllable. An example of this type of crisis is an act of terrorism. Crises in this quadrant are likely to be viewed by stakeholders quite sympathetically. Stakeholder communications in these cases should reflect the nature of the crisis and should convey a sincere commitment to recovering from this "horrible stroke of misfortune or unthinkable tragedy."

For Case 2, in the upper-left quadrant of the matrix, crises are not necessarily controllable by the organization, but there will be stakeholder attribution to some extent because the cause of the crisis originated inside the enterprise. In these situations, organizations must appreciate that stakeholders will want to know how the company "could allow this to happen." Stakeholder communications should include information on the nature of the event and how, in fact, this could happen. It should also include the steps being taken to prevent a similar event in the future.

For Case 3, in the lower-right quadrant, crises are caused by a source outside of the organization, but one that should have been predictable and controllable by the enterprise. In these cases, stakeholders will want to know why preventive measures were not in place and why they should trust that something similar will not happen again. Potential crises in this quadrant should inform pre-crisis planning efforts because stakeholders will rightfully expect these types of crises to be preventable.

Finally, for Case 4, in the upper-right quadrant, crises are caused by an internal source, and stakeholder perception is that the situation should have been preventable. This is the most difficult type of crisis for an organization to have to endure because stakeholder response will be negative and potentially extreme. As with crises that are described in Case 3, these crises are best prevented and managed through the pre-crisis scenario planning and resilience practices we explored earlier in this book.

There you have it: three examples of multi-dimensional, "four-area," matrix-based crisis typologies. How did these compare to the categorical list approach to crisis organization? Perhaps you found elements of both to be interesting and useful. Both methods can be effective, as researchers have claimed. The most important lesson here is that there are many ways to organize a collection of crisis types and the *best* one for you and your organization is the one that most effectively helps you develop plans for crisis prevention and, when necessary, crisis management.

- -

There are many ways to organize a collection of crisis types and the best one for you and your organization is the one that most effectively helps you develop plans for crisis prevention and, when necessary, crisis management.

- -

How have I found the two-by-two matrix approach to be useful in my own work? I was hoping that you might be wondering about that. When I work with executives to help them develop crisis response plans — particularly from the perspective of addressing the needs and interests of their various stakeholders — I suggest that they use the following matrix to inform their messaging. You'll notice immediately that it is a modified take on the third example I just shared with you.

SOURCE/ORIGINATION

	Not Controllable	Controllable
Internal	Not Our Fault, Internal Cause *Justify* Involvement, Not Fault; Commit to Resolving Crisis ASAP	Our Fault, Internal Cause *Confess;* Take Responsibility for Contributing to the Crisis
External	Not Our Fault, External Cause Remain *Silent* on Cause; Commit to Resolving Crisis ASAP	Our Fault, External Cause *Confess;* Take Responsibility for Contributing to the Crisis
	Not Controllable	Controllable

PERCEIVED CONTROLLABILITY

Figure 8

Rather than using the two-by-two matrix solely to differentiate categories of crisis, I use it to help executives proactively think through their communication plans. It also serves as a reminder for these executives of how vitally important it is to let stakeholders know how leadership is acting — and the responsibilities they are accepting as the situation moves forward. If the organization could have taken steps to prevent the crisis, then it is generally in the best interests of leadership to acknowledge some degree of responsibility for the situation at hand — regardless of the origin (i.e., inside or outside the company).

An important note here is that I am *not* suggesting leaders declare accountability for causing a crisis when the actual cause has yet to be determined. This would wrongly expose the business to potential harm. Rather, I *am* suggesting that leaders accept responsibility for being involved to some extent and for doing whatever is necessary to set things right as expeditiously as possible. What would that sound like? Something like this:

> "I want you all to know that a member of our team was directly involved in this afternoon's incident. All of us at XYZ corporation are deeply saddened by this tragedy and we are committed to doing our best to care for those involved. In partnership with local authorities, we are working to resolve this situation as quickly as possible. You have my commitment as CEO of XYZ that, regardless of what we learn about who or what caused this tragic event, I will keep you informed

and will do everything I can to not allow something like this to ever happen again."

We will explore the topics of leadership responsibility and accountability later in the book.

Combining a Categorical List with Other Dimensions

Having now looked at categorical lists and four-quadrant approaches to defining different varieties of crises, you may find it interesting that some crisis research experts (e.g., Dr. Timothy Coombs, whose work is referenced several times in this book) have determined that the two-by-two or *x*-by-*x* matrix approaches to crisis definition don't fit the results of their research, and that other sizes and shapes of matrices are worth consideration when designing a crisis typology framework for an organization.

Dr. Coombs wrote a paper for the *Journal of Business Communications* titled "Impact of Past Crises on Current Crisis Communication," in which he frames his discussion of crisis typologies in the context of Warner's Attribution Theory (referenced earlier).

According to Coombs, if attribution is such an important frame for leaders to consider in their responses to crisis, it would benefit them to cluster their crisis types into three groups based on the level of responsibility stakeholders are likely to ascribe to the organization. The three clusters offered by Coombs are labeled:

- Victim
- Accidental
- Intentional

Within these three clusters, he distributes 10 crisis types. Here is a great example of how a high-stakes leader might combine the benefits of a categorical list typology and a multi-quadrant framework.

The VICTIM cluster includes:

- *Natural disasters* — which are acts of nature that damage an organization

- *Rumors* — where false and damaging information about an organization is being circulated internally and externally

- *Workplace violence* — where a former employee injures or attempts to injure a current employee

- *Product tampering or malevolence* — where some actor outside of the organization has altered a product to make it dangerous.

The ACCIDENTAL cluster includes:

- *Challenges* — where stakeholders claim an organization is operating in an inappropriate manner. In these cases, a public challenge is based on moral or ethical, not legal, grounds.

- *Technical error accidents* — where a technology or equipment failure causes an industrial accident.

- *Technical error recalls* — where a product is deemed harmful to stakeholders.

The INTENTIONAL cluster includes:

- *Human error accidents* —where the cause of the accident is a person or people not performing a job properly

- *Human error recalls* — where the cause of a recall is a person or people not performing a job properly

- *Organizational misdeeds* — where stakeholders are placed at risk by management knowingly violating laws/regulations or by offering a product or service they knew could injure stakeholders.

The framing offered by Coombs provides a few valuable takeaways for us. First, he provides another example of a list-based typology, which is similar to those we have already seen, but he further organizes the crisis types by a critical dimension — in this case, attributability. As we have seen a couple examples of crisis-type lists that have been further distributed across another key characteristic, it seems as though lists, on their own, do not provide crisis leaders all the information needed to build effective response plans.

Second, Dr. Coombs makes explicit the importance of including stakeholder perspectives into a crisis-typology framework. Ultimately, as we have seen, the perception of stakeholders is perhaps the most important consideration for crisis leaders once the root cause or causes of a crisis have been identified and resolved.

And third, the framework is clearly designed to help crisis leaders develop and deliver stakeholder communications in the spirit of both fact-sharing (i.e., "here's where the fault should be attributed") and trust-restoration (i.e., "given the source of the crisis, here is what we are doing to fix things now and prevent recurrence in the future"). These are all valuable takeaways in the context of high-stakes leadership.[14]

Where Should You Begin?

My own preference for the design of a crisis typology is to begin with a list of crisis types that are most likely to be encountered by your organization. I find this starting point particularly useful because it provides tangible scenarios for your fellow leaders to consider. "OK team, if tomorrow we receive news that one of our products suffered a catastrophic failure that resulted in a serious injury, what would we do?" Every leader I have ever worked with has been able to identify at least a small handful of situations that were realistic threats to their enterprise (in most cases, they went on to say that they probably weren't as ready as they should be for any of them.) Once you have a few items on your list, you can then begin the process of working through how leaders at your organization will respond should any one of these become reality. During these discussions, you will determine whether or not it makes sense to add features or distinguishing characteristics to your list. In the exercise that follows, I will show you how this can be done.

---

14   W. T. Coombs, "Impact of Past Crises on Current Crisis Communication: Insights from Situational Crisis Communication Theory," *Journal of Business Communication,* 41, no. 3 (2004): doi:10.1177/0021943604265607.

Exercise #7
Crafting Your Own Typology

How can you make practical sense of the material we have covered in this chapter? Well, let's spend a few minutes taking what you have learned and crafting a custom typology for your organization. We won't strive for perfection here on your first attempt at developing a typology. But as the information in this chapter is still somewhat fresh in your mind, let's consider this a brainstorming session that might lead to the first formal typology for your organization.

Let's give this a try ...

Step 1

First, you will want a list of the stakeholder groups that have an interest in, or draw value from, your company or unit. You should already have this list on hand from Exercise #1.

Pause here for a moment to collect your stakeholder list. If you have *not* created a list of company stakeholders, you will want to do so now. Take as long as you need, then return to this section for the next step in our process.

_____   _____

_____   _____

_____   _____

Step 2

Refer to the various lists of crisis types that were shared in this chapter and create a hybrid list that illustrates the collection of crisis varieties that you believe might threaten the value propositions of your stakeholders in the future. Each of the lists shared in this chapter had a slightly different frame, but there was also quite a bit of overlap. Skim through the examples presented in this chapter and craft your own list of 5-10 crisis types that your organization may have to resolve. Keep in mind that while most specific crisis types impact multiple stakeholder groups, a particular type only has to impact one significantly to be considered worthy of inclusion on your list.

1. _____

2. _____

3. _____

4. _____

5. _____

6. _____

7. _____

8. _____

9. _____

10. _____

Step 3

Consider the collection of dimensions that we examined throughout this chapter. For your convenience, I will review what I consider to be a useful subset of these dimensions here. As I share each of these with you, what do your instincts tell you about its utility? Do you think that it could be useful for organizing crisis types by various levels or opposite extremes of that specific dimension? Again, we are not looking for exact science here. You should just be taking a crack at narrowing down the extensive list of options we explored in this chapter to a smaller subset that might serve your crisis-planning needs in the future.

Here are some of the dimensions that you might find useful:

- **Cause** — Man-made vs. Natural
- **Cause** — Internal vs. External
- **Probability** — From "Very Likely" to "Not Likely at All"
- **Predictability** — From "Hard to Predict" to "Easy to Predict"
- **Cost** — From "Potentially Very Expensive" to "Potentially Very Inexpensive"
- **Controllability** — From "Hard to Control" to "Easy to Control"
- **Attribution of Responsibility** — From "Beyond Our Control" to "Entirely Our Fault"
- **Safety Impact** — From "Major Injury or Fatality" to "No Injury or Only Minor Injury"
- **Level of Action** — From a Single Actor to a Supranational Group (Like the European Union)

Did you identify any dimensions that seem useful, given the organization you are using to frame your choices? Make note of them here.

_____

_____

_____

Step 4

Find the list you created in Step 2. Now, referring to your list, would it be helpful to further subdivide this list using one or two of the dimensions you identified in Step 3? Given our work in this chapter, it probably makes sense to do so. Having another dimension or two can help us more accurately organize crisis scenarios and will ultimately help us develop more effective response strategies. It is also possible that, at this point, you would prefer to abandon your categorical list — the list of specific crisis types — and create a matrix out of one or two or perhaps even three dimensions. If this is your preference, when you move on to Step 5 with your matrix, keep the list you created earlier, as these categorical items will provide specific cases that you should be able to plot somewhere on your matrix.

1. _____

    a. _____

    b. _____

2. _____

    a. _____

    b. _____

3. _____

    a. _____

    b. _____

4. _____

    a. _____

    b. _____

5. _____

    a. _____

    b. _____

6. _____

    a. _____

    b. _____

7. _____

    a. _____

    b. _____

8. _____

a. _____

b. _____

9. _____

a. _____

b. _____

10. _____

a. _____

b. _____

Step 5

Now, let's formalize your crisis typology. If you decided that a list was good enough as a starting point, great. You will now have a list and can use it to begin some crisis response planning. If you have decided to abandon or build upon your categorical list and create your own matrix out of one, two, or three dimensions, then prepare a graphic or a collection of summary statements that describes your dimensions and the different options for each dimensional characteristic.

It is possible that you have decided to keep your categorical list of crisis types *and* that you have elected to add a dimension or two to further differentiate crisis scenarios. For example, you may really like your categorical list, but you have recognized that by adding an option A and an option B to each item, you would be able to draw an important distinction between different scenarios. For example, you may want to differentiate between cases that include a fatality — which could be option A — and cases that do not have a fatality or serious injury—which could be option B. You could use any of the characteristics I mentioned earlier to further define your typology.

I recognize that digging into this concept of typologies can be time-consuming and headache-inducing, but I hope you'll remain open to doing the work ... even if the exercises feel over-engineered to you at first. Once you have a basic structure and some key thinking completed, it becomes easier (and sometimes breakthrough) to move on to versions 2.0 and 3.0 of your typology, where you may want a little more specificity than a simple list of different categories. The outcome of your efforts here are simply meant to be a starting point that will evolve as you begin to work with other leaders at your organization. Once you have something thoughtful enough to scribble onto the back of a napkin or onto a dry-erase board, it may be time to share it with your colleagues so they can help you take it further.

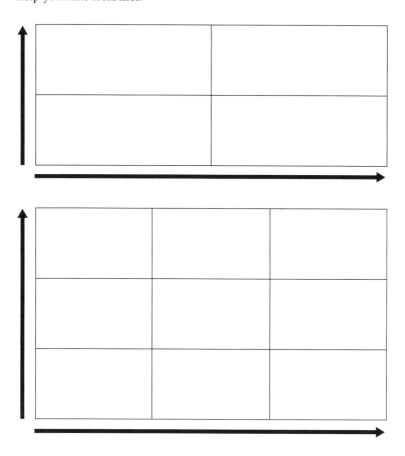

Step 6

As a final step in our process, you will find it useful to complete two additional exercises, each of which will allow you to test the utility of your typology.

First, if you created a multi-dimensional matrix without using the list of crisis types you created earlier, you should see if you can plot each of your crisis types somewhere in your matrix. This would serve as a litmus test for its validity. If an item from your list cannot be represented in some quadrant of your matrix, perhaps your matrix does not account for all the crisis variation you need it to.

Second, you might consider your stakeholders, one group at a time, and work your way through each item on your categorical list or through each quadrant of your matrix to define how each item or quadrant would impact each of your stakeholders. For example, if you consider your customer group and then step through each item on your crisis list or, alternatively, through each quadrant in your two- or three-dimensional matrix, you would be able to identify in which cases — and perhaps even to what extent — your customer group would be impacted by this type of crisis. This sort of exercise will make it much easier for you to develop specific crisis responses for a collection of well-defined scenarios.

That's it. You now have your own customized crisis typology. Nice work!

If you have taken the time to complete a typology of your own, you have just taken a significant step toward being able to construct basic crisis response plans that you will almost certainly require when you find yourself in a future high-stakes leadership scenario. No matter where you began this book — as a battle-weary crisis survivor or a new (or even aspiring) leader who has yet to wage war with his or her first big catastrophe — you are now well on your way to understanding the various ways the critical dimensions of a crisis could impact your organization ... *and* knowing what to do about it.

Tips for Talking to Your Leadership Team About Crisis Typologies

The insights in this book are only useful if you apply them at work. But what might that look like? Here are a few tips for taking what you've learned and sharing it with your colleagues ...

Initial Conversations — Use the typology you created in the previous exercise as a tool to inform an initial conversation with leaders at your organization on the topic of crisis readiness. For each of the items on your list, engage your colleagues in a high-level conversation focused on a single question:

> **"What would we do if we were faced with this type of crisis at our organization tomorrow?"**

This question will stimulate a broad range of responses. Some leaders will fully acknowledge your organization's lack of readiness and embrace the opportunity to improve in this area. If your organization already has some or many crisis prevention and management practices in place, the question will provide an opportunity to celebrate earlier efforts and find ways to update or improve existing practices. Other leaders will want to question the items on your list, perhaps dismissing many of them as "not going to happen here" or "we have more important things to worry about." Do not be discouraged. The most important outcome of your conversation is getting the members of your team to begin to think, collectively, about crisis readiness.

In time, your leaders will begin to embrace the notion of a crisis being an unavoidable chapter in the organization's future. Perhaps a silver lining of the COVID-19 pandemic (with all due consideration, of course, to the tragic impact and loss of life caused by this crisis) is the recognition that crises can come from sources we had not ever considered — and that without some degree of preparedness, our chances of managing them effectively are quite low. Your typology will give you and your colleagues a framework for some robust, healthy, and important initial conversations.

Deeper, Focused Discussions — After those initial conversations, keep the dialogue flowing. (Or consider an off-site leadership retreat focused entirely on crisis prediction, preparedness, and planning so those "initial conversations" can flow straight through to some deeper, focused discussions.) Be sure to share with your colleagues that your typology will not only help you think through crisis *preparedness* at your organization, but it can help you assess your current crisis *prevention* practices. "For this type of potential crisis," you might offer to your team, "what are we doing to look for early signs of trouble?" "How might our current practices expose us in this area?" "Should we make a few changes that could decrease our exposure?" These are all great questions for high-stakes leaders to consider. Now that you have an early version of a typology, you have enough specificity to sufficiently focus your discussions. And these discussions are crucial. Indeed, there are very few situations where leaders will be more challenged, more frustrated, more anxious, and less prepared than during a crisis. It behooves you to confront that reality and begin working to mitigate the potential fallout.

10

SWIMMING AGAINST THE TSUNAMI

Confronting the Arduous Nature of the Crisis Environment

One of the most challenging aspects of high-stakes leadership is having to assess situations and make decisions in an environment that seems custom-built to make a crisis leader's responsibilities extraordinarily difficult. In this chapter, we will look at the nature of the crisis environment and why it creates so many remarkable and unique challenges for high-stakes leaders.

First, **crisis situations will escalate at different rates**. Occasionally, crises build slowly over time and, despite our awareness of them, they become massive, complex predicaments. The COVID-19 pandemic and Hurricane Maria (2017) are examples of this type of crisis. Others, and these are much more common, erupt in an instant and immediately reach near-peak intensity. The events of September 11, 2001, the 2010 explosion on the Deepwater Horizon oil platform, and the 2019 fire at the Catholic cathedral of Notre-Dame de Paris are examples of crises that escalated rapidly, requiring crisis leaders to leap into action. Regardless of their escalation rate, crises will place enormous demands on the time, energy, focus, physiological

health, and psychological health of crisis leaders for extended periods
of time — and these demands may exceed anything ever experienced by
these leaders.

Crises will place enormous demands on the time, energy,
focus, physiological health, and psychological health of crisis
leaders for extended periods of time — and these demands
may exceed anything ever experienced by these leaders.

Second, in a crisis, **there will always be a degree of uncertainty — perhaps
a great deal — about the origin, the nature, and the potential consequences of the threat.** This uncertainty will create an initial sense of shock,
fear, and anxiety for everyone impacted by the crisis, and these concerns will
grow as the crisis continues. As time passes, the weight of this growing sense
of tension will increase, putting greater pressure on leaders to find solutions
and restore some degree of normalcy.

Third, **the crisis environment will present a threat to one or many stakeholders' value propositions.** Which stakeholders? Threatened how? To
what extent? Resolved by what? These are questions that will feel as though
they are coming quickly and furiously, particularly in the early stages of
a crisis. They underscore the benefits of having a crisis typology of some sort
to help crisis leaders respond more effectively to these very questions.

And fourth, because of the threats placed on these value propositions, **the
situation will call for, in the eyes of at least some stakeholders, urgent,
sometimes continuous, attention.** This will require crisis leaders to not
only scramble to resolve the immediate threat to the enterprise, but to do so
with continuously increasing pressure from its stakeholders. Resolving the
crisis and engaging stakeholders will put considerable demands on a crisis
leader's time, which is one of the most limited resources that a high-stakes
leader has at his or her disposal.

So, as we begin our exploration of the crisis environment, we can immediately see how important it is to have a sense of what will be required of
high-stakes leaders when they are called into action. We can also see how
important it is to be prepared to engage our stakeholders. Despite the

enormous demands placed on leaders to resolve the material aspects of a crisis, there will be relational aspects of the situation that will be just as challenging to manage.

In the book *The Politics of Crisis Management: Public Leadership Under Pressure* by Arjen Boin, Bengt Sundelius, and Eric Stern, the authors summarize the unique challenges facing today's high-stakes leader:

> "The very nature of the crisis environment creates a seemingly impossible task setting for high-stakes leaders: It requires urgent decisions, while essential information about causes and consequences remains unavailable; it requires effective communications to a variety of audiences with widely differing needs, views, and frames of reference. And it requires that leaders explain vulnerabilities in existing institutional structures, values, and routines as well as vulnerabilities in the leaders themselves."[1]

The crisis environment demands much of us. Being a high-stakes leader will require you to embrace vulnerability — the vulnerability of our systems and ourselves — and to lead almost entirely without a playbook.

Being a high-stakes leader will require you to embrace vulnerability — the vulnerability of our systems and ourselves — and to lead almost entirely without a playbook.

Observations and Lessons from the COVID-19 Pandemic

As the world watched and experienced the unfolding of the COVID-19 pandemic, we were able to observe and learn about the unique nature of the crisis environment in real time. The loss of life was overwhelming and tragic, the physical and emotional burdens placed on healthcare providers was unprecedented, and hundreds of millions of survivors were left to cope with diminished health and unknown long-term consequences. At the

---

1   Arjen Boin et al., *The Politics of Crisis Management: Public Leadership Under Pressure* (Cambridge: Cambridge University Press, 2019).

time of this book going to press, vaccinations were being administered at a rapid pace in the United States and beyond, and we were accepting the fact that it may be quite some time before we can ensure the health and safety of people around the world with adequate treatments and preventive measures for all the variants of the SARS-CoV-2 virus.

In the midst of it all was an opportunity for high-stakes leaders to learn from their observations and experiences — not so much to facilitate critique of those leading crisis-response efforts, but to draw lessons and insights from this crisis in order to help us deal more effectively with the next.

As we have already established, one way to think about a crisis is that it presents a threat of some sort to the value propositions of one or more stakeholders. Many different value propositions were threatened by the COVID-19 pandemic. Think about the various members of populations and organizations around the world, and ask yourself, "What should these people have expected of their business and community leaders?" Consider how these expectations *should* have been managed then think about how they actually *were* managed. I am not suggesting for a minute that the management of these expectations should have been easy. There is immense complexity here, and we have all struggled at times to determine which side of a contentious issue was right and which was not. For example, how should leaders have treated the tension between "stay-at-home" orders to slow the spread of COVID-19 and the support of local businesses, who desperately needed customers? This is why the crisis environment can be so challenging.

Let's take a moment to consider *your* perspective, as one of many stake-holders impacted by the COVID-19 pandemic. And let's use your perspective as representative of how others might have processed this crisis. This should give us a useful frame for appreciating the perspective of a single stakeholder, caught in an extremely challenging situation, living in our increasingly complex world.

I have suggested that a crisis calls for, in the eyes of at least some stake-holders, urgent (if not immediate) attention. Think back to the initial weeks and months of the pandemic. What were your own needs and expectations for action? Were you inspired or frustrated by the actions of federal or local government leaders? What did you see that helped you better understand the situation? What did you see that just made things worse? (Or more confusing? Or less certain?) From these observations, what can you take away as lessons that inform your own approach to crisis leadership? What did you see that you'd like to emulate in your own future actions (i.e., behaviors you want to *always* do when leading a team through a crisis)? What do you *never* want to do? Don't miss the opportunity to learn from your experience. Being an observant *stakeholder* during a crisis can inform your future performance as a crisis *leader*.

Being an observant *stakeholder* during a crisis can inform your future performance as a crisis *leader*.

The COVID-19 crisis has been one that required disparate and sometimes coordinated crisis-response efforts from leaders at every level and in every sector of society. We first looked to national and state or provincial leaders. Then we started paying attention to the words and behaviors of other community and business leaders — mayors, health department officials, small business owners, corporate executives, school boards and superintendents, and even homeowners' associations and heads of families. What did you see from the people around you that is worth building into your own crisis leadership toolkit?

How about the behaviors or opinions of your own family members? Were you inspired by how some of them rose to the occasion? Or perhaps you were stupefied by the way they processed or responded to the crisis. In either of these cases, there are lessons to be learned about how stakeholders perceive their circumstances and how we, as high-stakes leaders, might be able to address them more effectively. If you listen and watch closely enough, the perspectives of a sister can inform how you serve colleagues, and the words of a neighbor might spark ideas about how to calm and reassure your customers. Crisis response is utterly and imperfectly human — it's messy and it's unfolding in real time, but the lessons are everywhere.

I have no doubt that the words and behaviors of others during the COVID-19 pandemic repeatedly caught your attention — making you scratch your head, or smile and nod, or feel either encouraged or disappointed. There were many great moments of inspirational leadership, from both expected and unexpected sources, and many moments that produced immense frustration. I believe the driving force behind this broad range of actions — from admirable to atrocious — was simply the complex nature of the crisis environment.

Crises that are products of the VUCA environment in which we live and work can be, and quite often are, exactly like the environment in which they exist: immensely volatile, uncertain, complex, and ambiguous. Now that you have gained quite a bit of experience living through one, wouldn't you agree?

Crises that are products of the VUCA environment in which we live and work can be, and quite often are, exactly like the environment in which they exist: immensely volatile, uncertain, complex, and ambiguous.

Crises Are Typically the Result of Multiple Contributing Factors

Crisis investigators, typically assigned by a regulatory agency to determine contributing factors and root causes of a recent crisis, always include a summary of findings in their final reports. What is a consistent lesson in these summaries? Crises are almost always the result of *multiple* contributing factors, which interact or overlap across a period of time (sometimes very quickly and sometimes very slowly), and which eventually produce a chain reaction that results in a catastrophic outcome.

Why is this an important insight for high-stakes leaders to understand? It tells us that, in most cases, there are many warning signs before — often well before — there is a full-scale crisis. We have established that we can benefit greatly by engaging our stakeholders to serve as our early warning systems and to help us address potential crises before they become critical. This is a key aspect of resilience. But when these efforts are not successful, particularly when our stakeholders have been pointing out seemingly minor threats that have now escalated into a full-blown crisis, what was once an asset turns very quickly into a liability.

Consistent with the description shared earlier of the VUCA world in which we live and operate, *all* organizations are also facing growing levels of complexity. As complexity increases, early warning signals and subtle (maybe even not-so-subtle) vulnerabilities become more difficult to spot. Complexity makes solution-finding exceptionally difficult, as root causes are harder to identify, the scale and scope of both problems and solutions are more challenging to define, and solution implementation may feel almost impossibly arduous. Increasing complexity has enabled some incredible innovation and business outcomes, but a byproduct has been its often-debilitating impact on crisis leadership effectiveness.

Take the COVID-19 situation, for example, in the early moments of the crisis — in January, February, and early March of 2020. Even as we watched the development of the situation in Wuhan, China, the complexities of our tightly coupled world made it difficult even for healthcare experts to predict the potential of this now-historic pandemic. Regardless of your political perspective, we in the United States appear to have grossly underestimated an appropriate response, not because we did not see it coming — WE ALL WATCHED IT — but because we could not navigate the complexities of the various systems (political, social, economic, health and welfare, etc.) — that govern our lives.

Let's talk for a moment about some lighter-hearted crises — ones that, while they felt heart-sickening to those involved — didn't have fatal or far-reaching consequences. As an interesting example of system complexities coming together to produce a crisis, consider the events that led to the infamous moment at the 89th Academy Awards celebration on February 26, 2017, when *La La Land* was announced as the year's best motion picture, but *Moonlight* was the actual Oscar-winning film.[2]

---

2   Scott Feinberg, "'They Got the Wrong Envelope!': The Oral History of Oscar's Epic Best Picture Fiasco," *The Hollywood Reporter* (February 26, 2018), https://www.hollywoodreporter.com/features/they-got-wrong-envelope-oral-history-oscars-epic-best-picture-fiasco-1087829).

Image Credit: (Left) Chris Pizzello/Invision/AP; (Right) Al Seib/Los Angeles Times

Consider all the things that had to go wrong for the two hosts, Warren Beatty and Faye Dunaway, to announce the wrong movie. You don't have to be a student of the motion picture business to identify several factors that may have contributed to this crisis — some of which will be summarized below. What you should be a student of, however, is how complex systems or processes with many moving parts can create threats to an organization. Many of these threats start very small and are seemingly insignificant, but when a collection of small, insignificant issues come together in just the right way, the results can be explosive.

What are some potential root causes of the best-picture crisis at the 89th Oscars? Here are a few elements of the process that suggest potential problems, should things not go entirely according to plan. As you read each item in the following list, consider how observers (i.e., stakeholders who can help us identify threats and increase our capacity for resilience) might have been able to recommend process modifications to reduce the potential for a catastrophe.

1. *The secretive nature of the process.* PricewaterhouseCoopers (PwC) was responsible for managing vote tabulation and the determination of Oscar winners. In fact, only two people at PwC knew the actual winners before they were announced on live television.

2. *Dependence on the celebrity award presenters.* Warren Beatty and Faye Dunaway were instructed to announce whatever they read from the card in the envelope provided to them. They would have no way of knowing if they were announcing the correct winner.

3. *Dependence on the presenters being able to read what is printed on the card.* This particular year, a new combination of paper and ink colors were reportedly difficult to read. What if the presenters could not read the card, or could only partially read it?

4. *Dependence on show producers to get the correct envelope to the announcers.* For the announcers to reveal the actual winner, they would need to receive the correct envelope (it was later determined that Mr. Beatty was erroneously handed the envelope for the previous category winner, which was Emma Stone for her performance in *La La Land.*)[3]

5. *Dependence on the effective use of redundancy.* Show producers had elected to create two sets of awardee envelopes, with a set being available to presenters on each side of the backstage area. While this was done to provide redundancy and flexibility for producers, it was this redundancy that contributed significantly to the crisis.

6. *Overconfidence.* According to PwC interviews, prior to the event, there was no possibility that such an error could take place. The accounting firm had managed this process for years without an error, so it seemed almost unthinkable that an incorrect announcement could happen.[4]

7. *Lack of a crisis-management plan.* Finally, as the events played out on stage on that evening in the Dolby Theatre in Hollywood, CA, it was clear that neither PwC nor show producers had a way to deal with such a crisis when it did occur.

This list of potential "single points of failure" is provided as a way to illustrate that even in a system as simple as the one described here — the announcement of a Best Picture Oscar, which had been done 88 times previously without error — there are opportunities for things to go wrong in a significant way. This is why it's so important for high-stakes leaders

---

3   Scott Feinberg, "'They Got the Wrong Envelope!': The Oral History of Oscar's Epic Best Picture Fiasco," *The Hollywood Reporter* (February 26, 2018), https://www.hollywoodreporter.com/features/they-got-wrong-envelope-oral-history-oscars-epic-best-picture-fiasco-1087829).

4   Matthew Jacobs, "What Would Happen If A Presenter Announced The Wrong Winner At The Oscars?" Huffington Post (February 24, 2017), https://www.huffpost.com/entry/oscar-wrong-winner-marisa-tomei_n_58af326de4b0a8a9b780339f.

to understand that an important feature of the crisis environment is that threats can arise from many sources.

Complex Systems Make Threat Identification Difficult

Our environment is continuously increasing in its level of complexity. There are many ways we can think about this, all of which lead to a general agreement that it is nearly impossible to understand the outcomes or products of a system simply by looking at its individual parts and understanding what they do. "Systems thinking" evolved in response to this challenge and focuses on the way that a system's constituent parts interrelate and how systems work together, over time, within the context of larger systems. An entirely new way of thinking has emerged because the elements of complex systems can no longer be understood as a collection of linear processes. Instead, the elements of a system are interconnected in such a way that each element depends on others to function. And outcomes are produced not as outputs of each element, but rather, because of synergies between and among elements within the system. Why is this important to us? Because the way complex elements interact within a complex system are hard to understand. And because they are hard to understand, it is exceedingly difficult for high-stakes leaders to easily see where a weakness in their complex business system might generate an issue that could eventually become a crisis.

It is exceedingly difficult for high-stakes leaders to easily see where a weakness in their complex business system might generate an issue that could eventually become a crisis.

In 1979, Russell Ackoff, a Professor of Systems Sciences at the University of Pennsylvania, wrote in his now very well-known article, "The Future of Operational Research is Past," that:

> "Managers are not confronted with problems that are independent of each other, but with dynamic situations that consist of complex systems of changing problems that interact with each other. I call such situations messes. Managers do not solve problems anymore, they manage messes."

While I will not try to differentiate messes from crises here, I do agree with Ackoff's point — that managers of complex systems, such as those faced by high-stakes leaders every day, will find it exceptionally challenging to predict the source(s) of what he calls a mess, and what we will call a crisis.[5]

Charles Perrow, a Professor of Sociology at Yale, wrote extensively about the impact of challenges in large social systems. He believed that crises are an unwanted by-product of modernity. His theory of vulnerability in complex systems[6] identified two intersecting factors at the heart of both modernization and system vulnerability: complexity and coupling. He wrote:

> "As socio-technical systems become more complex and increasingly connected, in other words, more tightly coupled to other systems, their vulnerability to disturbances increases exponentially. The more complex a system becomes, the harder it is for anyone to understand it in its entirety. Tight coupling between a system's component parts, and those of other systems, allows for the rapid proliferation of interactions and errors throughout the system. In these complex, tightly coupled systems, we should thus expect periodic failures that have the potential to escalate out of control."

And, in fact, this is what we are seeing in our VUCA business environments. As organizations grow, the number of connections among their various stakeholders increases, making effective and consistent interactions more difficult to execute. As organizations grow, the number of products and services grow, making them more challenging to organize and manage. As organizations grow, the leadership structure becomes more complex, making effective management a more complicated endeavor. And as advances are made in hardware, software, corporate policies, business practices, regulations, etc., it gets increasingly difficult for the organization to keep up, to stay organized, to manage risk, and to avoid crises.

---

5   Russell L. Ackoff, "The Future of Operational Research Is Past," *The Journal of the Operational Research Society*, 30, no. 2 (1979): doi:10.2307/3009290.

6   Charles Perrow, *Normal Accidents: Living with High-Risk Technologies* (Princeton, NJ: Princeton University Press (1999). – Earlier edition published by Basic Books in 1984.

The point here is that our organizations and the environments in which we operate are constantly becoming more complex and more difficult to control. As high-stakes leaders, we need to recognize this new reality and become even more attentive to early indications of trouble. If we do not, not only will emerging threats be more difficult to spot, but they will be more challenging to resolve once they become crises.

In the quasi-immortal words of famous University of Michigan football coach Bo Schembechler, "Every day you either get better or you get worse. You never stay the same." In the context of our increasingly VUCA world, if we are not doing what we *can* to stay ahead of this added complexity, we are falling behind it. And if we fall too far behind, we may not have any chance to see our next crisis coming.

Complexity Makes It Harder for Stakeholders to Identify Threats

To this point, you've learned about the increasing complexity of business, how this complexity can generate a variety of threats to an organization, and how the nature of the crisis environment creates challenges for high-stakes leaders, particularly in the context of threat identification. You've also learned to lean on stakeholders to help you identify threats. Unfortunately, there is an inverse relationship between complexity and the ability of your stakeholders to spot potential sources of crisis. Therefore, finding ways to limit complexity can preserve your capacity for organizational resilience.

- -

Finding ways to limit complexity can preserve
your capacity for organizational resilience.

- -

Your business is unique, and it has a complexity unlike any other. As a high-stakes leader, your job includes finding ways to manage this complexity so that your organization can be as resilient as possible. How might you think about doing so? Here are a few considerations, first about managing the complexity itself, and second about working through the complexity to create avenues for continuous improvement and threat detection.

Managing complexity. The practical reality for business leaders is that as companies grow and expand their offerings, they will necessarily become more complex. As companies grow, hiring increases and organizational structures become more complex; product development, sales, and inven tory management processes become more involved; technology evolves, which can be both helpful and problematic; partnerships are formed across multiple geographies, which are difficult to manage; and competition spans the globe, making strategic choices more complex. Increasing complexity is not necessarily a bad thing, in and of itself. But increasing complexity is going to make it harder for you and your stakeholders to identify poten- tial threats.

What are some ways that leaders can reduce complexity?

- Get feedback from all levels of your organization about process prob- lems or inefficiencies.

- Identify and solve root causes of organizational problems, not just the symptoms that crop up.

- Elevate and rely upon managers who are particularly talented at managing complexity.

The first step in reducing complexity is examining it from different vantage points. Strong leaders look at complexity through the eyes of people at all levels of the organization. Many times, senior leaders see organizational design or product management or operational processes as perfectly appro- priate and logical from their perspective, yet organizational members two or more layers deeper in the enterprise don't see things that way at all. When developing and implementing new organizational structures or processes, get feedback from as many layers of the enterprise as you can. What you learn will help identify improvement opportunities.

When developing and implementing new organizational structures or processes, get feedback from as many layers of the enterprise as you can. What you learn will help identify improvement opportunities.

A second key step in reducing complexity involves clarity between "cause and effect." Focus, where you can, on causes. Do not allow yourself to attend only to symptoms; instead, identify and solve root causes of the complexity. It is easy to mistake symptoms for causes. When leaders do so, and then solve the symptom (instead of solving the problem), the problem almost always reappears. When you identify an area of opportunity for improvement, ask yourself: "What is *causing* this problem that I am seeing and that I want to solve?" This question will point you in the direction of a root cause, not simply a manifestation of the issue.

A final, third recommendation for leaders attempting to reduce complexity: remember that some managers are simply better at managing complexity than others, and having the right people in the right roles with the right responsibilities is crucial for your success. Some managers are exceptional collaborators, and some are not. Some managers are great at thinking in terms of process and structure, and others are not. When you are looking to attack complexity, make sure that you have the best possible people doing the job, then trust them to do it while supporting them appropriately.

Creating avenues for improvement and threat detection. You know that your best resources for threat detection are your stakeholders. If you create and maintain the right kinds of relationships with members of these groups, they will help you identify areas of opportunity for improvement as well as potential threats. In many ways, in fact, these two things (opportunities and threats) are often very closely related. As complexity increases in your organization, never lose sight of the fact that the burden you will be placing on these stakeholders to identify potential threats increases. In other words, the more complex your organization, the more difficult it will be for stakeholders to see challenges — to connect the dots among a collection of seemingly small issues that might, collectively, create a meaningful organizational threat.

The more complex your organization, the more difficult it will be for stakeholders to see challenges — to connect the dots among a collection of seemingly small issues that might, collectively, create a meaningful organizational threat.

To help your stakeholders serve more effectively in their observer roles, you should: 1) reduce or minimize complexity that does not add value, and 2) provide mechanisms that make it easier for your stakeholders to share what they are able to see. Do not force them to connect dots on their own, as they probably will not be able to. But you should make sure that, "if they see something, they say something." You and your team should be taking steps to help them do so. Because, in the end, if people don't sound the alarm bells, it's almost always because you didn't create a safe, welcoming space for such critical feedback. Culture is key.

The Need for Urgent Decision-Making with Limited Information

Another challenging aspect of the crisis environment is how the urgent need for decision-making is hindered by the limited availability of information. During a crisis, high-stakes leaders have to make decisions — decisions about whether or not they are actually in a crisis; decisions about whether or not to call the crisis team into action (are things bad enough to sound the alarm?); decisions about how to deploy limited resources, how to interpret limited data, and how to decide on option A or option B, when either could be right or wrong; and decisions about whether it's time to make a decision or if they should wait for more or better information before doing so.

Being a decision-maker during a crisis is a formidable responsibility. It takes character, competence, experience, courage, and — perhaps most importantly — an understanding that while many of your decisions will be right, many will be wrong. This is a difficult reality for decision-makers in a crisis. When confronting the arduous nature of the crisis environment, leaders often discover that each decision and each step forward feels like swimming against a tsunami. Exceptional leaders keep swimming.

- -

Being a decision-maker during a crisis is a formidable responsibility. It takes character, competence, experience, courage, and — perhaps most importantly — an understanding that while many of your decisions will be right, many will be wrong.

- -

Peter Drucker, often called the father of modern management, famously said: "Whenever you see a successful business, someone once made a courageous decision." His point being that, at some point, a leader was forced to make a difficult decision, with limited information and without a perfectly clear picture, and had the courage to make it anyway. Exceptional leaders know that if you wait until you have all the information before you act, you might find that someone else has seized the opportunity that was ready-made for you (if only you had acted sooner). With high-stakes leadership, decision-making is not about seizing opportunity, per se, but it is very much about having the courage to make decisions, with limited information and in a timely manner, in the best interests of everyone involved.

Michael Lewis, the author of *Moneyball* and several other bestselling books, had the opportunity to interview former President Barack Obama while he was still in office. One line of questioning had to do with the challenges of making decisions with limited information. When asked about this, Obama responded: "Nothing comes to my desk that is perfectly solvable. Otherwise, someone else would have solved it." He went on to say, from his experience: "Any given decision you make, you'll wind up with a 30 to 40 percent chance that it isn't going to work. You have to own that and feel comfortable with *the way* that you made the decision. You can't be paralyzed by the fact that it might not work."[7]

> "Any given decision you make, you'll wind up with a 30 to 40 percent chance that it isn't going to work. You have to own that and feel comfortable with the way that you made the decision. You can't be paralyzed by the fact that it might not work."
>
> — *President Barack Obama*

Obama's point was not that there is actually a 30–40% chance that a leader making decisions in a complex environment is going to be wrong. His point was that high-stakes leaders are going to have to make decisions in situations where there may never be enough information — enough clarity of the situation — to know exactly how to be right. This is the nature of the crisis environment. The information won't come as fast as you want it to come,

---

7   Michael Lewis, "Obama's Way," *Vanity Fair* (September 11, 2012), https://www.vanityfair.com/news/2012/10/michael-lewis-profile-barack-obama).

and sometimes it won't reveal itself at all. Regardless, crisis leaders will be charged with making decisions, for better or for worse.

Decision-making during a crisis is also significantly complicated by the VUCA environment in which we are required to make them. We lead through volatility, in uncertain times, with incredible complexity, and a foreboding sense of ambiguity.

The dynamics of crisis situations are *volatile*, and every decision can have dire consequences. Yet, decisions are necessary, and they must be made. A good one could make things much better; a bad one could make things much worse. But not making decisions can often be worse than making decisions that eventually turn out to be wrong. In fact, a failure to act is much more likely to move the process, the team, and the crisis *backward* than it is to move the situation forward or even hold the line.

We are almost always *uncertain*, to some degree, about what we *do* know, what we *could* know, and what we *wish* we knew to inform our decisions. Leaders must develop the instincts to understand when they know *enough* to make difficult choices.

- -

Leaders must develop the instincts to understand when they know *enough* to make difficult choices.

- -

The environment is typically incredibly *complex*, and confounding, and it can be exceedingly difficult to see how pieces of the puzzle fit together to clearly identify cause and effect relationships, or to know enough about a complex set of options and how they might best be deployed into a complex set of circumstances.

And there will always be a sense of *ambiguity* in the situation. It will rarely be clear how individual decisions will produce both intended and unintended consequences.

This is the environment of a high-stakes leader during a crisis. It will never be comfortable. You will never be as confident in your decisions as you will want to be. But decisions will have to be made. And in the end, whether those decisions prove to be right or prove to be wrong, it is always better to have made them than to have stood still. For many reasons, high-stakes leaders must be assertive and decisive. There are simply no better alternatives. And because most of these decisions will have to be made with limited information, they will be some of the most difficult — emotional, painful, even gut-wrenching — decisions you will ever have to make.

In the early years of your career or when you first encounter a major crisis, decision-making will be especially hard. The decisions you make and the words and actions you choose will not always be right. But they will have to be made. Over time, as you gain experience, your decision-making skills will improve. This will not resolve the issue of having to make decisions with limited information, but you will find that your ability to make sense of the situation and determine the best options to pursue under the circumstances will improve dramatically. You will develop a gut-instinct for high-stakes leadership, and your effectiveness will improve while the emotional stress you carry will diminish somewhat. Crisis leadership is an art and a science whose tenets are learned and whose skills are honed only over time.

Urgency Versus the Tendency to Wait for the Facts

In the book *Ulysses S. Grant: Triumph Over Adversity, 1822-1865,* author Brooks D. Simpson shares this story as an example of General Grant's perspective on the crucial role of decision-making in war:

> "That winter James Rusling, a colonel in the quartermaster's department, caught his first look at the hero of Chattanooga [Grant] and was disappointed. Here was no shiny general with brass buttons, sash and sword, but a rather common-looking man, just like 'a country storekeeper or a western farmer.' The general was 'evidently intent on everything but show.' But when it came to giving orders, Grant came alive, his 'clear and penetrating eye' and set jaw suggesting that he could 'dare great things, and hold on mightily, and toil terribly' in pursuit of his objective. He might be a man of few words, but 'he knew exactly what he wanted, and why and when he wanted it.' Nearly every night the general could be found using the telegraph to keep tabs on his command (and the enemy), as he pondered the next move.

"Once, the colonel approached Grant with a requisition order authorizing large expenditures. Briefly reviewing the report, the general gave his approval, catching the colonel by surprise. Might the general want to ponder the matter a little longer? Was he sure he was right? Grant looked up. 'No, I am not,' he responded, 'but in war anything is better than indecision. We must decide. If I am wrong, we shall soon find it out and can do the other thing. But not to decide wastes both time and money, and may ruin everything.'"[8]

As a high-stakes leader, you are going to have to determine when you have enough information to decide. Rest assured, it will never be as much as you would prefer to have. It will rarely be enough to give you confidence in your decisions. But decision-making in a crisis is not a matter of perfection — it is a matter of progress. As you have seen, choosing not to decide may occasionally be the best answer, but those cases are few and far between in a crisis.

Decision-making in a crisis is not a matter of perfection — it is a matter of progress.

In an article titled "Making Decisions with Limited and Imperfect Information," Professor M.S. Rao, PhD. acknowledges that: "Anybody can make decisions when complete information is available. Anybody can make decisions when partial information is available. But it requires immense imagination and intuition to make decisions when there is a dearth of information."[9]

Dr. Rao poses the following as a set of steps for making successful decisions, no matter the circumstances:

---

8   Brooks D. Simpson, *Ulysses S. Grant: Triumph Over Adversity, 1822-1865* (United States: Voyageur Press, 2014).

9   M.S. Rao, PhD, "Making Decisions with Limited and Imperfect Information," *Training Magazine* (April 4, 2017).

1. Find out the situation. Understand the issues from multiple perspectives.

2. Think of the best and worst that will happen.

3. Discuss with your close connections to create appropriate alternatives.

4. Choose the decision that is possible and feasible to execute with limited risk and maximum returns.

5. Obtain feedback to improve your decisions in the future.

Rao also reminds us that, regardless of whether one must rely on "head, heart, or gut" to make a decision, it is better to have made a decision (even a poor one) than to not have decided at all.

I recommend taking the time to find and read this article, considering the lessons and wonderful advice Rao shares that seems perfectly adapted for our study of the crisis environment and the challenges it creates for high-stakes leaders.

Exercise #8
Developmental Opportunities for Self and Team

Part 1: Urgent Decision-Making with Limited Information

The preceding pages described the requirement for crisis leaders to make urgent decisions with limited information. There is simply no way around it.

Given your takeaways from this discussion and the frameworks offered, record a few ideas for things you can do, skills you can learn, or other actions you can take, to help you develop your capacity to effectively make urgent decisions with limited information during a crisis.

The Demand for Effective Communication to Multiple Audiences

Another challenge for high-stakes leaders during a crisis is the requirement for effective communications with a variety of audiences who inevitably have widely differing needs, views, and frames of reference. Given what we know about the interests of our stakeholders, how do we figure out what they want to hear when we find ourselves mired in a crisis?

What makes this question so difficult to answer is that determining what they want to hear depends on several different variables, all of which make effective communication with each stakeholder group an exceptionally challenging responsibility.

We know that each of our stakeholders will be viewing the crisis from a different perspective. We also know, because we have taken the time to understand our stakeholders, how each group perceives its value proposition with our organization. During a crisis, it is these value propositions that are threatened, so it would make sense for us to frame our communications around the threat that each of our stakeholders is seeing. This is not the challenging part — unless, of course, you have not taken the time to understand how each of your stakeholder groups gains value from its relationship with your company. Then framing your communications *will* be a challenge. But if you understand your stakeholders and their interests, you're at a good starting point.

Communicating with stakeholders during a crisis is multi-faceted, to say the least. You are tasked with finding the time to deliver all the different messages that each of your stakeholders wants to hear, when they want to hear it, with the content that means the most to them, and through the medium that each wants to receive it. Think about that for a moment. There is a lot going on here.

Each of your stakeholder groups is going to be hyper-focused on collecting whatever information they can. They will be looking to you and your team for that information. How can a high-stakes leader make sure that all stakeholders are getting what they need, when they need it? This is why companies have a dedicated communications person or team. During a crisis, there will be too many unique messages to send, to too many different interested parties, for a single crisis leader to effectively manage. Now, if your organization is very small, or just getting started, you may not have a dedicated communications leader or team. In this case, you will want to appoint someone to this role during a crisis. Perhaps there is a member of your team who has exceptional communication skills and can take on this role. There are also professional service firms that can fill this role if you are in desperate need of a resource to help you in this area. Think of this spokesperson as your press secretary or your official mouthpiece. This job is critical and should only be entrusted to someone with strong experience, an approachable persona, and a level head.

The bottom line here is that your high-stakes leadership team will have an extensive collection of audiences to serve with communications during a crisis. Different groups will want and need to hear different things. Early in a crisis, you will be able to communicate with high-level, general communications that can be sent to all stakeholders simultaneously. We saw during the COVID-19 crisis that much of the messaging was designed to be informative to anyone who took the time to listen. But these general messages don't do much to acknowledge or address the interests of specific stakeholder groups, so general announcements and broad statements are just the beginning.

Eventually, in any crisis, communication efforts will have to transition from the macro to the micro. Your messages can be general at first, but they will need to become much more targeted and specific as the crisis proceeds. The burden to manage this increasingly specific and complex messaging will eventually become quite significant. Taking the time to build this reality into your crisis planning will pay significant dividends when the inevitable crisis appears at your organization.

Revisiting Stakeholder Perspectives
and Value Propositions

Let's return to the stakeholders who you identified earlier for your organization. Given what you have just heard about the requirement for crisis leaders to engage different audiences, in different ways and with different information, how should you be thinking about the information your different stakeholders might need during a crisis?

As a reminder of the relationships that high-stakes leaders form with their stakeholders — and the fact that the relationship is not simply one of unemotional value exchange — here is how author and stakeholder theory expert Ed Freeman describes these relationships:

> "To create value for stakeholders, executives and entre-preneurs must see business as fully situated in the realm of humanity. Businesses are human institutions populated by real live complex human beings. Stakeholders have names and faces and children. They are not mere placeholders for social roles. Most human beings are complicated. Most of us do what we do because we are self-interested *and* inter-ested in others. Business works in part because of our urge to create things with others and for others. Working on a team, or creating a new product or delivery mechanism that makes customers' lives better or happier or more pleasurable all can be contributing factors to why we go to work each day. And, this is not to deny the economic incentive of getting a pay check. The assumption of narrow self-interest is extremely limiting, and can be self-reinforcing — people can begin to act in a narrow self-interested way if they believe that is what is expected of them, as some of the scandals have shown. We need to be open to a more complex psychology — one any parent finds familiar as they have shepherded the growth and development of their children."[10]

---

10   R. Edward Freeman et al., *Stakeholder Theory: The State of the Art* (Cambridge: Cambridge University Press, 2014).

We have relationships with our stakeholders not simply to extract economic value (or to be well-prepared high-stakes leaders), but to make their lives better — to make their responsibilities more enjoyable. Interestingly, the Ross School of Business at the University of Michigan is known for, among other things, its Center for Positive Organizations, an academic unit dedicated to business that enriches the lives of its stakeholders. Their mission is quite consistent with the description shared by Dr. Freeman.

Do you remember the value propositions that your stakeholders have with your organization? We considered these earlier, but it might be helpful to briefly review them here.

- *Enterprise leadership.* This group — the C-suite and its counterparts — has a unique set of responsibilities and, in exchange for their leadership, they extract a great deal of value from the enterprise. During a crisis, their own interests are impacted in many ways.

- *Employees.* Their jobs and livelihoods are at stake in an organizational crisis. What do they want to know? When and how do they want to know it? During a crisis, high-stakes leaders will have their full attention, so it will be our responsibility to help employees understand the situation and the actions being taken to secure their futures.

- *Customers.* Customers and suppliers exchange resources for the products and services of the firm and, in return, receive the benefits of the products and services. These stakeholders will be expecting value in exchange for something of value that will be or may have already been exchanged for it. During a crisis, customers will be worried about the possibility that your organization will not be able to deliver the value they are expecting.

- *Investors.* Owners or financiers clearly have a financial stake in the business, and that stake might be stocks, bonds, and/or other currencies. Investors expect a financial return from their investments. In a crisis, however, their expectations are put in jeopardy; investors become concerned about the current state of their investment as well as the long-term value of it.

- *Regulators.* Governmental officials play a couple of different roles in their relationships with an organization, each of which will be threatened during a crisis. While regulatory officials are elected or appointed to serve the interests of their constituents, some look after the interests of communities (e.g., mayors, governors, etc.), while others look after enterprise compliance (e.g., safety or legal officials). In a crisis, both types of regulators will have concerns, and they will be looking for information to share with their constituencies.

- *Media.* Members of the media are driven by the interests (i.e., the questions, concerns, curiosities, and fears) of their viewers, readers, listeners, or followers. During a crisis, the media will want access to information as it becomes available and to developments as they occur. Journalists will feel a growing sense of pressure as a crisis evolves because of a continuous stream of news to be shared, and a worry that access to the most intimate and timely details will be difficult to secure.

- *Competitors.* As we have established, this may be an odd group to think of as a stakeholder. They are in many cases, however, impacted by the choices that a competing organization makes ... and the way it manages a crisis situation.

The unique and formidable nature of the crisis environment is colored by the endangered value propositions of your stakeholders, who are watching you swim against the tsunami and who are expecting that you'll act and speak in *their* best interests despite all that overwhelms you in the moment. As a high-stakes leader, you will be operating in that tenuous environment we reviewed at the top of this chapter — in a moment of complexity, where the crisis escalates at sometimes rapid and unexpected rates, where stakeholder values are threatened, and where people are demanding urgent and sometimes continuous action from you. Remember when seeking to address those stakeholder threats that the best way to engage stakeholders during a crisis or disruption is to do so in a manner the conveys to them (and others) that they are far more than instruments of economic value to you. Let them know that you think of them as members of your organizational family.

The best way to engage stakeholders during a crisis or disruption is to do so in a manner the conveys to them (and others) that they are far more than instruments of economic value to you. Let them know that you think of them as members of your organizational family.

What can you do, today, to gain a better understanding of what your stake-holders will want to hear during a crisis and to create plans to make sure that they get what they need when they need it?

Exercise #9
Developmental Opportunities for Self and Team

Part 2: The Demand for Effective Communication to Multiple Audiences

During a crisis, there is a persistent demand for effective communication to multiple audiences, each of whom will want different information, at different times, through different channels, and in ways that feel tailored to their specific concerns and needs. This will be truly challenging for high-stakes leaders.

Given your takeaways from this chapter and your fresh perspectives about the nature of the crisis environment in which you must rise to the challenge, record a few ideas for things you can do, skills you can learn, or other actions you can take, to help you develop your capacity for managing the demand for effective communication to multiple audiences during a crisis.

_____

_____

_____

_____

The Importance of Acknowledging Individual Vulnerability

When making decisions with limited information, we are going to make mistakes. Similarly, many crises are the product of vulnerabilities in the way we operate, the way we conduct business, and the choices we are forced to make as we create the greatest amount of value we can with limited resources. Businesses and other organizations are fallible because, quite simply, people are fallible.

Why does this become an issue in the crisis environment? Because during a crisis, leaders will have to deal with the reality of weak spots and vulnerabilities in existing institutional structures, values, routines, and people — all of which contribute some degree of responsibility to the crisis that is currently being dealt with. These very public displays of organizational imperfection will require leaders to acknowledge that they, themselves, are vulnerable and imperfect. For leaders, this is not a natural or comfortable act. But to be a high-stakes leader, it is a responsibility that you will have to accept.

- -

> Public displays of organizational imperfection will require leaders
> to acknowledge that they, themselves, are vulnerable and
> imperfect. For leaders, this is not a natural or comfortable act.

- -

On the issue of institutional vulnerability, I think today's organizations are gradually getting more comfortable with having to deal with their mistakes. There has been a movement over these past couple of decades to organizational philosophies that embrace a "learning fast, innovating, and always getting better" mindset, which is a considerable departure from that of "flawlessly excellent," which described the philosophies and branding messages at the turn of the century. This change has not been driven so much by companies' lack of interest in delivering exceptional quality, but the definition of quality has evolved a bit from "perfect" to "constantly evolving to meet stakeholder (typically customer) needs." The notion of perfection is becoming less of an aspiration as businesses try to keep up with their constantly changing landscapes. This should help us, at least to some extent, feel a little more comfortable about the expectations of our stakeholders.

On the question of leadership vulnerability, it is interesting how much research has been done recently. If you are reader of business literature — and I hope you are; I have a half-dozen books at the ready at any given time — Dr. Brené Brown has done some really nice work on this topic. In one of her recent books, *Dare to Lead*, she presents some wonderful and useful thoughts on the importance of leadership vulnerability.[11] And nowhere in her writing does she suggest that vulnerability is bad. In fact, in an earlier work, she shared that "vulnerability is a weakness" is a remarkably common myth that has led many leaders astray.

If you speak to any CEO, any military veteran, or anyone who is expected to perform under conditions that a high-stakes leader is required to face during a crisis, each will tell you that it is impossible to feel anything but vulnerable as you face challenging environments like these. Ultimately, we are all human, and we all make mistakes. Everyone knows it. So, high-stakes leaders must find a way to embrace, rather than avoid, this reality.

Stakeholders are *not* expecting you to be flawless, or perfect, or omniscient. They are, however, expecting you to be visible, courageous, and committed to the best possible path forward for all stakeholders, regardless of the origin of the crisis.

Stakeholders are not expecting you to be flawless, or perfect, or omniscient. They are, however, expecting you to be visible, courageous, and committed to the best possible path forward for all stakeholders, regardless of the origin of the crisis.

As a final thought on the topic of individual vulnerability, I'll share a quote from Theodore Roosevelt that I keep on a wall in my office. Full disclosure, I'm also drawn to the former President as I served a good portion of my US Navy sea duty on CVN-71, a nuclear-powered aircraft carrier named USS

---

11   Brené Brown, *Dare to Lead: Brave Work, Tough Conversations, Whole Hearts* (New York, NY: Random House, 2018).

Theodore Roosevelt. Here is what he had to say about those who hold back because they are anxious about the prospect of making a mistake:

> "It is not the critic who counts; not the man who points out how the strong man stumbles, or where the doer of deeds could have done them better. The credit belongs to the man who is actually in the arena, whose face is marred by dust and sweat and blood; who strives valiantly; who errs, who comes short again and again, because there is no effort without error and shortcoming; but who does actually strive to do the deeds; who knows great enthusiasms, the great devotions; who spends himself in a worthy cause; who at the best knows in the end, the triumph of high achievement, and who at the worst, if he fails, at least fails while daring greatly, so that his place shall never be with those cold and timid souls who neither know victory nor defeat."

As a high-stakes leader, it's imperative that you try not to be fearful of the fact that you will make mistakes. Without question, you will make them. But crises are the times when your team, your organization, and your stakeholders need you to step up and lead. Embrace the fact that when you fail, you will fail daring greatly. With luck, your stakeholders will ultimately recognize the incredible courage that it takes to lead during a crisis.

Exercise #10
Developmental Opportunities for Self and Team

Part 3: Acknowledging Individual Vulnerability

High-stakes leaders must recognize, acknowledge, and deal with the reality that the decisions they make and the actions they take during a crisis won't always produce great results. This will make them feel vulnerable — as if they let people down or aren't performing well for stakeholders under the circumstances. Sadly, there is no way to avoid these realities or these feelings. They will appear for every leader during every crisis.

Knowing and accepting this, record a few ideas for things you can do, skills you can learn, or other actions you can take to help you develop your capacity for recognizing, acknowledging, and dealing with vulnerability during a crisis.

_____

_____

_____

_____

Leading Through the Harshest of Environments

The nature of the crisis environment is harsh. Moments of crisis present us with a concentrated microcosm of the turbulent, VUCA world we are all attempting to navigate while facing the unrelenting headwinds of a raging tsunami. Each crisis you experience will feel as though it has been custom-built to make all your leadership responsibilities as difficult and challenging as possible. You are reading this book because you know this to be true. But you also know that the capacity for effective crisis leadership is no longer an option for leaders in the 21st century — it's a requirement. In the chapters ahead, I will help you understand how the very best high-stakes leaders take on these critical responsibilities.

Throughout this chapter, we've explored how our increasingly complex business environment will always create a great deal of uncertainty about the origin, the nature, and the potential consequences of a developing crisis — uncertainty that will manifest itself in a constantly escalating sense of anxiety and fear for everyone involved. And as time passes, the weight of this growing sense of tension will intensify, putting increasingly greater pressure on leaders to find solutions and right the ship.

Amid these remarkably hostile conditions, high-stakes leaders will be called upon to lead — to make decisions about what to do and how to do it — all with limited, often very limited, information. This will be hard, and it will be uncomfortable. We'll have to fight the instinctive urge to delay decision-making until more data is available, until the picture is clearer, or until we can make choices with a great deal of certainty. We must push through because, unfortunately, during a crisis, time, clarity, and even facts are often luxuries that we simply won't have. Leadership is about making difficult choices — about making decisions. And these decisions may never be more important to an organization than when it is facing a crisis.

The crisis environment is the perfect storm of dangerous and overwhelming conditions. It's daunting and much of what we face is utterly out of our control. So we control what we *can* and we focus our efforts on the right things at the right time, embracing our vulnerability, and trusting the people around us. High-stakes leadership is not for the faint of heart. But we can and will prevail ... as long as we recognize the merciless conditions of the crisis environment, courageously put ourselves out there, and commit ourselves to the best possible path forward for all of our stakeholders. After all, if we don't, who will?

11

STEPPING UP
How to Be, Know, and Do the Right Things as a High-Stakes Leader

During a crisis, what is a crisis leader actually expected to *do*? What are they expected to *know*? What and how are they supposed to *be* in the eyes of their constituent stakeholders?

Yes, there is a great deal of literature out there on the topic of crisis leadership (including, now, this book!). Some of it is very good. Much of it, however, makes it hard to know why, or when, or how, to apply the author's recommendations. As we embark on the final chapters of this book, it's important to me that I offer practical, actionable, inspirational guidance to you so that when crisis strikes — even it if arrives tomorrow — you will be able to jump into action feeling more confident than you did prior to reading this book.

Eight Roles Crisis Leaders Should Be Able to Assume

In an article titled "Crisis Leadership: A View from the Executive Suite," author and researcher Tony Jaques shares the results of an extensive study of leadership responsibilities in a crisis environment. Drawn from surveys and interviews with CEOs and other C-suite executives, Jacques presents eight roles that crisis leaders must be ready to assume in order to be truly effective in their efforts to prevent, prepare for, and manage crises.

In the following paragraphs, you will learn a little about each of these roles. For our purposes, they will each be covered at cursory level, simply to give you a sense of the underlying purpose of each role. As you read about these eight crisis leadership roles, you should consider two questions for each: 1) What level of capability do I currently have in each of these areas? And 2) What level of capability currently exists in the members of my leadership team? I recognize that these will be challenging assessments to make, but use your best judgment.

Here is the full list of roles that crisis leaders must be willing and able to assume at their organization. As you read through this list, do any stick out as particularly challenging or in need of improvement at your organization?

1. Encourage a proactive crisis culture.

2. Establish and enforce standards and processes.

3. Prioritize and set an example.

4. Properly assess the full range of risks.

5. Promote open upward communication.

6. Build relationships before the crisis.

7. Be ready to deal with the news media.

8. Encourage a learning environment and share experience .

Let me share a little more detail on each of these eight leadership roles so you can see why they are vital for the development of organizational resilience and equally valuable to your high-stakes leadership efforts. Each role will be presented first as it is was shared by Jaques, followed by a few thoughts of my own.

- - - - - - - - - - - - - - - - - -

(1) Encourage a proactive crisis culture.

By default, most leaders focus primarily on the pressing day-to-day issues that must be managed to effectively lead the business. Crisis preparedness, as you might have guessed, is not one of these pressing or high-priority issues unless there's already a crisis underway. And that creates a cultural constraint. When the boss isn't crisis-focused, why should you be? In order for people at all levels of an organization to dedicate time and energy to crisis prevention and preparation, Jacques argues in his list of eight roles for crisis leaders, the organization's senior-most executives must be encouraging such prioritization (and even demonstrating a commitment to crisis readiness by putting it on their own agendas).

Two things come to my mind when I think about a proactive crisis culture. First, I am reminded of the challenge associated with an organization's ability to continuously scan the environment for early warning signs of trouble. When leaders throughout the organization have a proactive crisis culture, they are more likely to spot opportunities for improvement well before they get out of hand. My second thought is that our senior-most enterprise leaders must be prepared to fill all the critical crisis leadership roles during a major disruption. Now, they may not ultimately actually *play* all those roles, but they should be prepared and willing to do so.

- - - - - - - - - - - - - - - - - -

(2) Establish and enforce standards and processes.

Within that crisis-ready culture, Tony Jaques contends that senior leadership must be committed to the creation and enforcement of standards and processes in pursuit of exceptional risk management and crisis prevention. Senior leaders from safety-sensitive industries such as aviation and nuclear power require significant commitments to safe policies, procedures, and practices as core elements of their company's strategy. In other industries, commitments to this extent are rare.

To be truly well-prepared for the inevitable crisis that will impact your organization, high-stakes leaders must find a way to inspire a commitment to standards and processes that facilitate the identification of potential organizational threats and the actions necessary to address them.

To be truly well-prepared for the inevitable crisis that will
impact your organization, high-stakes leaders must find
a way to inspire a commitment to standards and processes
that facilitate the identification of potential organizational
threats and the actions necessary to address them.

---

(3) Prioritize and set an example.

High-stakes leaders, according to Jacques, must not only make sure that
crisis preparedness is an element of the company's culture (see item #1 on
this list), but they must also make sure that capability development and
process improvement are priority requirements. Crisis-preparedness
training programs and regular crisis-management process reviews are
neither exciting nor simple exercises to administer — but they must
take place to ensure the appropriate levels of organizational readiness.
Additionally, crisis preparedness cannot be a "do as I say, not as I do" situation. Senior enterprise leaders need to commit themselves to participation
in these exercises to underscore their importance.

As someone who has spent much of my professional career creating developmental opportunities for working professionals, I have a great deal of
experience trying to build programs in environments where the senior
leader or leadership team was not visibly supportive of the effort. I know
first-hand that if the senior leaders are not behind an initiative, it is almost
impossible to be successful. The same applies to crisis preparedness. The
C-suite must get behind this effort. If they aren't there yet, you need to find
a way to get them there. If they are, you need to help them ensure adequate
participation in crisis training from leaders across the enterprise.

---

(4) Properly assess the full range of risks.

The underlying objective in this role, according to Jacques, is ensuring that
organizations are scanning widely enough to identify risks that are beyond
the obvious. It is common for organizations to look internally for things
that could go wrong and produce some sort of crisis-level event. But crises

can come from external sources as well. The COVID-19 pandemic is a great example. While most companies had not given a single thought to the potential of a global pandemic and its impact on their business, exceptional high-stakes leaders were thinking about scenarios where a significant health issue, such as a particularly difficult flu season, could create a challenge for their enterprise. This is because they were assessing an appropriately broad range of potential organizational risks.

The work you have been doing in this book has been focused on helping leaders understand the many sources of organizational risk. One of our most valuable lessons has been that external risks can be most effectively detected and managed through exceptional stakeholder relationships. And crises that develop internally are best detected by whom? Internal stakeholders, of course. Given the right culture and clear expectations, your employees will absolutely — without hesitation — help you determine sources of potential crisis. I am certain of it.

- - - - - - - - - - - - - - - - - -

(5) Promote open upward communication.

Many organizations struggle to create the necessary culture to motivate employees throughout the enterprise to identify threats and opportunities for improvement and share these observations up the chain of command. High-stakes leaders must establish the expectation that crisis prevention begins with vigilance and continues with a willingness to call out threats as they are detected. We all know from our experiences in organizations that this is much more easily said than done. Many forces are at work that inhibit this sharing of information, which is why Jacques includes "open upward communication" in his list of the eight roles crisis leaders must play. The removal of these spoken and unspoken inhibitors is a key element of promoting open upward communication.

Your internal stakeholders, your employees, have remarkably sensitive threat radars. Make it clear to them that they *must* serve as your front-line crisis detection unit, and that you will do whatever it takes to create mechanisms for the safe and effective communication of warning signals to the senior leaders who can act on them. Let them know that you're counting on them.

----

(6) Build relationships before the crisis.

In his research, Jacques discovered many connections between the notion of strong relationships with stakeholders — particularly internal stakeholders (i.e., employees) — and open upward communication. And a key element of these relationships, according to his findings, is trust. Trust must be earned.

This should certainly come as no surprise. Our work together in this book has focused a great deal on the importance of relationships - inside and outside of the organization. Strong stakeholder relationships are quite possibly the most valuable tool high-stakes leaders can have in their crisis management toolkit.

----

(7) Be ready to deal with the news media.

High-stakes leaders must be prepared to engage their media stakeholders. The appearance of this item on a list of critical crisis leadership roles suggests to us not only that such a readiness is important, but also that it is not always done particularly well. There is no denying that your team will ultimately be facing a crisis situation, so being prepared to engage the media — in fact, being prepared to face your full complement of stakeholders *through* the media — will demonstrate that you are appropriately aware of and engaged in your situation.

According to Jacques' interviews with C-suite executives, there was universal agreement that readiness to face the media was a critical capability for crisis leaders. Many stories were shared about leaders who weren't ready to do so, and their lack of preparedness was clear. Given the time we have spent in this book exploring the importance of readiness to engage with the media group (as well as others, of course), you should be appropriately motivated to find ways to develop your skills in this area. Many companies offer media training, just for such occasions. If you have an opportunity to attend this sort of training, do so. I am certain that you will find the experience exceptionally beneficial.

- - - - - - - - - - - - - - - - -

(8) Encourage a learning environment and share experience.

It is imperative that employees learn from their experiences not only from crises, but also from near misses. Additionally, it is insufficient to learn strictly from personal experience. The most effective organizations can leverage mechanisms and culture to learn from the experiences of others. High-stakes leaders must ensure the availability of these mechanisms and the nurturing of the appropriate culture to enable experience sharing.

The third stage of the resilience process, as we have discussed in this book, is that of Adaptation — the ability to adapt to and learn from critical situations. Our definition of this resilience stage includes having mechanisms to reflect and learn from the opportunities presented by crises and near misses, and to incorporate these lessons into organizational processes and procedures through formal change initiatives. In all these endeavors, shared experiences and insights are incredibly valuable.[1]

The Eight Roles and Their Validity During the COVID-19 Pandemic

Perhaps as you were reading through these eight leadership roles, you wondered how they might apply to the COVID-19 crisis. If you're anything like me, while you like to understand theory and research, you would much rather understand how to put concepts into practice. So, here are a few comments on how each of these leadership roles became practically valuable during the COVID-19 pandemic.

(1) Encourage a proactive crisis culture. The most important benefit of a proactive crisis culture is that it helps organizations overcome the "it can't happen to us" syndrome. An enterprise with a proactive crisis culture also makes sure that the urgent does not always get in the way of the important. Daily, there always seem to be more urgent things to do than "worry about safety" or "set aside some time to talk about what happens if this COVID virus has an impact on our business." I know finding time to

---

1   Tony Jaques, "Crisis Leadership: A View from the Executive Suite," *Journal of Public Affairs*, 12, no. 4 (2012): doi:10.1002/pa.1422.

focus on the important (e.g., crisis preparedness and strategy) and not the urgent (e.g., the ringing phones, the bills to pay, the meetings scheduled for today) is very difficult. The business practices that have become the norm at most organizations don't provide much time for anything but the urgent; we're all over-scheduled business "firefighters." Perhaps it is unfair to look in the rearview mirror and suggest that we should have done more to prepare for the pandemic, but I will still make the argument that organizations with proactive crisis cultures tend to be better at letting the evidence drive their decision-making, as opposed to their instincts, and finding a better balance between focusing entirely on the urgent and focusing on the important. And all we have to do is look around us to see examples of companies that have weathered the pandemic better than others — because they had the right culture in place.

(2) Establish and enforce standards and processes. As I mentioned previously, in safety- and security-critical industries, there tend to be strict standards and processes that have been designed to keep stakeholders safe. Organizations focused on safety and security spend more time preparing for crises. They are better prepared to scan their environments for signs of trouble. Organizations not as focused on safety and security tend not to be so focused on these processes. Irrespective of the extent to which your organization focuses on these things, the COVID-19 pandemic has taught us how important it is to have established standards and protocols for things like remote work, virtual meetings, collaboration technology, employee health and wellness, and "curbside service" for customers should our facilities become inaccessible. The very best organizations are able to find the resources and support necessary to prepare their organizations for a crisis. We now have a greater appreciation for the importance of these preparations.

(3) Prioritize and set an example. In my mind, some of the most beneficial takeaways from the COVID-19 pandemic are the lessons we learned by watching the behaviors of our leaders. Many of these leaders — in businesses and communities alike — set incredible examples. Perhaps you have seen or worked with people who were at their very best when the pandemic delivered its toughest blows. These leaders demonstrated care and compassion for everyone around them. They understood the decisions that had to be made for the short-, mid-, and long-term health and welfare of their people, as well as for the success of their organizations. They never claimed

to have all the answers and they didn't pretend to be perfect. But they did rely on data, evidence, and the experts who had valuable experience and expertise to offer. These leaders knew how to set an example.

(4) Properly assess the full range of risks. The COVID-19 pandemic illustrated how difficult it can be to understand the full spectrum of organizational risks. The nature of the crisis environment makes it incredibly challenging for any leader to gather all the information necessary to create a clear picture of all potential threats. So, in these situations, where an unforeseen risk has appeared on the short-range radar, exceptional high-stakes leaders find a means to explore and process the full extent of possible exposure. For most organizations, this means starting with the senior leadership team — pulling them together, and taking an inventory of how everyone is feeling, what they are thinking about the situation, and how everyone around the table believes the enterprise should proceed. When a situation like the COVID-19 pandemic presents a problem that has been previously given very little (if any) thought, this is where senior management as a whole needs to step up as a team. No single leader will have all the answers. In fact, it is quite possible that none of the leaders will have *any* of the answers. To fully assess the range of risks in a situation such as this, the leadership team needs to come together to determine what they know (and don't know), and to develop a plan for getting the information they need so they can effectively navigate the crisis.

(5) Promote open, upward communication. Your internal stakeholders, your employees, have remarkably sensitive threat radars. Make it clear to them that they *must* serve as your front-line crisis detection unit, and that you will do whatever it takes to create mechanisms for the safe and effective communication of warning signals to the senior leaders who can act on them. Also, once an enterprise finds itself in a crisis, such open, upward communication is critical to staying in touch with the status of the workforce. Be asking: "How is everyone doing? What needs to be resolved? How is our crisis response plan working?" The relationship between senior leadership and the organization's front line, with as much free-flowing communication as possible, will never be more important than it is during a crisis. Did your senior leadership team seek out your thoughts on these questions during the pandemic? Would you have been willing to share them if given the opportunity? Did you create a space for those on your team to do the

same? Our collective experience with COVID-19 has put a fine point on the importance of these practices.

Your internal stakeholders, your employees, have remarkably sensitive threat radars. Make it clear to them that they *must* serve as your front-line crisis detection unit, and that you will do whatever it takes to create mechanisms for the safe and effective communication of warning signals to the senior leaders who can act on them.

---

(6) Build relationships before the crisis. Once again, a pandemic is one of many crisis types that highlight the critical importance of strong relationships with stakeholders. As a stakeholder yourself, what relationship did you have with your leader (i.e., your boss) before the crisis? How did this relationship inform your interactions with this person throughout the pandemic? If you could turn back the clock to a time before the pandemic, what would you do differently in your relationship with your immediate supervisor? What would you do differently with the members of your team? In both cases, while we cannot turn back the clock, we can always make the effort to implement some changes going forward.

(7) Be ready to deal with the news media. While you may not interact directly with the media in the normal course of your job, consider how many "regular citizens" — not just government officials or business leaders — appeared on camera during a news cast for commentary on the pandemic. If you found yourself with a camera and a microphone in front of your face, what would you say about your company? Your team? The efforts underway to help your stakeholders navigate this tragic crisis? Your readiness to answer these questions is what this leadership role is all about.

(8) Encourage a learning environment and share experience. You have experienced the COVID-19 pandemic first-hand. I hope that you were spared the loss of a loved one, serious illness, or some other particularly difficult outcome. Sadly, millions were not spared. But as we began to emerge from this crisis and were able to look back upon all that transpired, what did we learn? What changes did we make? What did we do to make sure the next pandemic (or, for that matter, the next crisis) is better managed

— better led? If we don't learn from this experience and apply what we have learned in a deliberate way, we may be forced to repeat it. I, for one, hope never to endure something like the COVID-19 pandemic ever again.[2]

Crisis Leadership Through a "Be, Know, Do" Lens

We live and work in a world that is becoming more complex and volatile every day. There are greater levels of ambiguity in the information we receive and uncertainty behind the decisions we must make. The COVID-19 pandemic provided us with a tangible and, for many, frightening illustration of this reality. As the viral outbreak has undoubtedly had an impact on you and your family, you have likely paid a great deal of attention to how those around you have demonstrated — or have not demonstrated — effective leadership. What have you learned? Almost certainly, you have concluded that rarely has the need for exceptional leadership been so clear or so important. What should you expect from leaders in a crisis? As a crisis leader, what should your stakeholders — your families, your businesses, your employees, your communities, etc. — expect from you? A growing body of research offers some answers to these questions.

What do those looking for leadership want to see in a crisis leader? The United States Army has long used a framework known as "BE, KNOW, DO" to train and inspire its leaders. I believe the framework provides a practical structure for outlining the expectations of high-stakes leaders in the civilian world as well — and I am not alone. Other researchers and leadership experts have found this framework to be particularly useful as well. My experiences in the field — and in hundreds of classroom sessions with global executives who shared their crisis lessons with my students — suggest that crisis leaders should have a solid framework for what to *be*, what they need to *know*, and what they should *do* during a crisis. I will first provide a very brief overview of each element I've included in my "BE, KNOW, DO" framework. Then, throughout the rest of this chapter, I will provide much greater detail for each, making it easier for you to understand not only what's behind each element, but how to apply what you are learning.

---

2   Tony Jaques, "Crisis Leadership: A View from the Executive Suite," *Journal of Public Affairs*, 12, no. 4 (2012): doi:10.1002/pa.1422.

- - - - - - - - - - - - - - - - -

BE.

If you were asked to describe what a crisis leader should *be* during a crisis — in other words, if you had to describe the characteristics that you would like that leader to demonstrate in the midst of a crisis — what would you say? Think about that for a moment.

From your COVID-19 experience, what should a leader *be* to instill confidence and deserve the trust of stakeholders? From my experience and the many executives who have shared lessons from their own high-stakes leadership performances, the most effective crisis leaders are:

1. *Visible.* Stakeholders want to see leaders, in front of their teams, leading the response.

2. *Caring.* The most effective crisis leaders will demonstrate a great sense of care and concern for all stakeholders.

3. *Empathetic.* Not only must crisis leaders care for their stakeholders, they must also recognize that some have lost (or will lose) a great deal as a result of the catastrophe. Their loss deserves acknowledgment and empathy.

4. *Calm.* Stress and fear produce anxiety in stakeholders. The most effective crisis leaders can remain calm, think clearly, and, through their composure, help reduce stress and fear in others.

5. *Assertive.* Not only do stakeholders want to be able to see their crisis leaders, but they want to see them doing something, to be asserting themselves and working toward a solution to the crisis.

- - - - - - - - - - - - - - - - -

KNOW.

What do you want your crisis leaders to clearly understand — to *know* — to support your organization and its stakeholders during a crisis? Consistent with my own experience, dozens of my executive colleagues have expressed the importance of understanding with crystal clarity three foundational instruments for leading effectively during a crisis:

1. ***Organizational Vision.*** To be truly effective, crisis leaders should know the organization's mission and vision, be able to articulate them, and be able to align their crisis leadership efforts to the overarching mission and vision. A portion of every stakeholder's value proposition is attached to their belief in what an organization is trying to accomplish. Incorporating the organization's vision and mission into a crisis response will resonate with stakeholders.

2. ***Organizational Values.*** If an organization's vision describes *what* it is trying to accomplish, then its values describe *the way* it plans to get there. A great deal of research has been done on the extent to which employees aspire to work for a company that shares their values. New research indicates that other stakeholder groups — particularly customers — want values alignment as well. In a crisis, stakeholders will be looking for an organization to "walk the talk." This is best demonstrated through values-driven leadership.

If an organization's vision describes *what* it is trying to accomplish, then its values describe *the way* it plans to get there.

---

3. ***Guiding Principles.*** Crisis leaders will be required to make an incredible number of decisions with limited information. Many of these decisions will prove to be less than perfect over time, as new information becomes available. This is not typically a product of poor decision-making, but rather a function of the crisis environment. What can be done to improve this seemingly impossible situation for crisis leaders? We can help stakeholders understand how and why decisions are being made. The most effective crisis leaders create and share a set of guiding principles that can be used in the decision-making process. Examples of guiding principles include: *We will value, protect, and support our people. We will deliver on the vision and mission of our organization. We will communicate effectively and thoughtfully with our stakeholders throughout this crisis.* Principles such as these can help stakeholders understand *how* decisions will be made so they are less likely to judge them *after* they have been made.

DO.

What should crisis leaders be *do*ing during a crisis? Once again, from my personal experience and that of the many executives who have shared their own battle-tested lessons with my students, four primary tangible and courageous actions are core to effective crisis leadership.

1. *Communicate.* We know that stakeholders are anxious during a crisis because their value propositions are being threatened. Given these concerns, what do these stakeholders want and need? They need information so they can deal with their fear. They need clear, compelling, consistent, and reliable communication. As a crisis leader, you should establish a communication plan, inform stakeholders of your plan, and become their primary source of learning about your intentions, your actions, and the facts as they become available.

2. *Make Decisions with Limited Information.* A primary responsibility of every leader is decision-making. Unfortunately, during a crisis, leaders will be required to make urgent decisions with limited information. Therefore, guiding principles become very important. But these principles will not resolve the fact that decisions made by crisis leaders will typically produce as many poor outcomes as good ones. Exceptional crisis leaders embrace the reality that decisions made early in a crisis may have to be modified or even reversed as more is learned about the situation. This reality will make decision-making uncomfortable, but the alternative of not making decisions until all the facts are in and the choices are clear will almost certainly produce disastrous results.

Exceptional crisis leaders embrace the reality that decisions
made early in a crisis may have to be modified or even
reversed as more is learned about the situation.

----

3. *Take Responsibility.* Stakeholders want to know who is taking responsibility for leading the crisis response and resolution efforts. Once the enterprise has determined the person or team taking charge, it should be made clear to everyone involved. Stakeholders will also want to

understand what led to the crisis and who was ultimately at fault. As humans, we are wired to be extraordinarily curious about causation and the assignment of blame. When it is clear that the organization or a member of the organization is at fault in a crisis, the most effective crisis leaders communicate this reality to their stakeholders at the earliest opportunity.

4. *Engage Stakeholders.* As you know, stakeholder engagement may be the most valuable and important action a crisis leader can take. For a given crisis, exceptional crisis leaders take the time to determine how all stakeholder groups have been, or will be, impacted and will then engage each of them in a way that helps those stakeholders understand that organizational leaders care, that they empathize, that they are taking ownership of finding a resolution, and that they are committed to creating a stronger organization going forward as a result of what they have learned through this crisis.

During a crisis, stakeholders will be looking for tangible evidence of leadership. They will want and need leaders who they can believe in — leaders who understand and appreciate their perspective. They will not expect crisis leaders to be perfect or omniscient, but they will expect them to be visible, courageous, and committed to the best possible path forward. Are you doing all that you can to be ready for your next crisis? Your organization and your stakeholders will be depending on you.

What Stakeholders Need a Crisis Leader to BE

Now that you have a general sense of the "BE, KNOW, DO" framework, let's take a slightly deeper dive into each of the elements. We'll begin with BE. What should a leader *be* to instill confidence and deserve the trust of stakeholders?

Be Visible. During a crisis, the value propositions of organizational stakeholders are being threatened. This, of course, creates a great deal of concern for individual members of your stakeholder groups. Throughout the span of a crisis event, these stakeholders will be anxiously awaiting whatever information they can get to help them understand the extent of the threat, the outcome they should expect, and the amount of time they are going to have to wait before the threat has been eliminated and losses can be calculated. This is not new information, as you learned about this earlier in the book.

Only slightly less concerning to stakeholders than the anxiety created by the threat to their value propositions is a fear that the threat — and the potential damage that it may bring — has not attracted the attention of organizational leaders. When stakeholders feel threatened by something beyond their control, they will want to know that the threat is being addressed by someone or some team that should, from their perspective, have some degree of control — at least much more than they have. Not surprisingly, these stakeholders become hyper-sensitive to the appearance of an authority figure who demonstrates a clear awareness of the situation's gravity and seems, to an adequate extent (in a purely subjective sense), committed to resolving the issue with minimum impact on their value proposition.

Think about the last time you were impacted by a particularly troubling disruption of some sort that caused you a bit of anxiety. Perhaps you have been the unfortunate victim of a delayed flight that just keeps being delayed further, but no communication is taking place. Maybe you have even seen the poor customer service agents at the gate being tormented by angry customers — even though the customers understand that these agents probably don't have much better information than they do. If this was your situation, what did you want from airline leadership? Sure, you wanted the problem fixed. But in the process of getting it fixed, what did you want? You wanted to SEE someone in leadership. You wanted them to be visible. You wanted to be able to confirm that a company leader was aware of the situation and at least appeared to be working on your behalf to solve the problem.

What do you suppose the gate agents wanted to see? Yes, they wanted to see the problem fixed as well. But they also wanted their leader to be supportive of them. They wanted their leader to be visible — to come see the ugly position that the company put them in — and the gate agents want to see that their leaders are willing to roll up their *own* sleeves and help. This is what it means to be visible during a crisis.

Be Caring. Stakeholders want to know that organizational leaders are aware of the threat to their value propositions and that they are also committed to eliminating the threat as quickly as possible. In one sense, stakeholders don't really care why they are committed to resolving the threat or what they have to do to resolve it. "Just make it go away," some might think. But as this is a book that has continued to emphasize the value of stakeholder relationships, how *should* high-stakes leaders want their stakeholders to feel about the way they are approaching a resolution of the crisis? Leaders should want their stakeholders to know that they are committed to resolving the crisis because it is in the best interests of its stakeholders. In other words, high-stakes leaders should want their stakeholders to know that they genuinely care about making things right — that they genuinely care for them and recognize the stress and anxiety that has resulted, for the moment, at least, from the relationship. The most effective high-stakes leaders are able to communicate, through their words and their deeds, that they recognize the emotion the situation has produced and that, because they truly care about their stakeholders, they are committed to resolving the issue as quickly and painlessly as possible.

The most effective high-stakes leaders are able to communicate, through their words and their deeds, that they recognize the emotion the situation has produced and that, because they truly care about their stakeholders, they are committed to resolving the issue as quickly and painlessly as possible.

Be Empathetic. In similar fashion to the previous description of demonstrating care for stakeholders, high-stakes leaders must demonstrate empathy to their stakeholders as well. How is this different from caring? Caring for stakeholders means recognizing the unique interests of each and making a commitment that feels personal to resolving any value proposition threats that materialize. Being empathetic to stakeholders means recognizing and acknowledging that the threat has already resulted in, or is likely to result in, a meaningful loss. Perhaps this loss is monetary. Perhaps it is loss of life or limb. Regardless of the specifics, high-stakes leaders must find a way to demonstrate empathy. Ideally, the expressed empathy is genuinely felt and naturally shared. It should simply feel like the right thing to do. Perhaps, however, the empathy is symbolic. No value judgments here, as there are actually situations where it is appropriate to symbolically express empathy. When people suffer a loss, it is simply good form to do so. In either case, if you hope to fully regain the trust and loyalty of any stakeholder that has or will suffer a significant loss as a result of a crisis, an expression of empathy will go a long way to demonstrating that the relationship is truly important to you.

Sometimes what gets in the way of an expression of empathy is the notion that demonstrating such an expression somehow suggests guilt or an admission of responsibility. It does not. Do not let this worry stop you. When a stakeholder suffers a loss, *always* be empathetic. If you are, you will find these stakeholders to be much more understanding after the fact, and that their levels of moral outrage will be reduced, perhaps dramatically.

> Sometimes what gets in the way of an expression of
> empathy is the notion that demonstrating such an
> expression somehow suggests guilt or an admission of
> responsibility. It does not. Do not let this worry stop you.
> When a stakeholder suffers a loss, *always* be empathetic.

Be Calm. There are a number of reasons to stay calm during a crisis. Two that are particularly important for our purposes here are: 1) staying calm demonstrates to stakeholders that you are in control of yourself, and in so doing, you suggest that you are better prepared to take control of the situation; and 2) staying calm does actually allow you to more effectively think, process information, and make better decisions.

During a crisis, your stakeholders are going to be anxious. As we've established, stakeholders will be looking for tangible evidence of leadership, for leaders who they can trust, and who they can believe in. What characteristics are you looking for when searching for someone who *you* can believe in? If you're like most people, you want to see a leader who is calm, who appears confident, and who seems totally focused on helping everyone around them feel less stressed and less anxious. The importance of this should not be minimized. When stakeholders see a calm high-stakes leader, they will be much more likely to trust that progress is being made toward resolving the issue and restoring their confidence.

There is a great deal of science behind the detrimental effects of allowing a situation to produce a state of distress — a condition in which mental and physical performance is reduced — sometimes to the degree that a person is literally unable to perform anything other than basic life support functions. There has also been a great deal of recent science dedicated to the condition of what is called "eustress." This is a state of heightened alertness, mental and physiological performance, and energy. During a crisis, there will always be sufficient stimuli to reach a state of eustress. The key is to not allow those stimuli to overwhelm you to the point of distress. A good habit when exposed to the kind of environment typical of a crisis is to remember that you can only control those things in your personal power. This will not remove stimuli from your immediate vicinity, but it will allow you to regain a sense of control over how you respond to those stimuli.[3]

Stress is not necessarily a bad thing. A little stress can actually help you perform better. Just remember that too much stress will inhibit your performance. Preparation, a good plan, and a strong supporting team will do wonders for helping high-stakes leaders stay calm during a crisis.

Preparation, a good plan, and a strong supporting team will do wonders for helping high-stakes leaders stay calm during a crisis.

Be Assertive. Assertiveness is a characteristic that deserves an explanation. At first thought, it may not be clear why assertiveness is so important and why stakeholders will be looking for it. But it is a very important trait that high-stakes leaders will want to demonstrate during a crisis.

Assertiveness is a characteristic that falls between the extremes of passiveness and aggressiveness. It demonstrates a balance between being overly passive (and giving the impression to stakeholders that you are submissive or not in control), on one end of the spectrum, and being overly aggressive (and being perceived as hostile), on the other. Assertiveness is the ability to demonstrate a healthy confidence in knowing the right things to do — to stand up for one's self in the face of adversity. Assertive leaders are direct

---

3   "Eustress," Wikipedia, June 26, 2020, accessed July 14, 2020, https://en.wikipedia.org/wiki/Eustress.

and honest. They make it clear what they want and need from others to ensure the necessary actions are taken in a given situation.

Assertive leaders don't expect others to read their minds. When they want or need something, they say so. When they disagree with someone or something, they speak up. Assertive leaders stay calm and they typically demonstrate body language that is consistent with the messages they are delivering with their voices. Assertive leaders maintain eye contact; they confidently lean in to their conversations; and they speak simply and directly. These are the attributes of an assertive leader — and they are what stakeholders are looking for in their crisis leaders.

Assertive leaders don't expect others to read their minds. When they want or need something, they say so. When they disagree with someone or something, they speak up.

Visible, caring, empathetic, calm, and assertive. These are the five observable characteristics that stakeholders want their leaders to *be* during a crisis. How effectively do you demonstrate these attributes and what can you do to improve in each and every one of them?

What Stakeholders Need a Crisis Leader to KNOW

I suggested earlier that there are at least three things that stakeholders need their crisis leaders to KNOW during a crisis: 1) the organizational vision, 2) organizational values, and 3) a set of guiding principles that will inform the decision-making process. As a high-stakes leader, how are you supposed to think about these responsibilities and why will they become so important during a crisis? Here are a few thoughts to help you understand the benefits of having a very clear sense of your organization's vision, values, and a set of guiding principles to help you make decisions during a crisis.

Knowing the Organizational Vision. If you have studied the recent literature on guiding frameworks for organizations, you have almost certainly come across descriptions of vision statements, mission statements, purpose statements, and other instruments for communicating to stakeholders what the company is trying to achieve, why it exists, and what purpose it is trying to serve. For our purposes here, we are not going to conduct a deep dive into the differences between these statements or what they are trying to accomplish. In fact, if you conducted your own research in these areas, you would find that experts often disagree upon which statement serves what purpose. Here, it doesn't really matter.

What does matter is that your organization was created for some collection of reasons. It is likely that your executive team has crafted descriptions of these reasons. Whatever they are called, they serve to communicate to stakeholders what members of your organization believe they are trying to accomplish, what principles the company has organized around, how decisions will be made, what employees believe to be true, and what employees of the organization value. All of these, if you think about them, actually define some very important qualities of an enterprise. Do you know how your company leaders would respond to these questions if asked? Would all their answers, if given independently, be consistent? Have specific statements for each of these questions been crafted by company leaders? Have they been shared with employees? Have they been conveyed to other stakeholders? These are all useful questions and they are worth any time and effort that a leadership team could give to them — not only because the answers will become important during a crisis, but because they will always be important to enterprise stakeholders.

Why might clarity on organizational vision be important to high-stakes leaders? Because if the leadership team has taken the time to articulate why the enterprise exists and what it is trying to accomplish, then stakeholders will receive these articulations as promises in terms of what they should expect from the company. You learned earlier that JetBlue's vision statement is: "Bringing Humanity Back to Air Travel." This is a very simple but powerful statement. It was widely shared and embraced by JetBlue crewmembers. It was also shared with customers who, in the best of times, loved the edgy promise of JetBlue being better than its competitors. In the worst of times, however, such as during the Valentine's Day Operational Crisis, the vision statement became the punchline of a very bad joke: "Stranding customers on an airplane for eight hours? Where's the humanity in that?"

During a crisis, a high-stakes leader's efforts must align with both the word and the spirit (i.e., intent) of the promises that the company has previously made, or implied, to stakeholders — the brand promises, vision or mission statements, or even company or product taglines. If the words and actions of leadership do *not* align with those promises, not only will stakeholders hold it against the company, but they will also lose confidence in the organization's ability to live up to its promises and commitments in the future. If the ultimate success of a company can be measured in the value it creates for its stakeholders, then trust capital and stakeholder confidence are key results indicators. Misalignment between stated vision and demonstrated vision will not serve high-stakes leaders well in the eyes of stakeholders during a crisis.

> During a crisis, a high-stakes leader's efforts must align with both the word and the spirit (i.e., intent) of the promises that the company has previously made, or implied, to stakeholders.

Knowing the Organizational Values. What are organizational values? They are a collection of beliefs that define a company's identity. They support the company vision, shape the culture of the organization, and reflect the principles that every member of the company holds dear.

Ann Rhoades, a co-founder of JetBlue, author, and world-renowned expert on corporate culture, shared the following in her book *Built on Values: Creating an Enviable Culture That Outperforms the Competition:*

> "*Leaders drive values* by making the commitment to a values-based culture and leading by example. *Values drive behaviors* by acting as a mechanism for illustrating to employees (and all other enterprise stakeholders) what acceptable behavior in the company looks like. Values must be defined by behaviors that any employee can recognize and emulate. *Behaviors drive culture* because the collective behaviors of people in the organization are, by definition, the culture, for good or ill. Leaders must create the environment that encourages a high-performance culture based on values. *Culture drives performance* because people who are

committed to and understand the values and behaviors will take responsibility for performance."[4]

The research suggests that a clear set of organizational values can be immensely helpful in two ways that are worth calling out here (there are many more ways, but these two are particularly germane to our discourse). First, a clear understanding of values will help employees make better decisions over time. As values are aligned with company goals, and behaviors are the manifestations of the actions required to achieve those goals, employees who make decisions in line with organizational values are ultimately helping the company achieve its goals. In other words, when employees live and demonstrate the values of the enterprise, their choices, over time, will help to move the company forward. This is particularly important during a crisis, when decision-making is difficult, and there is rarely a clear path to "the best right answers." In a crisis, employees need a north star, something that serves as a guide for their choices. Here, the values of an organization meet this requirement remarkably well.

The second reason why organizational values are so important is that they communicate to your stakeholders what the organization stands for — a window into the company's soul, if you will. When a company can build relationships with stakeholders based on common beliefs and principles, a much deeper sense of connection and trust will develop. This trust will serve as a platform for a high-stakes leader's crisis-management efforts. On several occasions throughout this book, trust has been referenced as a very fragile connection between stakeholders and organizational leaders. During a crisis, whatever level of trust has been established is threatened. Greater levels of pre-crisis trust with stakeholders will provide a deeper well of resources that can be drawn upon while a crisis is being managed — either providing high-stakes leaders more time to work out the problem or accelerating the restoration of trust after a crisis.

---

4   Ann Rhoades and Nancy Shepherdson, *Built on Values: Creating an Enviable Culture That Outperforms the Competition* (San Francisco: Jossey-Bass, 2011).

Organizational values are a window into the company's soul.
When a company can build relationships with stakeholders
based on common beliefs and principles, a much deeper
sense of connection and trust will develop.

For these two reasons in particular, it is very important that an organization establishes and communicates a set of values to all stakeholders and incorporates them into every aspect of organizational activity. Once this has been done, high-stakes leaders must know these values cold and then align every decision they make with them to fully leverage their incredible potential.

Knowing the Guiding Principles. A clear understanding of the organization's vision and values is crucial for high-stakes leaders. Vision and values provide a platform upon which decisions can be made and actions can be taken. What they do not provide, however, is a mechanism for setting priorities or clarifying specific critical objectives for a given high-stakes scenario. This is where guiding principles become so important.

In Bruce Blythe's book *Blindsided: A Manager's Guide to Crisis Leadership*, the author describes guiding principles as "a crisis leadership roadmap throughout the organization for strategic crisis decision-making." Blythe describes a starting point for a set of guiding principles that could be adapted to benefit any organization during a crisis:

1. Wellbeing of people first, with caring and compassion.

2. Assume appropriate responsibility for managing the crisis.

3. Address needs and concerns of all stakeholders in a timely manner.

4. All decisions and actions based on honesty, legal guidelines, and ethical principles.

5. Available, visible, and open communication with all impacted parties.[5]

---

5   Bruce T. Blythe and Kristen Noakes-Fry, *Blindsided: A Managers Guide to Crisis Leadership* (Brookfield, CT: Rothstein Pub., 2014).

Bonus Materials and Tools You Can Use!

Check out **www.IISLResources.com** to get your hands on some real-world materials that you can learn from and emulate. Bonus materials for readers include:

- The guiding principles used by the University of Michigan to guide its COVID-19 crisis decision-making
- The story behind how JetBlue Airways developed its corporate values, and how those values drove everyday decision-making and crisis management
- The case of a sub-organization (the Ross School of Business) realizing that its guiding principles for crisis might need to be different from, though aligned with, the parent organization's (University of Michigan's) guiding principles
- And much more!

If your organization does not have a set of guiding principles for crisis decision-making, this is a good place to start. You can see in this example how a company's vision and values could help frame the way decisions are made by a high-stakes leader during crisis, but that a set of principles, such as these, is necessary to define priorities and key actions that are required of leaders *during this specific situation*. This is why a set of principles, such as those shared here, are just a starting point. For each crisis situation, the principles must be modified to accurately fit the disruption at hand.

During a crisis, high-stakes leaders must KNOW their organization's vision and mission, live by its values, and have a set of guiding principles at the ready to support decision-making. When a crisis appears at your organization, will you be able to leverage the work that has been done to develop and communicate the company's vision and values? Do you have a "starter set" of guiding principles ready to tailor for the unique circumstances of the crisis at hand? To each of these questions, your answer should be a resounding "Yes!" If your answer is "no" or "I'm not sure," I would say that you have identified an opportunity for improvement.

What Crisis Leaders Must DO

Let's consider what high-stakes leaders must DO during a crisis. While there are literally hundreds of books and thousands of articles, both scholarly and practitioner, that provide recommendations to crisis leaders for optimum behaviors and actions during a crisis, I have found these four key elements offer a great foundation for your own development as a high-stakes leader.

Crisis leaders must:

- Communicate
- Make decisions with limited information
- Take responsibility
- Engage stakeholders

Let's take a brief look at each one of these actions. But before we do, let me take a moment to address a question that may have come to your mind regarding what crisis leaders must DO during a crisis.

You may be thinking, "Hey Mike. There's a lot more for a crisis leader to do during a crisis than communicate and engage stakeholders. Where are all of your recommendations for things like assembling the leadership team; activating the crisis response plan; resolving the cause of the disruption; building and executing a recovery plan; and things like that?" I have two responses for you.

First, in the next and final chapter of this book, I will provide several recommendations for preparing your team and your organization to accomplish all these things. As you will see — and as the list above implies — there will be an extensive list of issues to consider, decisions to make, actions to take, and people to care for during a crisis. As a high-stakes leader, you're simply going to have to work through these challenges as the situation requires. I'll help you with a framework, but the details will be up to you to provide. Second, the recommendations I am sharing here are framed as they are to underscore the critical importance of engaging stakeholders every step of the way — to leverage the potential contributions of stakeholders as you grapple with and recover from the crisis (and as you seek to retain and regain as much trust as possible). I'm not giving you an all-inclusive list of things that must be done by high-stakes leaders in the midst of a crisis because, frankly, the list will be massive and it will be different for every situation. Rather, I'm providing a short list of key responsibilities that crisis leaders consistently fail to execute during a crisis. I believe that a vital ingredient missing from most high-stakes leaders' approach to crisis management is their commitment to stakeholders. Therefore, I've focused my list of recommendations accordingly. Now, let's get back to the four things high-stakes leaders must DO during a crisis.

Communication. First, crisis leaders must do what they can to ensure effective communication throughout the course of events. Ideally these leaders are great communicators as well, but we have all seen great leadership from those who may not be the best or most compelling public speakers. During a crisis, stakeholders are anxious and they need clear, compelling, consistent, and reliable communication. In fact, given what we know about the nature of the crisis environment and the different media, modes, and frequencies of communication that are necessary during a crisis situation, in many ways it does not matter that any particular individual on the leadership team is a spectacular individual communicator or speaker. This is normally a core competence of a senior leader but, in a crisis, communication is not about individual communication skills — it's about effective communication between the organization and its stakeholders.

That said, every high-stakes leader must be able to assemble the necessary resources and then communicate effectively with stakeholders. As we know from our understanding of stakeholder value propositions, our communications must do what they can to address the:

- Anxiety of stakeholders
- Nature of the threat to their value propositions
- Plan to resolve the threat
- Expectations that stakeholders will need to recover lost value and lost faith in the organization.

Beyond this, communications should include the appropriate care and empathy, and they should be distributed through the preferred channels of the different stakeholder groups.

Communications should include the appropriate care
and empathy, and they should be distributed through the
preferred channels of the different stakeholder groups.

One soundbite about communication that has always stuck with me because it was constantly reiterated by my brother Dave, who was a fellow co-founder, President, and eventually CEO of JetBlue Airways, was this: "When you are absolutely certain that you have communicated enough, triple the effort, because you're only a third of the way there." I have always loved that quote — mostly because I have yet to see the practical reality of this statement be disproven. During a crisis, high-stakes leaders shouldn't only do their best to communicate with stakeholders, they should assume that whatever communication efforts they have planned and executed will probably be less than what stakeholders had expected or hoped for. I'm not going to tell you to "over-communicate," which has been widely overused. I am, however, going to suggest that whatever you do, your stakeholders probably won't think it was enough — a practical reality worth keeping in mind.

Making Decisions With Limited Information. A crisis leader is also going to have to make decisions with limited information — with less certainty and less confidence than they would like. It's not hard to see why this is the case — it's simply a function of the crisis environment. In a crisis, new information is always coming in. Leaders are constantly learning more about the situation. So, as this new information contributes to new insights, new and different decisions will have to be made.

I will offer what I believe are two universal truths about decision-making during a crisis:

1. **To have any chance of making progress toward a resolution, crisis leaders are going to have to make decisions that they are uncomfortable making.** This discomfort will largely be a function of

limited information and the lack of clarity regarding what has already happened, what is happening now, and what is going to happen in the future. There is simply so much going on during a crisis that it will be nearly impossible to have a crystal-clear picture of everything that has taken place prior to a given moment and what is going on right this second. The best leaders have a sense of these things, but nobody will have perfect clarity. Ever. So don't expect that you will have it either. Nonetheless, even without the clarity we would all love to have, decisions are going to have to be made.

2. Universal truth number two is that **most of these decisions will need to be reversed or modified as new insights are learned**. This is not going to be comfortable either, and it may appear to threaten the credibility of the leader who made the decisions in the first place. How does a leader deal with this tension? You should be as transparent as you can with what you know, when you know it, and your understanding of the situation at the time of the decisions. If decisions must be made early in a crisis, make it clear that there is much yet to be learned. When decisions need to be modified, be transparent about course corrections and share some detail about what has been learned to warrant the change. It's not rocket science, but it's also not natural for most leaders to speak and make decisions about situations where so little is known. It's a skill that high-stakes leaders must develop to be effective in their crisis leadership roles.

Take Responsibility and Engage Stakeholders. The final two things that a crisis leader must be prepared to DO are take responsibility and engage stakeholders. I won't expand on the notion of engaging stakeholders because I have covered this topic in great detail throughout this book. I'll simply summarize by saying: Engage your stakeholders throughout the crisis. Help them understand that you care, that you are empathetic to their situation, and that you are doing everything that you can to keep them apprised of progress toward the best possible solution.

In terms of responsibility, I will say this. A course on high-stakes leadership has been taught at University of Michigan's Ross School of Business for more than 40 years. A core element of the course all along has been the weekly inclusion of executive guests, most of them chief executive officers. At some point in every class session, the question is asked of the visiting executive,

"What is one thing that you would have done differently during a crisis that you wish you could go back and do over, if given the chance?" In almost every case, the answer has been something along the lines of: "I wish that we would have taken responsibility earlier."

There will be great pressure put on crisis leaders to avoid taking responsibility and exposing the company to liability — particularly if there is not absolute clarity regarding who was actually at fault. I am not suggesting that you should ever admit to doing something that you did not do. This would put the company at great risk for no reason. Do not do that. But when you know that a member of the team was responsible, at least to some extent, or you know that your company played a significant role in the crisis, own it. Own the fact that you or a member of your team was involved. Own that you are deeply concerned about the situation. And own that you and your leadership team are taking responsibility for getting through these difficult times to be a better company going forward. This is not an admission of fault — it is a commitment to taking personal responsibility for action and resolution. That is what stakeholders want to see and hear from enterprise leadership. That is what our visiting executives at the Ross School have consistently said that they wish they would have done sooner and more effectively. So, I will echo their admission here. Take responsibility when you should. It is the right move.

- -

> When you know that a member of your team was responsible,
> at least to some extent, or you know that your company
> played a significant role in the crisis, own it. This is not
> an admission of fault — it is a commitment to taking
> personal responsibility for action and resolution.

- -

During a crisis, stakeholders want to see four actions from leaders — four things they want and need to see them DO: communicate, make decisions (with complete or limited information), take responsibility (as soon as it is appropriate to do so), and engage stakeholders. Do these well, and you will find that your high-stakes leadership efforts will have the greatest probability of success.

Leadership During Challenging Times

Not long ago, my friend Robert "Bo" Brabo — who was a decorated combat veteran in the US Army and who worked for a decade inside the White House Communications Office — asked to interview me for a book he was writing on values-based leadership. Bo thought that some insight from JetBlue (a company known for its values-based culture) might be worthy of a mention in his book about values-based leadership. As it turned out, he enjoyed our conversation so much that not only did he share a number of JetBlue lessons in the book, but he also asked me to write the book's foreword. Bo's book is entitled *From the Battlefield to the White House to the Boardroom: Leading Organizations to Values-Based Results*. I think it is a pretty good read. If you have enjoyed the lessons in this book, I think you would enjoy Bo's book as well.

The foreword that I wrote provided some insight on the challenges of leadership during difficult times. I thought it would be helpful here as well. Here is a portion of what I shared at the beginning of Bo's book:

> As a Professor at the University of Michigan's Stephen M. Ross School of Business, I have the privilege of teaching a unique and wildly popular MBA course entitled *High-Stakes Leadership*. This course has been a fixture at Michigan Ross for more than 40 years and offers students the opportunity to explore — through real interactions, not just case studies or textbooks — the experiences of seasoned C-suite executives and the lessons each of those leaders has learned from guiding their organizations through a major crisis. To date, *High-Stakes Leadership* has welcomed, as our esteemed guests, hundreds of chief executives from many of the world's most recognizable brands. A fundamental lesson that has been shared by nearly every visiting executive is the vital importance of understanding our own personal values and then consistently behaving in ways that demonstrate them. When students inevitably ask why values matter, our guests generally respond with something like this:

Today's business environment is remarkably complex. While we aspire to deliver exceptional value to all our stakeholders, we don't always succeed. When we fall short, our ability to effectively lead is questioned. It can be hard for stakeholders to see and appreciate how our enterprise is trying to create value for them, especially when we're failing to meet their expectations. It is, however, easy for them to see the way we behave and the effort we put forth — or don't — to engage with them.

To earn and maintain the trust and confidence of stakeholders, we must consistently and sincerely demonstrate our commitment to their interests. When our behaviors are aligned with our personal values, our actions are more consistent, they are executed with greater energy, and they are much more likely to be accepted as genuine.

Everyone knows when your actions are (or are not) true to what you really believe.

During each class, as students probe further into these claims, executives invariably describe two reasons why values-based actions are so important for today's leaders. First, they consistently point to the level of effort required to run a successful enterprise. Exceptional execution in any environment takes an incredible amount of dedication and energy. Clear alignment between the mission of an organization and the personal values of those leading it is imperative for maintaining the requisite level of effort over an extended period of time. It is this sustained effort, our guests contend, that ultimately enables an organization to remain highly competitive.

Second, the visiting executives point to the challenges of what I simply refer to as "the messiness of business" — often described by military leaders as the *volatile, uncertain, complex,* and *ambiguous (VUCA)* environments in which today's military units are typically required to operate. In these environments, resources are always constrained, information is never complete or perfect, and decision-making quality is paramount. In complex scenarios like these, leadership efforts must be focused on the implications of constantly changing conditions. This is *not* the time to be weighing the differences between *what needs to be done* and *what the organization wants me to do.* In high-performance organizations, the alignment of personal and organizational values takes place well in advance of having to face a crisis or even the everyday "messiness of business."[6]

Today's operating environments are, indeed, remarkably complex. To execute effectively, organizations must have leaders whose actions consistently earn the trust and confidence of their stakeholders. According to a growing body of research, the best way to ensure this consistency is the thoughtful and explicit alignment of organizational values and the personal values of the leaders who guide it.

I would be remiss not to mention that several of the esteemed leaders who have been guests in that MBA course were kind enough to write endorsements for my book (see the Praise section before the table of contents). As I think about my recent interactions with them and the insights they have provided in my classroom, I am in awe of how much I have learned from them collectively. I have taken the liberty of presenting the spirit of their remarks here because I hope that you find their perspectives about values-based crisis leadership helpful as you think about developing your own competencies as a high-stakes leader. I certainly have — and I refer to these lessons every day as I continue to build on my own capabilities in my pursuit of being the very best high-stakes leader I can be.

Three Quality Examples of High-Stakes Leadership Communication

Throughout this chapter on crisis leadership, I have shared a great deal about the roles crisis leaders should be prepared to assume, how crisis

---

6   Robert Brabo, *From the Battlefield to the White House to the Boardroom: Leading Organizations to Values-Based Results* (Kenosha, WI: Silver Tree Publishing, 2020).

leaders should BE, what they should KNOW, and what stakeholders expect them to DO during a crisis. We have focused very little, however, on crisis communication. Still, it is a critical high-stakes leadership skill — one that you should make a commitment to develop.

During the COVID-19 pandemic, I saw quite a few examples of quality leadership communication. While there also were many no-so-great examples, a few struck me as particularly well done. I'd like to share three that I found to be exemplary.

Please read very slowly and deliberately through each of these messages. As you do, consider first the responsibilities of a high-stakes leader during a crisis. What do you see in each of these messages that demonstrates a clear commitment to these responsibilities? How effectively does each of them demonstrate how leaders should BE during a crisis? What they should KNOW? And what they should DO?

- - - - - - - - - - - - - - - - -

Military Leaders McChrystal and Fussell — Action, Visibility, Honesty, Compassion

On March 24, 2020, just days after the World Health Organization declared the SARS-CoV-2 outbreak a global pandemic, the *New York Times* ran an opinion piece authored by Stanley McChrystal and Chris Fussell. McChrystal is a former US Army general best known for his command of Joint Special Operations Command in the mid-2000s, and Fussell is a former US Navy Seal. The two leaders now work together at the consulting firm McChrystal Group. The editorial, entitled "What 9/11 Taught Us About Leadership in a Crisis," describes post-9/11 military leadership lessons that can also serve as lessons for business leaders as they cope with the impact of COVID-19 on their organizations.[7]

Below is an excerpt from that article. What lessons can we draw about crisis communication from these words written *by* experienced and decorated leaders *for* other leaders in the midst of a pandemic?

---

7   Stanley Mcchrystal and Chris Fussell, "What 9/11 Taught Us About Leadership in a Crisis," *The New York Times* (March 23, 2020, accessed July 14, 2020), https://www.nytimes.com/2020/03/23/opinion/coronavirus-mcchrystal-leadership.html.

"In any crisis, there is a natural temptation to simply wait it out. Today's leaders cannot give in to this instinct. We're facing a perfect storm of economic downturn, social isolation, and a fast-spreading pandemic. The answer to this problem will not suddenly reveal itself; leaders must create solutions. Here's what that means.

First, don't hunker down. Today's leaders must also stand and be visible to their organizations, their communities, and their families.

Second, demonstrate candor — and demand it from the leaders below you. Today's leaders must be honest with their people to a level that will and should feel uncomfortable.

Third, give up more authority than feels natural. Fighting through complexity requires quick and informed action at the edge. This is dependent upon fast, transparent, and inclusive communication.

Finally, be more compassionate than you think you need to be. As your organization disperses to remote-work status, the loss of personal interactions will quickly sink in. It will be easy for leaders to overlook or undervalue the fear and stress their people are feeling because of this isolation. You must immediately take your culture online, and learn to reinforce camaraderie, esteem, and compassion, via digital platforms.

We are now weathering a once-in-a-hundred-year event, and Americans are hurt — physically, emotionally, financially, and spiritually. Leaders at all levels in society need to embrace the changes this crisis brings rather than struggle against it. Your people need you. This is your moment, and you can rise to it."

- - - - - - - - - - - - - - - - - -

JetBlue Leaders Hayes and Geraghty — Sharing the Facts, the Plans, and the Hope

This second example is a message that was distributed to the 23,000 crewmembers of JetBlue Airways from CEO Robin Hayes and President/COO

Joanna Geraghty on March 18, 2020, just one week after the COVID-19 pandemic was declared. I'm sharing this message with you in its entirety and unedited. As you read through these remarks and reassurances from the two highest-ranking corporate executives, consider what you have learned about crisis leadership and how this letter to crewmembers illustrates some of the *roles* crisis leaders are expected to assume as well as elements of the "BE, KNOW, DO" framework that was presented.[8]

"Dear Crewmembers,

It has been a very tough few weeks. We are so proud to see once again how the JetBlue culture brings us together during times of crisis. Thank you for continuing to serve our Customers and deliver the JetBlue experience, particularly when your own lives are being disrupted in so many ways.

With safety our #1 value, we continue to take the measures necessary to protect your health. But as it relates to our business, we are not going to sugarcoat it. Demand continues to worsen, and the writing is on the wall that travel will not bounce back quickly.

We'd like to give you some color on what we are seeing. Last year on a typical day in March we took in about **$22 million** from bookings and ancillary fees. Throughout this March, our sales have fallen sharply and in the last several days we have taken in an average of less than **$4 million** per day while also issuing over **$20 million** per day of credits to Customers for canceled bookings. This is a stunning shift, which is being driven by fewer new bookings, much lower fares, and a Customer cancel rate more than 10 times the norm. If you do the math, $4 million per day does not come anywhere close to covering our daily expenses. It is hard to predict how long these conditions will last and how much more challenging the environment may become.

---

8   "JetBlue Provides Update Related to Coronavirus," JetBlue (accessed July 14, 2020), http://mediaroom.jetblue.com/investor-relations/press-releases/2020/03-18-2020-113459855.

We are not alone. Virtually every major carrier is taking actions that were almost unthinkable a few weeks ago, making huge schedule reductions and parking significant portions of their fleets.

Even though we entered this from a position of strength with a strong balance sheet and cash in the bank, because of the dramatic fall-off in bookings, we need to reduce our spending immediately so that we can continue to fund JetBlue's operations and ensure your jobs are protected. **We have already announced an initial capacity reduction, pay cuts for our officers (VPs and above), voluntary time off programs, re-negotiated Business Partners agreements, and other spending reductions.**

We've taken swift and decisive actions to protect you, but we must do more and do so quickly to weather this storm.

Reducing Our Flying to Reflect Demand

We are reducing our capacity in the coming months, with a reduction of at least 40% in April and May. We also expect substantial cuts in June and July, and given the unpredictability of this event, we will ground some of our aircraft. We know this is not an easy move — it will impact hours for many frontline Crewmembers, but it is also essential that we reduce capacity in the face of dramatically falling demand.

We will be notifying Customers of their specific cancellations in a phased approach so that we do not overwhelm Customer Support as they continue to receive exponentially more calls than they ever have before.

Reviewing Our Fleet Plan

One of our most substantial capital expenses is the purchase of new airplanes. In collaboration with Airbus, we are looking at our order book for opportunities to slow deliveries and reduce aircraft pre-delivery payments (PDPs). We will also defer the four previously used airplanes that we announced earlier this year.

Cutting Our Capital and Operational Spending

We will reduce spending wherever we can to preserve our cash, and both of us will be taking a 50% pay reduction during this crisis.

We entered the year with a list of major initiatives to invest in our infrastructure, technology, and real estate. As of today, we have paused or stopped more than 75% of these projects and will continue to stand down work wherever we can.

Increasing Our Cash Reserves

The dramatic loss of revenue in recent days means we will have to start dipping into our cash savings. Although we came into this with about $1.2 billion, our expenses total millions of dollars each day. The good news is we have secured a new liquidity facility — an extra credit line — which allowed us to borrow $1 billion. This is not free money — it's a band-aid solution that holds us over and we have to pay it back with interest. Even with these cash reserves we, like the rest of the industry, will need significant government support to help us through these losses.

Calling for Government Intervention

The governmental warnings and actions taken to manage this health crisis have hit both domestic and international travel hard. We have been coordinating with Airlines for America (A4A) and other U.S. airlines to ensure government leaders understand the threat to our global economy if air travel is not supported. When this pandemic passes — and it will — air travel will play a major role in getting life back to normal and supporting economic recovery. We are going to need significant government help to do that. This is not a position we'd like to be in, but government assistance will help us protect our

23,000 Crewmembers who are our most important priority as we navigate these turbulent times.

From the beginning we have faced many challenges and, against all odds, we have thrived through some incredibly difficult events. Now we are faced with what is by far the biggest challenge our company and our industry has ever seen. While we know this is an incredibly difficult time for all of you as you work to juggle your own concerns around coronavirus, we have come through other challenges in our 20 year history and we can — and will — come through this together.

The next few months won't be easy, but please know that all the steps we're taking today are focused on protecting the health and safety of our Crewmembers and Customers and ensuring JetBlue remains a great place for you to work well into the future."

- - - - - - - - - - - - - - - -

Amazon CEO Jeff Bezos — Confronting the Crisis and Rallying the Troops

The third example is a message from Amazon CEO Jeff Bezos to his nearly 850,000 "Amazonians" on March 21, 2020 — 10 days after the pandemic was declared. The following example of crisis communication is exemplary. Once again, you should be able to see in this message a commitment to transparency, gratitude, focus, and several examples of items from the "BE, KNOW, DO" framework.[9]

"Dear Amazonians,

This isn't business as usual, and it's a time of great stress and uncertainty. It's also a moment in time when the work we're doing is its most critical.

---

9   "A Message from Our CEO and Founder," US Day One Blog (March 22, 2020, accessed July 14, 2020), https://blog.aboutamazon.com/company-news/a-message-from-our-ceo-and-founder.

We've changed our logistics, transportation, supply chain, purchasing, and third-party seller processes to prioritize stocking and delivering essential items like household staples, sanitizers, baby formula, and medical supplies. We're providing a vital service to people everywhere, especially to those, like the elderly, who are most vulnerable. People are depending on us.

I'm not alone in being grateful for the work you are doing. I've received hundreds of emails from customers and seen posts on social media thanking you all. Your efforts are being noticed at the highest levels of government, and President Trump earlier this week thanked this team profusely.

Across the world, people are feeling the economic effects of this crisis, and I'm sad to tell you I predict things are going to get worse before they get better. We're hiring for 100,000 new roles and raising wages for our hourly workers who are fulfilling orders and delivering to customers during this period of stress and turmoil. At the same time, other businesses like restaurants and bars are being forced to shut their doors. We hope people who've been laid off will come work with us until they're able to go back to the jobs they had.

Much of the essential work we do cannot be done from home. We've implemented a series of preventative health measures for employees and contractors at our sites around the world — everything from increasing the frequency and intensity of cleaning to adjusting our practices in fulfillment centers to ensure the recommended social distancing guidelines. We are meeting every day, working to identify additional ways to improve on these measures.

We've placed purchase orders for millions of face masks we want to give to our employees and contractors who cannot work from home, but very few of those orders have been filled. Masks remain in short supply globally and are at this point being directed by governments to the highest-need facilities like hospitals and clinics. It's easy to understand why the incredible medical providers serving our communities need to be first in line. When our turn for masks comes, our first priority will be getting them in the hands of our employees and partners working to got oooontial producto to poople.

My own time and thinking is now wholly focused on COVID-19 and on how Amazon can best play its role. I want you to know Amazon will continue to do its part, and we won't stop looking for new opportunities to help.

There is no instruction manual for how to feel at a time like this, and I know this causes stress for everyone. My list of worries right now — like yours I'm sure — is long: from my own children, parents, family, friends, to the safety of you, my colleagues, to those who are already very sick, and to the real harm that will be caused by the economic fallout across our communities.

Please take care of yourselves and your loved ones. I know that we're going to get through this, together."

Crisis communication is a critical skill for high-stakes leaders. A true measure of crisis-communication effectiveness is the ability to demonstrate a readiness to respond to the interests and needs of stakeholders. These three messages provide wonderful examples of these objectives in action.

You, Too, Can "Be, Know, and Do" Well During Crisis

This chapter has focused on the places where the proverbial rubber meets the road during an organizational crisis — presenting you with detailed guidance about the ways in which good leaders must behave, the mindsets they must adopt, and the actions they must take when the going gets tough.

There is so much to learn about crisis leadership, and we have only touched upon a few areas here in this chapter. But if you take these lessons and spend some time with them, particularly in the context of all the other things you have learned in this book, you will find that you have built a strong foundation of capabilities for becoming an effective high-stakes leader.

These lessons will surely NOT go to waste. As we have said, the question is not "if" your organization will find itself in the midst of a crisis some day; the question is "when." Keep building on what you have learned here, and you will be more than ready to play an invaluable role in the response to a future crisis that your organization will undoubtedly have to face. You, too, can "be, know, and do" all the right things when you are called into service during turbulent times.

Crisis leaders need to BE: *Visible, Caring, Empathetic, Calm,* and *Assertive.*

Crisis leaders need to KNOW: The organization's *Vision and Values,* and, when making decisions during a crisis, a set of *Guiding Principles.*

Crisis leaders need to DO these things exceptionally well: *Communicate, Make Decisions with Limited Information, Take Responsibility,* and *Engage Stakeholders.*

Exercise #11
My Personal Crisis Leadership
Philosophy: "I Must Be, Know, Do ..."

As we bring this chapter on crisis leadership to a close, you might want to spend some time on a task that is potentially uncomfortable and may take more time than you want to dedicate to it right this moment. At a minimum, you should take some first steps — any steps — to formalizing your own personal approach to crisis leadership. You would benefit immensely from having such an invaluable tool.

Here, should you choose to do so, you can begin the development
of a Personal Crisis Leadership Philosophy. Take as much time as
you'd like and make an effort to address all of the items that stakeholders expect of their leaders during a crisis. Grab a notebook or
a device to type on, or scribble some starting notes on the lines
below. Don't write more than a single page at this point. It will help
to reinforce the material presented in this chapter and give you an
opportunity to personalize your lessons in a way that will be useful
for many years to come.

As a high-stakes leader, what do you personally want to BE, to
KNOW, and to DO, when called upon to lead a team through
a future crisis?

12

READY OR NOT

Strategies, Roles, and Practice for Optimal Crisis Preparation

Welcome to this final chapter of *High-Stakes Leadership in Turbulent Times*! Here, we will bring everything together and further help you and your organization prepare for the inevitable significant disruption or crisis that is apt to appear in the not-too-distant future.

In the pages that follow, I will walk you through a method for helping your company leaders come together and organize around a crisis-preparation and crisis-planning process. You will be using many of the notes and lists that I hope you have been developing as you've made your way through this book. You may not have felt as though you were creating elements of a high-stakes leadership toolkit, but you were. If you are really looking to begin, or significantly improve, the process your organization has in place to prepare for and deal with crises, get ready to do some really interesting and creative work. As you pour yourself into this final chapter, I would like to invite you to treat these final pages as a workbook rather than simply an informative guide. If you *haven't* been taking notes or making lists along the way, that's quite OK, too. Either way, I think you'll enjoy this summary of how to prepare your organization for a crisis.

Whether you are planning to use this last chapter as a workbook or simply a review, I suggest that you read all the way through once before returning to complete the activities that I'll be sharing. Don't let yourself get bogged down here before you've read all the way to the end of the chapter, but please feel free to look through any notes that you've taken prior to this point in your reading when you see references to previous activities — just don't let them slow you down much during this first read-through.

The process we'll follow in this chapter looks a little like this:

- First, we'll revisit your crisis typology — that list or matrix or hybrid solution that you crafted back in Chapter 9.

- I am going to ask you to review your typology, edit it, and have it at the ready for the exercises that follow.
  - If you didn't put any time into that exercise, I'll create some space for you to do so shortly, if this is something you think would be helpful — I certainly think it would be. To help you in this effort, I will be sharing with you a JetBlue example of how a typology was used to help my company build a crisis readiness plan.

- Then I'll ask you to take your typology and work through each crisis type as it would be perceived by each of your primary stakeholders. Remember back in Chapter 4 when you identified and listed the primary stakeholders for your business? Well, this is where the work you did then is going to pay off.

- Then we will explore a way to develop and organize the roles and responsibilities of the crisis management team. In Chapter 11, we completed a deep dive into the general expectations of crisis leadership, but we did not go over the specific tasks that crisis leaders would have to perform during a crisis. That's what we'll explore here in this final chapter. And we won't just think about the full range of tasks for a single crisis leader; we'll look at a way to define the roles and responsibilities of every member of the crisis management team. (Completion of all these definitions is something you and your colleagues can do after you finish reading this book, because you'll be well-armed with a mechanism for doing so.)

- Finally, we'll wrap up this book by examining some exercises that you can complete with your new crisis management team — or the existing team, if you already have one in place — that will accomplish a number of objectives necessary to truly prepare your team for action.

- First, we'll look at a way to collaborate and fine-tune every member's role on the team and the responsibilities that they must be ready to perform during any crisis.
- Second, you'll learn a way to help team members discover for themselves what they need to be doing for each scenario in your crisis typology.
- And third, I'll introduce you to some ways to provide real-world training for your crisis management team by having them participate in exceptionally effective crisis-response simulations. (And, of course, I'll throw in a JetBlue example or two along the way to illustrate how the tools and exercises explored in this chapter can be prepared and executed in the real, high-stakes world.)

Whew! We have a lot to cover in this final chapter. I hope you are excited to see how everything you have learned so far can be put into practice, and how you can take what you have learned and use it to create an actual, robust, ready-to-execute crisis management team — really exciting stuff. And it couldn't be more important. Think back to the "By the Numbers" infographic in Chapter 5, where I shared the facts and figures — the painful impact — of the JetBlue Valentine's Day Crisis. $44M and 150,000 impacted customers. And we actually had a strong culture, meaningful crisis plans, and pretty admirable execution under fire. Imagine how much worse a crisis like that could be — for your organization — if you're not prepared. Luckily, you're getting prepared!

OK, readers (and leaders!) ... You are almost there! There is light at the end of the tunnel, and it is not a train! (*That* would be a crisis, wouldn't it?!)

Revisiting Your Crisis Typology

Earlier in this book, you crafted a typology of your own — a mechanism for differentiating the types of crises your organization may encounter. You crafted this list after having learned about different crisis types and methods of formulating a typology. Lists and grids and matrices, oh my! At the time, it was your best guess at a collection of distinct threats to your enterprise.

Now, you are to return to the typology you created. Review it. Edit it, if appropriate, and get ready to use it later in this chapter. Take your time. Do not rush back into this final chapter. You have learned a lot over these last couple of chapters and you may want to make some adjustments to your previously documented typology. Keep track of its location in your notes. You will be referring to it again shortly.

Airline Crisis Typologies in Action

We have spent a great deal of time considering crisis leadership from an airline perspective. We did this largely because of my personal perspectives from my years as the leader of the Emergency Command Center at JetBlue Airways. But I have also been told by my students that airline examples are particularly useful because most people are familiar with the basics of how airlines work. At a very high level (pardon the pun), airlines move people and other things from place to place. To do so, they need airplanes and people and a route system, as well as sources of capital, customers, and operating partners. I bet you could probably sit down right now and sketch an airline stakeholder map on the back of a napkin. And I bet that you could have done so even before you read this book.

So, with your fundamental understanding of how airlines operate, how would you think about the types of crises an airline might prepare for? The airlines provide a great example of companies that spend a significant amount of time planning for crises, establishing emergency command centers, identifying crisis team members, defining roles and responsibilities, preparing tools and support materials, providing crisis training, and performing exercises to test processes and systems — all while building experience for the crisis leadership team. There is a lot to this crisis preparation, isn't there? Rest assured that as we move through this chapter together, we'll go over all the items I just mentioned in a context that can help you think through what might be appropriate at *your* organization. But for now, with all that said, I would like you to consider: *How might a typology be helpful for an airline, and how might it be used?*

As I have mentioned several times in this book, typologies are helpful for many reasons — perhaps the most important of which is that our typologies provide a framework for pre-crisis brainstorming, planning, and preparation. They can be used for discussing the likelihood of — and our readiness for — each situation that we have identified, for:

- Examining the potential impact of each situation were it to occur
- Planning responses so we won't have to create our crisis-management efforts from scratch when we need them
- As guides for our crisis-response practical training.

Every airline in the world has a crisis-response plan, and they typically have a dedicated safety or crisis-response team that spends a great deal of time monitoring the crisis preparedness of the enterprise. These people help identify the types of crises an airline might encounter and how they should respond in each case. To facilitate their planning, most identify a collection of crisis types to organize their efforts.

Here are two different typologies that have gained popularity in the airline industry. You will notice that both are categorical lists.

List # 1 was produced by a company called SimpliFlying. Their typology includes:

- Accidents
- Incidents
- Terrorism (real or presumed)
- Natural Disasters
- IT Malfunctions
- PR Disasters

List # 2 was produced by a company called F24, a crisis management company. Their typology includes:

- Foreign Object Debris (FOD)
- Collisions
- Aircraft Sabotage
- Pilot Error
- Mechanical Failure

- Adverse Weather Conditions or Events

- Bird Strikes

I share these lists for a couple of reasons. First, you should see again how useful it can be to have a list of crisis types to guide your thinking, planning, and preparation. Second, these lists present very different levels of focus. The first one is focused broadly across all departments in an airline, and the second is focused on flight-related crises. Is one better than the other? Not necessarily. But they do serve as a reminder that perspective matters and that you would be wise to define the most appropriate typology for your unique planning and readiness needs.

Perspective matters and you would be wise to define the most appropriate typology for your unique planning and readiness needs.

Why share another discussion of typologies here, when I have already asked you to create your own earlier in this book? The reason to create a typology is not simply to *have* one. Just having one doesn't do you much good. Having one and using it to improve your crisis preparedness, however, now *that* is the reason to have one. Sharing a new one here reminds you that even these typologies can be a matter of perspective and that they can become quite focused on a particular aspect of the business — right or wrong — if you are not constantly stepping back and ensuring that you are applying the appropriate frame for your efforts.

In the next section, I'm going to ask you to retrieve the typology you created back in Chapter 9 and complete an exercise in which you predict the likely impact of each crisis type on different stakeholder groups. You might have done a bit of this earlier in the book, but I'm going to ask you to formalize the work here.

By the end of this chapter, I expect you to have the beginnings of a basic crisis management plan. Given that you have already created a crisis typology — which is one of the best first steps for any organization when developing crisis response plans — the next step is to determine how these crisis types will impact different stakeholder groups. So that is your next task. Follow the instructions in the next exercise. Take your time. And good luck.

Exercise #12
Testing Your Crisis Typology with Your Organizational Stakeholders

Early in the book, you spent some time defining your organization's key stakeholders. It's now time to revisit that list. In this activity, you are going to conduct an exercise where you work through each of the crises in your typology from the perspective of each of your stakeholder groups. Here's how to proceed ...

Step 1

Refer to your *list of stakeholder groups* for your enterprise. Review it and update it, if necessary.

Step 2:

Retrieve the *typology* that you reviewed earlier in this chapter. Now consider your stakeholders, one group at a time, and work your way through each item on your categorical list or through each quadrant of your matrix, to define how each crisis type or crisis defined by the characteristics of each quadrant would impact each of your stakeholders. Scribble on the papers you've created or type on the documents you've been working from. (Or grab a fresh sheet of paper or notebook!)

By way of example regarding what you should be doing here, consider your Customer group and step through each item on your categorical crisis list or, alternatively, through each quadrant of your multi-dimensional matrix. For each item, you will be considering whether a crisis of "this type" would impact your Customer group. If they would be impacted insignificantly or not at all, then move on to the next crisis type. If they would be impacted significantly, then record in your workbook that Customers should be considered a primary stakeholder group for the given type of crisis. Each time the Customer group seems likely to be a primary stakeholder, take a moment to consider the potential impact on this group. Ponder: "To what extent would our Customers be impacted by this type of crisis?" Then ask, "What should we be doing, early in this type of crisis, to engage our Customer group to let them know that we recognize the threat and that we're doing our best to resolve it?"

Step 3+

Repeat this process for *all* crisis types on your lists or matrices, and for *all* your stakeholder groups. Yes, this will take a while, so don't attempt to be surgically precise or strive for perfection. Ideally, you will be repeating this exercise — at least once more — with other leaders at your organization at a later date. Just try to capture some basic information about each crisis type and the stakeholder groups most likely to be impacted by each.

Tip: Also, to help you move a little more quickly through this exercise, you may find it useful to limit your list of "primary stake-holders" to no more than three for each crisis type.

This exercise, when ultimately completed with a collection of senior organizational leaders, will make it much easier for the leadership team to develop specific crisis responses for a collection of well-defined scenarios.

Frameworks and Checklists: Organizing Your Crisis Response

You just completed an exercise that had you work through each category in your crisis typology and consider how each one could impact each of your primary stakeholder groups. What did you learn in the process? Perhaps you learned some things about your typology. Perhaps you were able to better understand the interests of your stakeholders. Perhaps you were struck by this realization: "OK, now that I have this list of horrible things that could happen at my organization and a sense of how significantly my stakeholders would be harmed by any one of these situations, I really don't like any of this. Crises suck, and I don't want them to happen."

Yes, you are correct. Crises are absolutely brutal, in every way one can imagine — and that's why it's so important that you and your fellow leaders do all that you can to prevent them, that you build relationships with your stakeholders to let them help you identify potential sources of crisis before they become critical, and that you address these issues when they are minor — not *after* they have erupted into a full-blown crisis. Yes, crises suck, and we do not ever want them to appear. Unfortunately, at some level, they will. So, let's prepare ourselves, which is our goal here. Let's take a look at how crisis-ready organizations proactively organize their crisis response plans.

 Now, before I go further, I am going to suggest that if you have been stepping through this book without completing each exercise, you won't find this exercise (or the following exercises) nearly as useful to you as more active readers might. It is particularly important, in my opinion, that you have developed a sense of how various potential crises at your enterprise would be perceived by stakeholders. So, if you didn't complete the previous exercises in this chapter, I encourage you to go back to the beginning and please do so now. The rest of the chapter will be here waiting when you come back.

Where should you begin in your efforts to effectively organize a crisis response? Start with a documented crisis-management process. What does that mean? In the following exercises, you will see some examples of elements of a crisis-management process. You will learn about:

- Checklists
- Roles and responsibilities
- The development of proactive crisis responses
- Practice sessions to test your processes and build expertise within your crisis response team.

In no way, however, will the materials that follow be sufficient for you or your organization. The following has been designed to raise your awareness of how to think and plan and prepare for a crisis — but, on its own, it will not be enough to get you ready. There is an abundance of resources — consultants, tools, readings, exercises, simulations, etc. — that can help you build upon what you are about to learn. Hopefully, this book has inspired you to seek out these additional resources. For now, here are some core elements of all effective response plans.

We will start with a collection of sample crisis-response checklists. Exposing you to these checklists will get you thinking about the elements you'll want to include when you craft your own (which, by the way, I will ask you to do once you have read through the following).

You have already crafted a typology. And you have thought through how each of these crises will impact your stakeholders. Now let's start thinking about how we can prepare our organization to deal with one of these crises and engage our stakeholders, should the need present itself.

Sample Crisis-Response Checklists

Let's break down the items that are worthy of inclusion in a crisis-response checklist (CRC). It's worth noting that if you perform some investigation on the topic of CRCs, you might find references to crisis *management* checklist (CMC). For our purposes, whether you call it "response" or "management," the lists are really the same thing. You may find, if you do some serious digging, that CMCs can be much more detailed, as they may be designed to provide guidance through an entire crisis, not just the initial response. Don't let this confuse you. Let's consider the terms and documents interchangeable. You can decide how detailed and for what specific purpose you would like your CRC/CMC to be.

Generally, a CRC will contain the following information:

1. **Guidance for taking immediate action.** What initial steps should be taken when someone is confronted with a crisis?

2. **Documentation.** How should early responders begin to capture information?

3. **Contact information for key people and organizations.** Who needs to be informed about the developing crisis situation?

4. **Specific guidance for specific crisis-response roles.** What initial steps should be taken by individuals with specific responsibilities?

5. **Guidance for stakeholder engagement.** Most checklists provide guidance for engaging members of organizational leadership, the media, and regulatory authorities.

I encourage you to find some CRCs (there are several available online, including a few of my favorites, which you can find at www.HSLresources. com. Review them with an eye for how they are similar or different in terms of content, scope, organization, and level of detail. None of the samples you find will be perfectly suited to your organization, but all can serve as useful examples for the exercise that follows, which will ask you to craft a very high-level CRC for your enterprise. Don't worry, you will be creating

Bonus Materials! Real-World, Sample CRCs

It can be helpful to get your hands on some actual crisis-response checklists from admirable, savvy organizations. Visit **www.HSLresources.com** to download CRCs from:

- The U.S. Department of Health and Human Services, Centers for Disease Control and Prevention
- The Insurance Thought Leadership Group
- The Destinations International Foundation

Spending some time looking at the CRCs of other organizations can help you fully appreciate the typical content, scope, organization, and level of detail you might want to put into your own CRC. Remember that none of these are perfectly suited to your organization, but all can serve as useful examples. Each of the sample checklists available at **www.HSLresources.com** has a different way of presenting guidance to crisis leaders.

something very simple for now. Later on, when your crisis-management team is ready, you will be developing something much more detailed for use at your organization. This online exploration and the next activity are simply warm-up exercises for that time.

Exercise #13
Drafting Your Own Crisis-Response Checklist (CRC)

You've just learned about the elements that typically are included in a crisis-response checklist (CRC), and you may have even visited my website to review some sample CRCs from different types of organizations. Now, it's time to draft a checklist for your own organization.

As with many of the activities in this book, the goal here is not to craft a perfect, ready-to-implement version of a crisis-management instrument. Instead, think of this as an outlining exercise, where you are simply beginning to create a skeleton upon which you can add as much detail as you would like later.

Step 1

Here is your challenge for this activity. Review the list of typical CRC elements on pages 316 and 317, and visit www.HSLresources.com to check out some sample checklists. Then, identify a set of headings or sections for your CRC. The online samples provide many options from which you can choose.

If this is as far as you would like to proceed at this point, that's fine. If, however, you would like to make a bit more progress on your CRC, continue to the next step.

Step 2

Under each heading or section title, add three to five steps (or more) that you believe should be completed or attended to if you were called to execute your CRC. Feel free to add as much detail to these steps as you would like.

Step 3

You now have a good starting point for a customized CRC for your organization. To further develop the work you have done here, it would be best to assemble a group of leaders at your organization and conduct a workshop with this instrument to include the content and level of detail most appropriate for your enterprise. Workshopping this CRC with a collection of your colleagues is also a great way to make sure everyone appreciates the contents and purpose of the CRC. Good luck with the creation of a final product, ready to deploy when it's necessary to do so.

Defining Roles and Responsibilities

If you took the time to complete the previous exercise, you have just drafted a relatively simple version of a crisis-response checklist. As noted during the exercise, this is not something that a single individual is typically expected to do alone. This is best accomplished as a collaborative exercise with fellow organizational leaders who have different areas of responsibility. But the exercise should have given you some useful insight on general categories of importance and perhaps even some specific steps that should or could be completed in each category. These checklists are instruments that will probably never be 100% complete. You should return to them frequently for updates and additions.

Who is going to implement this new checklist of yours? Once again, there is an incredible amount of literature out there to provide some guidance for defining crisis-management roles and responsibilities for your organization. This book doesn't cover all the considerations you should make when identifying and assigning organizational leaders to your crisis management team. If you are serious about setting up the right team and creating a world-class crisis response capability, then I would suggest engaging a consulting company with expertise in this area. If there is limited expertise in your company and your leadership team has begun to realize the importance of crisis readiness — in fact, the COVID-19 pandemic may have been the driving force in helping them draw this conclusion — then an engagement with a team of experts would be money well spent. They can serve as a one-stop shop to help you build a robust plan.

But you may not be ready for an elaborate plan just yet. Or maybe you don't have the resources to make that commitment right now. So, your organization will have to depend on you and your freshly acquired expertise. Here is how I suggest that you go about defining crisis-management roles and responsibilities at your company.

The first order of business is to think about the size and complexity of your organization and determine how different levels of leadership would typically support a company crisis. If your organization is relatively small and your leadership team is very well connected with the work being done throughout the enterprise, then perhaps this team will support both your strategic and tactical crisis-leadership requirements — a distinction I will describe in a moment. If your organization is large, it may be best to have your senior executives serve as members of your strategic crisis-leadership team and have the next layer in your organization serve as your tactical crisis-management team.

If your organization is large, it may be best to have your senior executives serve as members of your strategic crisis-leadership team and have the next layer in your organization serve as your tactical crisis-management team.

How do these roles differ? In his book *Blindsided: A Manager's Guide to Crisis leadership* — which would serve you well as a useful field guide to preparing for and dealing with a crisis at your firm — author Bruce Blythe describes the differences between these two teams like this:

- The **strategic crisis-leadership team** consists of executives and senior managers who focus on issues that threaten the viability of the organization. They are charged with maintaining a strategic perspective over the crisis, remaining largely removed from the tactical management of the situation. This group will focus primarily on decisions regarding threatened core assets, managing the concerns and interests of key enterprise stakeholders, authorizing significant decisions, expenses, and communications, and overseeing the effectiveness and well-being of the crisis-management team.

- The more **tactical crisis-management team** is charged with actually directing the crisis response of the organization. This is the team that staffs the company crisis command center and is comprises leaders from every function within the organization. In some publications, this team is known as the Crisis Action Team.[1]

At JetBlue, I was the director of our Emergency Command Center, and I was responsible for leading the crisis-management team for the company. On my team was a vice president or director from every company function. In our Command Center, each of these departmental leaders had a designated workstation and, for each crisis type in our typology, was responsible for a set of processes and procedures that they were expected to execute during a crisis.

At a minimum, whether you separate the strategic and tactical crisis-response teams or combine them, you will require designated leaders to fill key decision-making roles and tactical action roles.

- - - - - - - - - - - - - - - - - -

The Crisis Team, at a Glance

Across the various expert recommendations for establishing a crisis-management team, a few required roles are suggested as a starting point for your organization. If you have nothing in place today, begin with these:

---

1   Bruce T. Blythe and Kristen Noakes-Fry, *Blindsided: A Manager's Guide to Crisis Leadership* (Brookfield, CT: Rothstein Pub., 2014).

- First, a **crisis manager**. Do not let the title fool you. This should be a very senior member of the organization with the experience, expertise, and full authority to make decisions and represent the best interests of the company during a crisis. Who in your organization should lead your crisis-management team? Start here.

- Next, **point-people from key functional areas.** These will be the primary members of your crisis team. You should appoint senior (if not the senior-most) leaders from the following units as permanent members of the team:
  - **Finance**
  - **Legal**
  - **Human Resources**
  - **Public Affairs**
  - **Media/Corporate Communications**
  - **Operations**
    - Appoint a head or heads of operations for your primary business or businesses. If you have a COO, operations officer, or general manager, this is probably your ideal candidate.
  - *(Optional, depending on the structure of your organization)* **Information Technology** and **Safety or Safety/Security**

From this list of suggested crisis management team members, can you think of leaders in your organization to fill these roles? As I mentioned earlier regarding the creation of a typology, the filling of roles on a crisis management team is not the responsibility of a single leader. If you believe that your organization should have a strategic crisis-*leadership* team, then that group should select the members of the crisis-*management* team. If not, then members of your C-suite should identify the appropriate leaders at your organization.

Once you have identified the roles and people to fill them, you will need to define a set of specific responsibilities for each of them. There are a few ways to begin the "responsibility definition" process. First, you can engage an external expert to help. This may be expensive, but it would be fast and effective. Alternatively, you can assemble the crisis management team and brainstorm the responsibilities they believe they should have during a crisis. As departmental leaders, they will understand their normal responsibilities, so they should be able to help the team think through the added responsibilities they will assume during a crisis.

You may also find it helpful to use some crisis examples from your typology to facilitate the responsibility brainstorming. Sometimes having a place to start is all that the team will need to put pen to paper on "Who is going to be responsible for what during *this* type of crisis?" See, once again, your typology comes in handy.

The truth is that there is an almost infinite number of ways to organize and prepare your team for your next crisis. I hope that what I have shared will be enough to get you started. Then, over time, with a little bit of further preparation and practice, you will make some adjustments to your initial ideas. That should be expected. It is all a function of learning as you go, which is, of course, a key element of resilience and a characteristic of organizations that are truly committed to crisis readiness.

Developing Proactive Crisis-Response Strategies

You have developed a crisis typology for your organization and have thought through how each of these crises might impact your different stakeholder groups, as an exercise to both "pressure-test" the validity of your typology and to begin the process of identifying priority stakeholders — those who are likely to be impacted most significantly by each crisis type.

You then spent time crafting a crisis-response checklist, with at least enough specificity to be able to identify the key areas of action that need to be addressed during a crisis. You considered the question of who would actually be using these checklists, and that led you to the definition of roles and responsibilities for your crisis-*management* team and, if appropriate, crisis-*leadership* team. Now, you should be asking yourself: "How can I create a way for this new team of crisis managers to learn how to serve the organization in their new capacities and help us prepare for future crises?" Great questions — and here are my suggestions for addressing them.

Begin by asking the team to talk about their confidence in the organization's ability to deal with a crisis were the company to find itself in one. Perhaps a great place to start is to ask how the company recently dealt with the COVID-19 pandemic: "What did we do well, and what should we be doing better in the future?" This will help everyone get comfortable with some open discussion.

At this point, you have a couple options for your conversation. You might decide to continue the discussion in the context of how the crisis-management team could help the enterprise if there is a future COVID spike that causes significant disruption again or during the next similar crisis. Or, if there is not an appetite for another COVID discussion, you could pull out your crisis typology and use it to stimulate some discussion with the new crisis-management team.

If you choose the second option, explain how you arrived at the list and make it clear that it is not a finished product, but rather, simply a good place to start. Share what you have learned about the value of quality stakeholder engagement throughout all the stages of a crisis and then get some feedback on the team's alignment around the importance of this guiding principle. There is that "guiding principle" idea again — good one to note. With some discussion, the team will agree.

Return to your typology and ask the team to choose the scenario that they believe the company will most likely face someday. In my experience, they will be drawn to one or two items on the list. Select one, then collectively decide on an example of what a crisis of this type would look like at your firm. Once you have your example, the team should work their way through it. Ask the team: "OK, let's image this happens 30 days from now. What will we do?" Let the group talk about how they would formulate a response. You will quickly see how difficult it would be to align around a consistent response without some structure. This is a good time to pull out the checklists and have all team members weigh in on what they (i.e., their crisis-management role) should be doing to ensure the accomplishment of each step in the list.

You may prefer to have team members work through their checklists on their own before a group discussion of their actions, or you may choose to brainstorm through the checklists together as a team. Either way, you want to use this exercise to accomplish several objectives:

1. First, you want the team to **get comfortable working together**. During a crisis, tensions will be high and the members of your

crisis management team must be able to work very well together under pressure.

2. Second, you want to **test your checklists**, so use this exercise to add, subtract, or modify steps to be completed. You will also, at this stage, be able to start crafting individual checklists for each role. Having a single checklist is a great place to start, but you eventually want every member of your team to have their own checklist — ideally for each type of crisis in your typology (i.e., multiple checklists per person because of all the crisis types). Do not let that scare you, as most of the items on each person's list will remain unchanged regardless of crisis type.

3. Third, you want to **identify resource strengths and gaps**. Get the members of your team thinking about the resources, capabilities, and expertise already in place to be able to deal with a crisis, as well as gaps that may exist in these areas. As gaps are identified, it is important that the team discusses the need to address these gaps and, if necessary, how resolving them should be accomplished.

4. Then, as a final objective, you want the team to **begin to view crisis preparedness not as a burden, but as a critical necessity for the firm**. You want them to accept that crisis readiness is not optional; it is required.

If you can accomplish all these things with your new crisis management team, you will be well on your way to building the kind of organizational resilience truly necessary for an enterprise to survive and thrive in today's volatile, uncertain, complex, and ambiguous (VUCA) environment.

Exercise #14
Action Plan: Next Steps Toward a Crisis Response Strategy

There was a lot going on in the previous activity. If you are working through this book on your own, you are probably not ready to sit down with a group of fellow leaders at your organization and tackle all the suggested activities. That's OK. You do have an opportunity at this point, however, to begin the construction of a plan for helping your organization develop some pre-planned or proactive crisis response strategies, based on what you have learned in this course.

In this exercise, I'd like you to create a list of action steps that you would like to take to begin (or continue) the development of a robust collection of crisis-response strategies. Given the current state of crisis-response planning and crisis-leadership experience at your organization, you can make your list of action steps as simple or as aspirational as you would like. Your primary objective here is to create a list of steps that you can actually accomplish — that you would feel comfortable committing to.

Assume that any progress would be good progress if it helped your organization improve its ability to deal with the next inevitable crisis. With this in mind, create a list of action steps that are appropriate for helping your organization make progress in any of the areas examined in this module, particularly those described earlier.

Action Steps

1. _____   6. _____

2. _____   7. _____

3. _____   8. _____

4. _____   9. _____

5. _____   10. _____

Conducting a Tabletop Exercise as a Test of Readiness

A great way to test your crisis-management procedures is to run what is called a tabletop exercise. Tabletop exercises will allow you to practice and assess your plan, as well as to observe the performance of your crisis-management team (collectively and as individuals).

During a tabletop exercise, a facilitator — who could be an experienced professional crisis expert or an organization's internal crisis manager — leads a step-by-step walkthrough of a hypothetical crisis scenario and an organization's likely response. At every step during the exercise, members of the crisis management team are expected to use all available tools and support resources — such as checklists and procedural manuals — to determine and then share the appropriate action steps. Along the way, the facilitator asks probing questions of the group and encourages participants to challenge each other. The goal of the tabletop exercise is to review best practices, roles and responsibilities, areas for potential improvement, and new ideas that can be incorporated into response plans.

To create and execute a successful tabletop exercise and contribute to the organization's higher state of crisis readiness, the exercise must convincingly simulate a crisis scenario. It must give participants a taste of the chaos that would be an inevitable part of any crisis. Take this seriously; let blood pressures rise; use words that denote danger or catastrophe; create pressure in terms of timing or urgency; hold yourselves accountable not to be causal or dismissive or joking during this simulation. Feeling and reacting to some pressure and anxiety during a practice session will enhance the team's performance during an actual crisis.

If your organization is committed to vastly improving or seriously testing its existing crisis-response plans, you may want to engage an expert who can deliver an exceptionally high-quality exercise. If you choose to go this route, the expert will help you craft a realistic scenario, complete with a collection of progressive updates, that will allow you to test all aspects of your plan — from the leaders themselves, to their processes and tools, to their decision-making, and so on. You can run these exercises for a duration of just a couple of hours or over much longer periods of time, such as days or even weeks.

At JetBlue Airways, as the leader of our Emergency Command Center, I would partner with our Office of Safety and Emergency Response (now called Business Continuity) to plan and execute tests of our crisis readiness. Sometimes these exercises would be as simple as a short tabletop exercise for a single element of our crisis-management team (e.g., the media team or onsite "go team") or a single aspect of a crisis (e.g., activating the Command Center). Other times, such as with our biennial major crisis-response exercise, we would partner with one of the airports in our route system — we frequently partnered with our good friends at the Fort Lauderdale/Hollywood International Airport in south Florida — to run a full-scale, multi-day emergency exercise. These were incredible productions that included partnering with the airport to tow a JetBlue airplane into an unoccupied area of the field; partnering with local college theater programs to create simulated injured passengers that were positioned in or near the airplane that just experienced a simulated crash; partnering with local emergency response and hospital facilities to treat, deliver, and accept our "injured customers;" partnering with Fort Lauderdale local and New York-based media facilities to simulate the media frenzy that would appear during a crisis, including the production of simulated news reports, onsite tweets, and press releases; and everything else required to create the most authentic crisis scenario possible. These were truly amazing and important productions.

Why share these details with you? Because in some safety-critical industries, crisis preparedness is not just a luxury. It is an absolute requirement. And the best way to ensure a company's readiness is to test the processes, procedures, and people that will be deployed to manage a crisis, should they ever be needed.

> In some safety-critical industries, crisis preparedness is not just a luxury. It is an absolute requirement. And the best way to ensure a company's readiness is to test the processes, procedures, and people that will be deployed to manage a crisis, should they ever be needed.

Now, the example that I just shared with you was an exercise that we would manage ourselves. We did so because we had world-class crisis-response experts on our staff (my good friend Penny Neferis has run the Emergency Response [ER] team at JetBlue since the company was founded and is quite possibly the most knowledgeable ER expert on the planet). Your organization may, but probably does not, have people with this level of expertise And that is OK. Just know that experts do exist, they are happy to partner with you, and they can be very helpful in testing your crisis-response capabilities.

That said, this does not mean that you cannot conduct a tabletop exercise of your own. In the next exercise, you will learn how to do just that.

You may find the execution of these tabletop exercises to be some of the very best training that has ever been done at your organization. What makes these experiences particularly valuable is that your crisis-management team will be using actual crisis-response procedures and checklists as their training materials. As you know, this means that not only will the exercises be wonderfully useful for skill development, but they will provide opportunities to validate procedures, onboard new members of your crisis-management team, earn the confidence of your governing board

Bonus Materials! A Tabletop Exercise for You to Try

Tabletop exercises are wonderful experiences that can accomplish several different objectives, from raising awareness of readiness, to identifying opportunities for improvement, to training new members of a leadership team.

Head on over to **www.HSLresources.com** to download a tabletop exercise provided by the EduRisk unit at United Educators. While the sample exercise you'll find at my reader-resources website was developed to help academic institutions prepare for a crisis likely to happen in a higher-education environment, the structure of the tabletop exercise guide can be easily adapted to any organization in any sector. I suggest spending 30 minutes with it to inspire your own planning.

and senior executives, and contribute to your culture of resilience and crisis readiness. These are all great wins for the long-term future success of your enterprise.

Exercise #15
Action Plan: Next Steps Toward an Assessment of Readiness

You just read about the value of tabletop exercises, which can help leaders at any organization explore their current level of crisis readiness, test the validity of current practices, identify gaps in crisis-response plans or tools, or any number of other benefits that only an experiential exercise can help bring to light. And if you headed over to www.HSLresources.com, you've looked at a sample exercise too.

There are many reasons that you might choose to conduct a tabletop exercise at *your* organization — all of them beneficial for developing an increased capacity for resilience.

In this next activity, you are simply asked to document some ideas for using or conducting a tabletop exercise(s) at your organization.

Why would the team benefit from performing one (or more) tabletop exercises?

_____

_____

_____

_____

What would it help them see or learn?

_____

_____

_____

_____

Who should be involved?

_____

_____

_____

_____

What should be the focus?

_____

_____

_____

_____

Where would you begin to look for partners or materials for the exercise?

_____

_____

_____

_____

Who would facilitate?

_____

_____

Other key considerations:

_____

_____

_____

_____

Just take a few minutes to record your thoughts on how a tabletop exercise might be helpful at your organization and what it would take to conduct such an exercise. I think you would find such an exercise to be one of the most valuable and worthwhile learning experiences that could possibly be created for the team of high-stakes leaders at your organization.

Preparing for the Next Crisis

You have just about reached the end of this final chapter on crisis preparation. **How are you feeling about the readiness of your organization should it find itself in the midst of a major disruption or crisis? In your view, given all that you have learned, is your company light years away from being ready to handle a crisis, or do you feel as though a few tweaks would get them to a pretty healthy state of readiness?**

Well, regardless of your answers to these questions, I hope that you have come to the same conclusion that I have during my 35+ years of crisis-leadership experience — that readiness is not optional. It is really a matter of survival. Every organization is going to find itself in some sort of crisis — perhaps relatively minor on a global scale but monumental for a team within the company, or perhaps massive as we saw with BP and their Deepwater Horizon crisis. Big or small, crises will appear. Our job, as high-stakes leaders, is to help our organization prepare for the inevitable. The lessons we covered in this chapter should have painted a clear picture for you — of not only how to create checklists and a team of crisis managers, but much more than that. This chapter was ultimately about a collection of mechanisms designed to help your leaders look in the mirror and admit to themselves that, "We're not really ready for the next crisis, and now we have a much better sense of where and how we need to improve." That level of self-awareness creates opportunity and safety, a sort of insurance and organizational strength.

If your organization is like most others around the world, your leaders aren't spending enough time thinking about the next organizational crisis. And, really, it is hard to blame them. In this VUCA world of ours, leaders are dealing with so many *urgent* things on a daily basis that sometimes it's hard to consider the truly *important*. Crisis preparation is important. When crises strike, they strike hard. Now you know enough to understand why being underprepared can be catastrophic for an organization.

When crises strike, they strike hard. Being underprepared can be catastrophic for any organization.

This was the point of this chapter and, for that matter, this entire book. There are many steps that organizational leaders can take to be better prepared for the next crisis, but it takes a conscious effort to make these a priority. Hopefully, in this chapter, you learned a few different ways that you can help your leaders see them as such.

As we all should have learned during the COVID-19 pandemic crisis, threats can appear from just about anywhere — literally out of the thin air and sometimes originating oceans away. If we can build the muscle memory to view crisis readiness not as a luxury but as a hard requirement, our organizations and all our stakeholders will benefit immensely from our decision. COVID-19 exposed many areas of opportunity for improvement in our governmental and business processes, in the capability of our leaders to navigate the crisis environment, and in our general readiness for a crisis.

If you can use the approaches shared in this chapter to get your leaders to appreciate the gaps that exist between your current state of readiness and the ideal future state of readiness, consider your learning a great success. The path will be hard, but oh, so worth it … if you can make it happen.

Keep pushing and creating opportunities for your leaders to discover for themselves what I know to be true: **We can and should be much better prepared for our next crisis.**

Exercise #16
Three Key Opportunities to Better Prepare Your Organization for the Next Crisis

In this final activity, you are asked to think back across your entire learning journey on *High-Stakes Leadership* and to identify three key opportunities for helping your organization become better prepared for its next crisis. These don't have to be remarkably ambitious, but you have learned so much in the pages of this book (and during your times of reflection) and have identified so many areas of opportunity for improvement in the way leaders at your organization think about and prepare for (or *don't* prepare for) crisis. Take a few final moments to answer the following questions.

Which of these areas of potential improvement deserve immediate attention?

_____

_____

_____

Which could have the greatest impact if you could help your fellow leaders give them the appropriate amount of attention?

_____

_____

_____

_____

Within these questions rests the invitation for you to fully leverage what you have learned in the process of reading this book.

What are your three greatest opportunities for helping your organization better prepare for its next crisis? *(Write a paragraph for each.)*

1. _____

   _____

   _____

   _____

2. _____

   _____

   _____

   _____

3. _____

   _____

   _____

   _____

Now, ask yourself: **"What can I do to take action on all three of them?"**

_____

_____

_____

_____

Your answer to this last question will establish a platform for the next step in your journey of becoming a truly exceptional high-stakes leader at your organization.

CONCLUSION

We have sure covered a lot of ground together. I am so happy that you've reached the conclusion of a book that I've spent an entire lifetime preparing to write. Hopefully, the hours, days, weeks, or months you've spent working through this book have been — as you reflect upon the experience — time well spent. I've enjoyed it immensely and hope you will keep in touch (see page 345 for details on how to do that!). I can assure you that if you've embraced the lessons I have shared and completed all the exercises to the best of your ability, you now have an incredibly powerful set of tools and capabilities that can help you prepare yourself and your organization for our tumultuous and unpredictable world. Thank you for your energy, your thoughtfulness, and your commitment to being prepared for the inevitable when (not if) the next crisis appears at your enterprise.

> You now have an incredibly powerful set of tools and capabilities that can help you prepare yourself and your organization for our tumultuous and unpredictable world.

This book was written, as you are now well aware, to help developing and seasoned leaders effectively navigate the challenges of significant disruptions that have become increasingly common in today's constantly evolving business environment. This book was written for *you*, to support you in the vital work you do right now and to prepare you for what's around the corner.

We have explored so much. I really hope that you have developed an appreciation for the breadth of the topics we have examined. We started with a deep dive into the stakeholder theory of management, and you now clearly understand why stakeholder perspectives can and should inform and dramatically improve a leader's response to events that threaten their organization's very survival. Always remember to "love your stakeholders" — to give them every bit of attention and support that you can — whenever you can. That love and attention and respect makes a world of difference — in good times and in bad.

We also learned how understanding and developing individual and organizational resilience is such a vital capability. You might recall that we defined resilience as the ability to anticipate potential threats; to cope effectively with adverse events when they do occur; and to adapt to changing conditions to ensure the best possible path forward for ourselves, our teams, and our organizations. Resilience, we agreed, is not simply the ability to pick ourselves up after we have stumbled. It begins by eliminating the things that might make us stumble ... well before they have had a chance to do so. We also explored several ways that we could improve our company's capacity for resilience and our own personal capacity for resilience. In fact, we saw threads of these opportunities throughout the remainder of the book.

Resilience is not simply the ability to pick ourselves up after we have stumbled. It begins by eliminating the things that might make us stumble ... well before they have had a chance to do so.

We examined a model to help us better understand and predict stakeholder reactions to crises. We then applied what we learned to a discussion of crisis typologies. These typologies, including the one you have just created for your own organization, are immensely valuable mechanisms for both crisis preparation and crisis management. I hope that you feel really good about the time you spent crafting such an invaluable tool.

We then explored the nature of the crisis environment itself and how challenging it can be to navigate. Leaders, I suggested, will face very few situations more stressful, complex, frustrating, and vitally important than what they experience during a crisis. The very nature of the crisis environment is working against us (even before we know we're in a crisis in the first place) and it never gives us a break — even well after the cause of the disruption has been extinguished and our enterprise has moved on. Stakeholders have long memories and they will remind you, in some cases for years to come, how you let them down. It is simply how the crisis environment works. "Praemonitus, Praemunitus," I learned in a Latin course I took as an undergraduate at the University of Michigan many years ago — "Forewarned is forearmed." And now that you understand the crisis environment much better, you will be ready for it. You have been forewarned and are taking the steps to be fully forearmed for whatever may come your way.

The very nature of the crisis environment is working against us (even before we know we're in a crisis in the first place) and it never gives us a break — even well after the cause of the disruption has been extinguished and our enterprise has moved on.

We spent our final two chapters exploring the topics of crisis leadership and crisis preparedness. In terms of an operating framework for crisis leadership, you now have an appreciation for the value of "BE, KNOW, DO" during a crisis. Become a student of these and challenge yourself to BE: *Visible, Caring, Empathetic, Calm,* and *Assertive.* KNOW your organization's vision and values, and, when making decisions during a crisis, make sure that you have a set of guiding principles. They will be incredibly helpful. And then DO these things exceptionally well: *Communicate, Make Decisions with Limited Information, Take Responsibility,* and *Engage Your Stakeholders.* These are much harder to do than to say, but you have taken a great step forward with your commitment to working through this book.

As this book comes to a close, consider the value of bringing all the lessons you have learned together in an effort to prepare yourself and your organization for your next crisis. That dreaded crisis *will* come. And you now have a remarkable set of tools to help you navigate it. You will not, of course, navigate it flawlessly, but you will be much better prepared than almost anyone else at your organization could be. Your preparation, I can say with certainty, will make all the difference.

Your stakeholders will not expect you to be perfect or
omniscient, but they will expect you to be visible, courageous,
and unwaveringly committed to the very best possible path
forward. Your preparation will make all the difference.

Finally, I will remind you that, in our VUCA world, things can go sideways in an instant. When they do, the importance of leadership becomes very clear. In these stressful times, leaders must be willing and able to step up and lead because, in these moments, the stakes are high and leadership is needed most.

In a crisis, people — all your stakeholders — will look to high-stakes leaders, like you, for tangible evidence of leadership. When they look, they want and need leaders who they can believe in. They will not expect you to be perfect or omniscient, but they will expect you to be visible, courageous, and unwaveringly committed to the very best possible path forward.

High-stakes leadership (i.e., crisis leadership) is one of the most difficult capabilities any leader could master. But with the right mindset and an unwavering commitment to learn a little every day about how to do it better today than you did yesterday, you can undoubtedly make a difference. I suspect you already have.

Thank you for joining me in our exploration of *High-stakes Leadership in Turbulent Times: Why Stakeholders Are Your Greatest Assets ... in Good Times and Bad*. I wish you the very best in your own crisis-leadership journey. Thank you for being one of *my* stakeholders and for trusting me to travel at your side, even if only briefly, during this important learning odyssey.

ACKNOWLEDGMENTS

As this book has been written to summarize a lifetime of crisis leadership experience, it will come as no surprise that I have many people to thank for their love and support — of not only this project, but for so much of the success I've enjoyed over the years. I have always felt blessed to have so frequently found myself in the right place at the right time, with opportunities to do inspired, challenging, and satisfying work. We all have so much to offer, but not all of us find ourselves in our places of most potential. I have been presented with many opportunities to bring my best self to moments and teams that needed me, taught me, and inspired me. For the record (and formally memorialized here), my successes have always been a product of the incredible talent, passion, and courage of those with whom I have had the privilege to dare greatly. To all of you, I am certain that I have failed to adequately share my sense of gratitude and pride in the work that we have done together; the sacrifices made to accomplish things that have never been done before; and the selfless commitment to excellence that truly inspired greatness in all of us. Thank you, my friends.

Now, as I owe a debt of gratitude to so many people for the lessons and experiences that fill this book, I will do my best to acknowledge them here.

First and foremost, to my incredible wife, Anne. Thank you, honey, for giving me the time and space — what would have otherwise been *our* time and space — to work through this process. You are wonderful and I love you with all my heart.

To my daughters and sons — Amanda, Joseph, Brendan, Hannah, Kate, and Sam — thank you for the inspiration to share what I've learned in the hopes of creating a better world for you and your own children.

To my mother, Ann (Toni, to most who know her), thank you for your love, a lifetime of support, and your enthusiastic encouragement for whatever crazy ideas I chose to pursue. You have clearly overcome the disadvantages afforded you by that school down south. Thank you again, Mom, for suggesting that a few years in the military just might help shape my future. It appears that your instincts were spot on.

To my brother, Dave, fellow co-founder of JetBlue Airways, and life-long supporter of my efforts. Joining you to launch JetBlue was the most professionally fulfilling experience of my life. Thank you for everything you have done for me, my family, and so many others who have benefited from your leadership and generosity. You have been and continue to be an inspiration to thousands.

To my sister, Lauri Baker — and to her husband, Jim, and their son, Ben — thank you for your support over the years and your constant interest in my endeavors.

To the rest of my family — Glenn, Connie, Bob, Rob, nieces, nephews, cousins, and so many branches on our extensive family tree — thank you as well for your love and encouragement.

The journey of publishing a business book has involved the talent and support of many people. Many, many thanks to my outstanding editorial board — Anne Craig, Phil Price, Mary Simkins, Hannah Craig, and Jason Rowland. Your transparency, ideas, compliments, and questions were immensely helpful. The generous donation of your time and effort is something I will never forget.

To my new best friend, exceptional thought-partner, master editor, and President of Silver Tree Publishing, Kate Colbert, I cannot thank you enough for taking my manuscript of stories and ideas and turning it into a remarkable piece of literature. Your time, effort, dedication, and commitment to the important messages I had to share have been truly inspirational. *You*, Kate, are *my* hero.

As this is my first book, I had no idea how involved the production process would be and the number of people who I would meet at Silver Tree and who would lend their talents to the endeavor. To my extraordinarily capable art director, Courtney Hudson, thank you so much for designing incredible covers and typesetting the book to create such an engaging reading experience — even while recovering from a devastating injury. You are incredibly resilient and you have made everything, front to back, look fantastic. And to my eagle-eyed proofreader, Gwendolyn Blanc, thank you, as well, for making sure that I never missed the chance to more clearly articulate a key concept or vital lesson for our readers.

To my book publicist, Stephanie Feger, Founder of emPower PR Group, thank you for allowing me to meet your family and for believing that we had a valuable message to share. While our journey together is just beginning, I am so looking forward to a collaboration that will help thousands of leaders confidently face the messiness of our VUCA world.

To my endorsers and early readers — those incredible men and women who lent their time, opinions, and names to the Praise section of this book, Dave Almeda, Cathy Bessant, Robert "Bo" Brabo, André V. Branch, David Brandon, Russell Chew, Warren Christie, Derek Kerr, Marcy Klevorn, Andy Kozak, Ram Krishnan, Tom Lewand, Doug Lynch, Teresa Mackintosh, DeWolfe "Chip" Miller, Derek Newberry, Philip Price, Jennifer Sherman, Lang Sias, Al Spain, John Sznewajs, Alan Todd, and Pope Ward. I am honored and deeply humbled that you would so generously give of yourselves in support of this work. I thank you, and I look forward to somehow returning the favor.

To the many members of my Navy family who helped me learn how to lead and to embrace the challenges of strike-fighter combat and tactical readiness, thank you, my friends. Condo, Bullet, Pops, Hock, Hogg, Elvis, Creature, Scorch, Fuzzy, Snooze, Lurch, Noggin, Troll, Mole, DD, Tip, Pepe, Rolls, and many others, I learned so much from all of you. As I wrote this book, I reflected so much on our time together; doing so helped me realize how much of who I've become was forged, right beside you, in the crucible of carrier aviation. Speed is life.

To the members of my JetBlue family, together we created something a century-old industry had never seen before. What an honor and a privilege it was to spend so many indescribable and wonderful years creating the embodiment of Safety, Caring, Integrity, Fun, and Passion. David, John, Tom, Dave, Ann, Al, Brian, Usto, Chris, Tom, Rob, Amy, Alex, Frankie, Troy, Hitesh, and Amir, I hope that you find the stories in this book to be heart-warming reminders of the truly special things we accomplished together. And to my incredible colleagues who worked with me to launch and grow JetBlue University — Chris, Raul, Chuck, Ken, Steve, Shelley, Dean, Deb, LeeAnn, Stephen, Paul, Warren, Andy, Woody, Brian, Patty, Jeff, Chris, Brian, Kim, Trudy, Allison (I could keep going) — JetBlue is the company it is today because of your tireless commitment to the success of every learner who trusted us with their future.

To my fellow Chief Learning Officers, particularly those who joined me in a journey through the first-ever Doctoral Program on Work-Based Learning Leadership at the University of Pennsylvania, I so appreciate your friend-ship and your dedication to helping those you serve to perform at their very best. The impact you are having in organizations around the world is game-changing and worthy of much more praise and recognition than you will ever receive. Doug Lynch, my friend, thank you for creating a vehicle that elevates the role of the CLO to its rightful place at the leadership table.

To my friends and colleagues at CorpU. Thank you for the inspiration to tell *my* story just as you have helped so many tell *their* stories. The work you do each day empowers businesses to grow smarter and harness their collective genius to be the best they can be.

To the leadership team at Michigan Ross, my thanks to you as well. I am grateful for the opportunity to formalize the lessons I have learned about leading through crisis, bring them to bear on one of the most popular MBA electives at our wonderful institution, and to translate them into this book, which will help leaders everywhere make a positive difference in the world.

And to all those companies and professionals whose stories I shared in this book, thank you. If you have read through this book, you know that your example is simply illustrative of the messiness of business and a product of an environment that has never been more volatile, uncertain, complex, or ambiguous. Cheers to you, for having the courage to keep fighting and for recognizing that every stumble provides an opportunity to learn.

Forever and always, Go Blue!

KEEP IN TOUCH

🌐 **Learn more about High-Stakes Leadership and quickly connect with Dr. Barger on his website:**

www.MikeBarger.com

✉️ **Send an email:**

MBarger2525@Gmail.com

MGBarger@UMich.edu

Find, follow, and share on social media:

in LinkedIn.com/in/MGBarger

f Facebook.com/MBarger2525

🐦 Twitter.com/MGBarger

📕 **Inquire about bulk discounts or custom-edition books, speaking engagements, or consulting services:**

MBarger2525@Gmail.com

ABOUT THE AUTHOR

Dr. Michael (Mike) Barger is
a Clinical Assistant Professor of Business
Administration and Executive Director,
Ross Online, at the Stephen M. Ross School
of Business, University of Michigan. In his
teaching role, Dr. Barger leads courses in
entrepreneurship, early-stage business
development, and leadership during
organizational crisis. In his staff role, he
facilitates the design and execution of the
School's digital education initiatives and
oversees the operation of Ross Online.

Dr. Barger grew up in Howell, Michigan, just north of Ann Arbor, in an
airline family. His father was a United Airlines captain and his mother was
a flight attendant. Immersed in aviation and travel from the day he was
born, Mike began to fly at a very early age. When he graduated from the
University of Michigan in 1986 with an undergraduate degree in economics
and psychology and a bit of varsity baseball experience, he joined the
United States Navy and became a naval aviator.

Dr. Barger (callsign "Crusher") served most of his 13 years in the carrier
Navy as an FA-18 pilot and flight instructor, completing three, six-month
deployments aboard USS Theodore Roosevelt (CVN-71) and USS Dwight
David Eisenhower (CVN-69). These deployments included combat action

in Iraq during Operation Desert Storm, over Bosnia, and in the skies above Kosovo. The highlight of Dr. Barger's naval career was a three-year tour as an Instructor and then Chief Instructor at the U.S. Navy Fighter Weapons School (known to many as TOPGUN). Throughout his naval career, he was a widely published author, speaker, and educator on combat strategy and tactics, training techniques (particularly in advanced simulation), and complex weapons systems employment. He achieved the rank of Lieutenant Commander.

Dr. Barger left the US Navy in 1999 to become a founding member of JetBlue Airways along with his brother Dave — an airline industry veteran who held several senior leadership positions at Continental Airlines. Mike and Dave found the family approach to the JetBlue startup particularly satisfying, having both grown up in the airline business. While at JetBlue, Dr. Barger held many different leadership positions as the company received FAA certification, launched, and rapidly grew into the fifth largest airline in the United States. He created JetBlue University, the award-winning corporate training function that provides learning and development to all members of the JetBlue workforce; to this day, JetBlue University remains the only single-source provider of company education in the airline industry worldwide. Dr. Barger also served as the senior captain on both varieties of JetBlue aircraft (the Airbus 320 and Embraer 190) and served as the senior leader responsible for all Flight Operations, Maintenance Operations, Talent Management, and Enterprise Strategy at the company. Also, and perhaps most instructive to this book and his passion for crisis leadership, Dr. Barger led the company's Emergency Command Center, which guided JetBlue through events such as the 9/11 crisis, the 2003 Northeast US Blackout, and dozens of other major disruptions and crises.

Following his 13 years at JetBlue, Dr. Barger translated his passion for education into a leadership role at CorpU, an education technology company based in Philadelphia, Pennsylvania. As COO, he oversaw all CorpU operations, including the design, creation, and delivery of all CorpU Academy courses, educational offerings built on the wisdom and insight of the brightest minds in academia and business. Dr. Barger has a deep passion for helping leaders solve their most complex business challenges with knowledge and tools that help them harness the collective genius already present in their organizations.

After six years at CorpU, Dr. Barger joined the faculty at the University of Michigan's Ross School of Business, where he has been since 2017. Despite the fact that his sons have jokingly described his professional career as a "meteoric plummet from coolness," Dr. Barger has found teaching undergraduate and graduate students from across the University and thousands of business leaders from around the world to be some of the most satisfying work that he has ever done. When he is not teaching, he is writing, presenting conference keynotes, and researching crisis-leadership best practices to help high-stakes leaders at all levels within their organizations to become more effective in their roles ... in good times and in bad.

Dr. Barger received his Master's Degree in Learning Leadership in 2008 and his Doctor of Education degree in 2009 from the University of Pennsylvania. He currently lives with his wife and children in Novi, Michigan, USA.

Made in the USA
Monee, IL
29 October 2021